Drawn into the Heart of Reading

Teacher's Guide

Written by Carrie Austin, M.Ed.

Editor:

Julie Grosz

Cover Designer:

Merlin DeBoer

Heart of Dakota Publishing
www.heartofdakota.com

Special Thanks to:

- Julie Grosz for her patient editing and inspirational ideas.

- Cindy Madden for her willingness to pilot this program with her own children.

- Mike Austin for his encouragement, loving support, and continual help to do whatever is needed.

Copyright 1998 by Houghton Mifflin Company. Adapted and reproduced by permission from *The American Heritage Children's Dictionary.*

Scriptures taken from the HOLY BIBLE, NEW INTERNATIONAL VERSION. NIV. Copyright 1973, 1978, 1984 International Bible Society. Used by permission of Zondervan. All rights reserved.

Copyright 2001, 2004 by Carrie Austin
Heart of Dakota Publishing, Inc.
1004 Westview Drive
Dell Rapids, SD 57022

Website: www.heartofdakota.com
Phone (605) 428-4068

Printed in the U.S.A.

ISBN 0-9747695-0-9

Table of Contents

INTRODUCTION

Drawn into the Heart of Reading is designed to help you guide students toward becoming better readers. The instructions and activities were written to develop readers who successfully comprehend and analyze the meaning of what they read.

Drawn into the Heart of Reading is unique because it is a literature-based curriculum specifically written to use with multiple ages at the same time. Students of multiple ages are united by focusing on a similar topic. Yet, learning is individualized through book selections and daily activities that are developmentally appropriate for the reader.

Another important distinction of *Drawn into the Heart of Reading* is that the instruction and activities can be used with <u>any</u> literature, and are not limited to a prescribed or recommended reading list. This flexibility allows you to use your own discretion in selecting literature for your students to read. The structure of the program also allows you to individualize the pace at which each student completes the reading of the literature you select.

Drawn into the Heart of Reading incorporates a variety of methods to facilitate greater understanding of the text. These methods include the following:

- prereading activities
- lessons on nine key story elements
- guided literature discussions
- evaluation of character's actions in light of the Bible using lessons on Godly character traits
- creative projects with a unit study flavor
- exposure to a variety of literary styles

The instruction and activities are meant to enhance the reading experience, without dissecting the text until the pleasure of reading is lost. It is my prayer that *Drawn into the Heart of Reading* will minister to the needs of your family by making the teaching of reading a joyful experience.

PROGRAM GOALS

The goals for students who participate in *Drawn into the Heart of Reading* are as follows:

- To make connections within the text and raise questions prior to reading, creating a purpose for reading as students seek answers to their questions.

- To develop higher-order thinking skills through analyzing the key elements that make a story work.

- To participate in literature discussions with people of various ages, in order to gain a deeper appreciation for the text.

- To weigh book characters and philosophical issues raised in the text using a Christian standard that focuses on Godly qualities and values.

- To apply various vocabulary strategies in order to know how to discover the meanings of unfamiliar words in the text.

- To create a variety of projects that emphasize visual, auditory, and kinesthetic learning styles and demonstrate what was learned in the unit.

- To foster an appreciation for a variety of literary styles and inspire an enthusiasm for reading.

PROGRAM STRUCTURE

Drawn into the Heart of Reading is arranged into nine literary genre units. The glossary in the Appendix provides a definition for each genre. The nine units include the following:
- Historical Fiction
- Adventure
- Biography
- Fantasy
- Mystery
- Folk Tales
- Nonfiction
- Humor
- Realistic Fiction

This program is very flexible. It can be used as your entire reading program, or as a supplement to an existing program. You can use as many units as you choose each year. The nine units can also be used in any order. It is appropriate for students in levels 2 through 8.

Each of the nine units contains 20 days of instruction. Using all nine units in one year provides 36 weeks of instruction, which is equivalent to the common 180 day school year. The program is written to use year after year, as you move students through the various levels of instruction.

UNIT OVERVIEW

Each unit focuses on one literary genre. The lessons within each unit emphasize one story element and one major Godly character trait, with 3 subqualities. The glossary in the Appendix provides definitions of the story elements and the major Godly character traits.

The story elements that are emphasized in the nine units include the following:
- Character
- Setting
- Problem or Conflict
- Mood
- Prediction and Inference
- Compare and Contrast
- Cause and Effect
- Main Idea and Theme
- Perspective and Point of View

The major Godly character traits emphasized in the nine units include the following:
- Faith
- Fear of the Lord
- Responsibility
- Brotherly Love
- Loyalty
- Virtue
- Obedience
- Joy
- Integrity

The 20 days of instruction in each genre unit utilize the following format:
- a kickoff, or introduction, to the genre
- 15 days of leveled lessons
- assigned reading of literature you select to match the genre
- 5 days to work on one of three project options at the culmination of the genre

GENERAL DAILY FORMAT

The daily plans are divided into the three following levels of instruction: level 2/3, level 4/5, and level 6/7/8. The numbers correspond to approximate graded instructional levels. The program intends for students to remain in the same level of instruction for two years, before moving up to the next level. However, the design of the program, allows you to shorten or extend the number of years students remain in the same level to suit your specific needs.

Each level in the daily plans is labeled with one of the following lesson formats: *meet with the teacher, all levels together,* or *independent.* If 2 formats are listed, then the level will use both formats in the order they are listed for that day's lesson.

A clock icon under the level in the daily plans, indicates an emergency option is available for those students to complete independently. This option is for use in emergencies when you are unable to direct a lesson that is based solely on discussion.

The directions for the emergency options are found in the Appendix of the *Student Book* for each level. Directions are listed by genre and by day to coordinate with the clock icons in this guide.

GENERAL DAILY FORMAT:

LEVEL 2 / 3	LEVEL 4 / 5	LEVEL 6 / 7 / 8
Prior to Day 1: Kickoff: Introducing the genre. (All levels together.)	**Prior to Day 1:** Kickoff: Introducing the genre. (All levels together.)	**Prior to Day 1:** Kickoff: Introducing the genre. (All levels together.)
Day 1, Day 6, Day 11: Prereading Activities: Making connections within the text and raising questions prior to reading; setting a purpose for reading the text. (All levels together.)	**Day 1, Day 6, Day 11:** Prereading Activities: Making connections within the text and raising questions prior to reading; setting a purpose for reading the text. (All levels together.)	**Day 1, Day 6, Day 11:** Prereading Activities: Making connections within the text and raising questions prior to reading; setting a purpose for reading the text. (All levels together.)
Day 2, Day 7, Day 12: Story Discussions: Utilizing guided questioning to describe the text and make associations. Optional Phonics or Vocabulary Work (Meet with the teacher.)	**Day 2, Day 7, Day 12:** Story Element Lessons: Identifying and analyzing a different story element for each genre. (Meet with the teacher.)	**Day 2, Day 7, Day 12:** Vocabulary Builders: Applying one vocabulary strategy for each genre to discover definitions for unknown words in the text. (Complete independently.)
Day 3, Day 8, Day 13: Story Element Lessons: Identifying and analyzing a different story element for each genre. (Meet with the teacher.)	**Day 3, Day 8, Day 13:** Story Element Extensions: Demonstrating understanding of the story elements from the previous lessons. Optional Vocabulary Work: See Appendix for activities. (Complete independently.)	**Day 3, Day 8, Day 13:** Story Element Discussions: Evaluating and explaining the text through discussion and assignments focusing on the various story elements. (Meet with the teacher.)
Day 4, Day 9, Day 14: Godly Character Lessons: Relating personally to 2 Godly traits, comparing Biblical and book characters, and selecting one area to improve. (Meet with the teacher.)	**Day 4, Day 9, Day 14:** Godly Character Lessons: Relating personally to 3 Godly traits, comparing Biblical and book characters, and selecting one area to improve. (Meet with the teacher.)	**Day 4, Day 9, Day 14:** Godly Character Lessons: Relating personally to 4 Godly traits, comparing Biblical and book characters, and selecting one area to improve. (Complete independently.)
Day 5 and Day 10: Comprehension Check: Recalling and showing an understanding of important information from the text. (Meet with the teacher.)	**Day 5 and Day 10:** Comprehension Check: Recalling and showing an understanding of important information from the text. (Complete independently or all levels together.)	**Day 5 and Day 10:** Comprehension Check: Recalling and showing an understanding of important information from the text. (Complete independently or all levels together.)
Day 15 through Day 19: Culminating Genre Project: Selecting one of three project options and completing that project according to the listed requirements. (Meet as needed.)	**Day 15 through Day 19:** Culminating Genre Project: Selecting one of three project options and completing that project according to the listed requirements. (Meet as needed.)	**Day 15 through Day 19:** Culminating Genre Project: Selecting one of three project options and completing that project according to the listed requirements. (Meet as needed.)

Biography

GENRE: BIOGRAPHY

Definition:
    The true story of a notable person's life written by another person.

Common Characteristics:
1. Describes the person's surroundings.
2. Shows how the person affects other people.
3. Provides examples that demonstrate the person's behavior.
4. Supplies details that illustrate the person's individuality.
5. Implies or notes how the writer feels about the person.

Story Element Emphasis: Character

Definition:
    The people or individuals portrayed in a story.

Godly Character Trait Emphasis: Responsibility

Definition:
    Being accountable to God and to others as you carry out your duties or obligations in a faithful way.

Subqualities:
1. cautiousness
2. diligence
3. initiative

Teacher Directed   **All Levels Together**

Focus: Genre Kickoff

Preparation:

1.   The goal of the kickoff is to introduce students of all ages to the upcoming genre in a fun and entertaining manner.

2.   Decide how much time you want to spend on the kickoff. You can spend one normal reading class period, several hours, or even a whole day. After the kickoff, you begin with day 1 in the teacher's plans.

3.   Read through the list of ideas below and choose those that interest you for this genre's kickoff. You are welcome to add your own ideas that fit within this genre. Refer to the cover page for a definition and common characteristics for each genre. Introduce the name and definition of the genre to begin the kickoff.

Possible Kickoff Ideas:

1.   Brainstorm a list of biographical questions as a group from the following categories: facts about you, facts about your family, facts about where you live, important memories. Interview your assigned partner using the questions the group listed. Write down your partner's answers.

2.   Look through family photographs and instruct each student to choose 2 or 3 photographs that show an important time in their own lives. Have students share the photographs and explain why they selected them.

3.   Hand each student a sack or a box. Give students a limited amount of time to find 5 items to put in their sack or box that tell something about themselves. Have students share their items and explain their reasons for choosing each item.

4.   Sit in a circle and have students take turns finishing the following sentences:
      a) *I'll always remember the time when . . .*
      b) *One of my happiest memories is . . .*
      c) *I worked very hard at . . .*
      d) *I felt the saddest when . . .*
      e) *I hope people remember me as . . .*

5.   If you have any information about your family history or family tree, explore the information to discover your relatives' pasts.

6.   Cook a family recipe that has been passed down for several generations. Discuss what you can learn about your family heritage from the ingredients in the recipe, the name of the dish, the occasions when it was used, the person who passed it down, and the culture from which the dish came.

7.   Select pictures of several family members or relatives that show their personalities, hobbies, interests, and environment. Show the pictures to the group or give each student several pictures and have them discuss what they can discover about each person from looking at the photographs.

8.   Visit the historical home of a person that is no longer living. Discuss what you can discover about the person from that environment.

9.   Choose biographical facts to read about various individuals. Post a list of names of people that the facts could match. Have students guess which fact matches which person on the list.

10.   Tour your own house as a group and note what you discover about each family member from looking at their rooms or environment. Remember: During a tour, you may not touch anything. You may only make observations.

11.   Have students make their own scrapbook page with biographical information about themselves.

Questions to discuss at the end of the kickoff:
1.   What is a biography? (Refer to the definition on the cover page for this genre.)

2.   What can we find out about a person by reading a biography?

3.   What is the difference between a biography and an autobiography?

4.   What did you learn about biographies from today's activities?

5.   Why do we read biographies, or what is the purpose?

Teacher Directed   **All Levels Together**

Focus: Prereading Activity - Secret Passages

Preparation:

1.   Prior to meeting with the students for day 1, follow the directions for *Getting Started* listed in the back of this guide.

2.   Have the first book and one *Assigned Reading Calendar* ready for each student.

3.   You will need a folder or barrier of some sort between you and the students, so you can hide the covers of the books with the passages for today's lesson. If you have only 1 student, you will need to have several books from this genre beside the book he or she will be reading.

Lesson:

1.   Say, *Today we will be doing a prereading activity to help you think about the next book you will be reading.*

2.   Set out the books the students will be reading, but <u>do not tell</u> them who will be reading which book.   Allow the students to <u>briefly</u> look at the titles, covers, and illustrations for a few minutes.

3.   Say, *I will be reading several sentences from one of these books to you. Your job will be to guess which book has that passage.*

4.   Hide all the books behind your "barrier" and read a few sentences from one of the books. Then, set out the books in front of the students and have them guess which book had that passage. Have students give reasons for their choices.

5.   After each student has guessed, show students which book contains the passage.

6.   Continue steps 3, 4, and 5 until you have read several parts from each book.

7.   Give students the books you have chosen for them. Allow them time to carefully read the title, look at the front cover, read the synopsis, and look at the illustrations.

9. Discuss the following questions with your students:
    a) *What question(s) would you like to ask the person in your book?*
    b) *What made you think of that question?*
    c) *What makes your book a biography?*

10. Have students open their *Student Books* to the *Assigned Reading Calendar* for this genre. Help each student fill in the page numbers to be read for days 1-5.

11. Have students read the assigned pages for day 1 on their own.

Teacher Directed   **Level 2/3**

Focus: Story Discussion and Optional Phonics <u>or</u> Vocabulary Work

Preparation:
1.   You may choose to have students at this level review phonics <u>or</u> complete a vocabulary assignment. Use your own program for the phonics review. Refer to the Appendix for a reproducible vocabulary assignment. The lesson on this day is much shorter to compensate for the additional time you may spend on phonics or on vocabulary work.

Lesson:
1.   Optional phonics or vocabulary work

2.   Listen to your students read the assigned pages out loud to you. Use the Reading Strategies list and the Qualities of Good Reading list provided in the Appendix to help you know what to emphasize.

3.   Discuss the following questions with your students:
       a) *How would you describe this person?*
       b) *What problems does this person have up to this point in the biography?*
       c) *Where is this story taking place? Describe the place.*

Independent / Teacher Directed   **Level 4/5**

Focus: Story Element Instruction - Character Web

Lesson:
1.   Tell the students to read the assigned pages on their own, leaving 3-4 pages to read aloud to you.

2.   Listen to your students read several pages. Use the Qualities of Good Reading list provided in the Appendix to help you know what to emphasize.

3.   Work with the students to complete the Character Web on day 2 in the *Student Book*. List at least 3-4 examples for each category on the web. You may want to write answers on a marker board as you discuss them, so the students can copy them. Then, the students can concentrate better on the discussion.

4.   Discuss the following question with your students:
       a) *How are you similar to the person in this biography?*

Biography - Day 2

Independent   **Level 6/7/8**

Focus: Vocabulary Builder - Prediction Practice

Preparation:
1.   Have a dictionary available.

Lesson:
1.   The students complete the activities in the *Student Book* and read the assigned
       pages for day 2 on their own.

2.   The directions instruct students to come and show you the completed
       Prediction Practice vocabulary assignment.

Unit 1

Teacher Directed   **Level 2/3**

Focus: Story Element Instruction - Character Traits

Lesson:
1.   Listen to your students read part or all of the assigned pages out loud to you. Use the Reading Strategies list and the Qualities of Good Reading list provided in the Appendix to help you know what to emphasize.

2.   Work with the students to complete the Character Trait Web on day 3 in the *Student Book*. On the lines, write a quality describing the character. Then, give an example from the book that illustrates that quality. You may want to write the answers on a marker board as you discuss them, so the students can copy them. Then, the students can concentrate on the discussion rather than on spelling and capitalization.

3.   Discuss the following question with your students:
        a) *How are you similar to the person in this biography?*

Independent   **Level 4/5**

Focus: Story Element Extension - Character Profiles

Lesson:
1.   Tell the students to read the assigned pages for day 3 on their own.

2.   Tell them to complete the Character Profiles on day 3 in their *Student Books* when they finish reading.

3.   The directions instruct students to come and show you the completed assignment.

Teacher Directed / Independent   **Level 6/7/8**

Focus: Story Element Discussion - Character Attributes

Lesson:
1.   The students read the assigned pages for day 3 on their own.

2.   The students meet with you to discuss the following questions:
        a) *Describe the physical traits of the person in this biography.*
        b) *Describe this person's feelings and any actions that portrayed those feelings.*
        c) *How is this person similar to you?*
        d) *How is this person different from you?*

3.	Introduce Character Attributes in the *Student Book* under day 3.

4.	Have the students work to complete Character Attributes on their own.

5.	The directions instruct students to come and show you the completed assignment.

Teacher Directed   **Level 2/3**

Focus: Godly Character Traits - Examples

Preparation:
1.   Think of examples you can share from your own life for each of the following
        traits: *responsibility* and *diligence*. (Definitions are listed in the lesson below.)

Lesson:
1.   Introduce the following definition and scripture passage for *responsibility*:
        a) *Responsibility is being accountable to God and to others as you carry out
           your duties or obligations in a faithful way.*
        b) *Key Scripture verse: Each one should use whatever gift he has received to
           serve others, faithfully administering God's grace in its various forms.
           1 Peter 4:10*

2.   Share an example of *responsibility* from your own life.

3.   Help the students think of an example of *responsibility* from their own lives.

4.   Introduce the following definition and scripture passage for *diligence*:
        a) *Diligence is continuing to work at something without giving up.*
        b) *Key Scripture verse: Let us not become weary in doing good, for at the
           proper time we will reap a harvest if we do not give up. Galations 6:9*

5.   Repeat steps 2 and 3 for the trait *diligence*.

6.   Instruct your students to search for examples of *responsibility* and *diligence* as
        they read part or all of the assigned pages out loud to you. Use the Reading
        Strategies list and the Qualities of Good Reading list provided in the Appendix
        to help you know what to emphasize.

7.   Discuss the following questions with your students:
        a) *How does this character show responsibility? Or diligence?*
        b) *Did the character show the opposite traits of irresponsibility and
           slothfulness? Explain.*
        c) *What could the character do differently to be more responsible or diligent?*

Independent / Teacher Directed   **Level 4/5**

Focus: Godly Character Traits - Examples

Lesson:
1.   Tell the students to read and complete the Godly Character Sheet on day 4 in the *Student Book* on their own.

2.   The students need to silently read the assigned pages for day 4, leaving 3-4 pages to read aloud to you.

3.   The students should come and show you when both are completed.

4.   Review the Godly Character Sheet on day 4 in the *Student Book*, so the students and you will know what traits you are searching for in the biography. *(responsibility, diligence,* and *initiative)*

5.   Listen to your students read 3-4 pages aloud. Use the Qualities of Good Reading list provided in the Appendix to help you know what to emphasize.

6.   Discuss the following questions with the students:
       a) *How did the characters show responsibility?*
       b) *How did the characters show diligence?*
       c) *How did the characters show initiative?*
       d) *Did the characters show the opposite traits of irresponsibility? Or slothfulness? Or unresponsiveness? Explain.*
       e) *What might Jesus have done differently if He had been the character in the book?*

Independent   **Level 6/7/8**

Focus: Godly Character Traits - Examples

Lesson:
1.   The students complete the activities in the *Student Book* and read the assigned pages for day 4 on their own.

2.   The directions instruct students to come and show you the completed Godly Character page.

Teacher Directed / Independent   **Level 2/3**

Focus: Comprehension Check - Personal Points

Lesson:
1.   Go over the directions for Personal Points on day 5 in the *Student Book.* Students complete this assignment on their own after reading the assigned pages.

2.   Listen to your students read part of the assigned pages out loud to you. Use the Reading Strategies list and the Qualities of Good Reading list provided in the Appendix to help you know what to emphasize.

3.   The students finish the assigned reading and complete Personal Points on their own.

4.   The directions instruct the students to come and show you the completed assignment.

Independent   **Level 4/5**

Focus: Comprehension Check - Biographical Collage

Preparation:
1.   Have magazines available for this level's assignment, unless you plan to have the students draw the pictures instead.

2.   You may choose to have a large sheet of paper for this level's assignment.

Lesson:
1.   Tell the students to complete the Biographical Collage on day 5 in the *Student Book* on their own.

2.   The students also silently read the assigned pages for day 5 on their own. You may choose to have the students leave 3-4 pages to read aloud to you.

3.   The directions instruct the students to come and show you the completed assignment.

Independent   **Level 6/7/8**

Focus: Comprehension Check - Memorable Moments

Lesson:

1.   The students complete the activities in the *Student Book* and read the assigned pages for day 5 on their own.

2.   The directions instruct students to come and show you the completed Memorable Moments assignment.

Teacher Directed   **All Levels Together**

Focus: Prereading Activity - Questions and Answers

Preparation:
1.   If students are beginning new books today, make sure to have the number of pages to be read each day calculated and have those books ready to hand out. (See the *Getting Started* section, item #7, in the back of this guide for details.)

2.   If students are not beginning new books today, they use the books they are currently reading for today's activities.

Lesson:
1.   Say, *Today we will be doing a prereading activity to help you think about the next book you will be reading or the next part of the book you will be reading.*

2.   Give students a little time to look at the cover, read the synopsis, and quickly page through the book.

3.   Discuss the following questions with the students:
       a) *How do you punctuate a question?* (with a question mark at the end of the sentence)
       b) *How do you know if a sentence is a question?* (It ends with a question mark, and it asks something.)
       c) *What kinds of words do you find at the beginning of a question?* (asking words - such as *how, where, when, what, who, why*)
       d) *What would be a question you could ask about the person in your biography?* (Have students share ideas. Guide the students to see that questions should be about something important.)
       e) For example, *A question asking, "What color eyes does this person have?" is not a well thought-out question. An example of a better question might be, " What does this person look like?"*

4.   Tell students they will be writing questions about the people in their biographies. Students should get ideas from looking though the book. Students will answer as many of the questions as possible on day 10.

5.   Have students open their *Student Books* to the Question and Answer page for day 6 and write their questions.

6.   Help students update their *Assigned Reading Calendar* for days 6-10. Have students read the assigned pages for day 6 on their own.

Teacher Directed   **Level 2/3**

Focus: Story Discussion and Optional Phonics <u>or</u> Vocabulary Work

Preparation:
1.   You may choose to have students at this level review phonics <u>or</u> complete a vocabulary assignment. Use your own program for the phonics review. Refer to the Appendix for a reproducible vocabulary assignment. The lesson on this day is much shorter to compensate for the additional time you may spend on phonics or on vocabulary work.

Lesson:
1.   Optional phonics or vocabulary work

2.   Listen to your students read the assigned pages out loud to you. Use the Reading Strategies list and the Qualities of Good Reading list provided in the Appendix to help you know what to emphasize.

3.   Discuss the following questions with your students:
      a) *What problems does the person in the biography have right now?*
      b) *What advice would you give the person?*
      c) *What settings, or places, have been mentioned in the biography?*

Independent / Teacher Directed   **Level 4/5**

Focus: Story Element Instruction - Character Descriptive Details

Lesson:
1.   Tell the students to read the assigned pages on their own, leaving 3-4 pages to read aloud to you.

2.   Listen to your students read several pages. Use the Qualities of Good Reading list provided in the Appendix to help you know what to emphasize.

3.   Work with the students to complete Descriptive Details on day 7 in the *Student Book.* Each category should have short answers. You may want to write the answers on a marker board as you discuss them, so the students can copy them. Then, the students can concentrate on the discussion rather than on spelling and capitalization.

4.	Discuss the following questions with your students:
	a) *Which characters would be good influences? Explain.*
	b) *Which characters would be bad influences? Explain.*

Independent	**Level 6/7/8**

Focus: Vocabulary Builder - Prediction Practice

Preparation:
1.	Have a dictionary available.

Lesson:
1.	The students complete the activities in the *Student Book* and read the assigned pages for day 7 on their own.

2.	The directions instruct students to come and show you the completed Prediction Practice vocabulary assignment.

Teacher Directed / Independent   **Level 2/3**

Focus: Story Element Instruction - Character Information

Lesson:
1.   Listen to your students read the assigned pages out loud to you. Use the Reading Strategies list and the Qualities of Good Reading list provided in the Appendix to help you know what to emphasize.

2.   Discuss the following questions with the students:
       a) *Would you like to be friends with this character? Explain.*
       b) *Do you approve of the character's behavior? Why, or why not?*
       c) *Does the character remind you of someone you know? Explain.*

3.   Assign the students Information Please on day 8 in the *Student Book* to complete on their own. The students do not have to answer all of the questions. Instead, students choose several ideas to focus on from the ideas list.

4.   The directions instruct the students to come and show you the completed assignment.

Independent   **Level 4/5**

Focus: Story Element Extension - Personal Opinion

Lesson:
1.   Tell the students to read the assigned pages for day 8 on their own.

2.   Tell them to complete Personal Opinion on day 8 in their *Student Book* when they finish reading.

3.   The directions instruct students to come and show you the completed assignment.

Teacher Directed / Independent   **Level 6/7/8**

Focus: Story Element Discussion - Character Chart

Lesson:
1.   The students read the assigned pages for day 8 on their own.

2.   The students meet with you to discuss the following questions:
       a) *What is unique or important about the person in this biography?*
       b) *What important things has this person done?*
       c) *What caused this person's behavior?*

3.   Introduce the Character Chart on day 8 in the *Student Book*. Make sure the
       students understand what to do. Then, have the students work on their own.

4.   The directions instruct students to come and show you the completed
       assignment.

Teacher Directed   **Level 2/3**

Focus: Godly Character Traits - Biblical Comparisons

Preparation:
1.   Find a short children's book of the Bible story about Joseph and his brothers. Otherwise, you will need to read the story directly from the Bible in Genesis chapters 39-45.

Lesson:
1.   Review the following definitions and scripture passages:
   a) *Responsibility is being accountable to God and to others as you carry out your duties or obligations in a faithful way.*
   b) *Key Scripture verse: Each one should use whatever gift he has received to serve others, faithfully administering God's grace in its various forms.*
   1 Peter 4:10
   c) *Diligence is continuing to work at something without giving up.*
   d) *Key Scripture verse: Let us not become weary in doing good, for at the proper time we will reap a harvest if we do not give up. Galations 6:9*

2.   Read the children's book, or the Bible passage in Genesis chapters 39-45, about Joseph and his brothers. Instruct your students to listen for examples of *responsibility* and *diligence* in the story being read.

3.   Discuss the following question with your students:
   a) *How did Joseph's actions show responsibility and diligence?*

4.   Record the students' responses in the *Student Book* on day 9 under the Biblical Character column. (Possible answers include the following: *Responsibility* to Potiphar in his honest work and in his refusal to do what Potiphar's wife wanted; *Responsibility* to Pharaoh by interpreting his dreams for him; *Diligence* to store up grain for 7 years to prepare for the famine that was coming.)

5.   Listen to your students read the assigned pages for day 9 out loud to you. Remind the students to be searching for examples of *responsibility* and *diligence.*

6.   Using the questions listed below, compare Joseph with the person in the biography. Record the responses on day 9 in the *Student Book* under the Book Character column.
   a) *How does the character in your book show responsibility and diligence?*
   b) *What would the Biblical character, Joseph, do differently from the character in your book?*

Independent / Teacher Directed   **Level 4/5**

Focus: Godly Character Traits - Biblical Comparisons

Preparation:
1.   Find a short children's book of the Bible story about the boy, David, and his battle with Goliath. Otherwise, the students read the story directly from the Bible in 1 Samuel chapter 17.

Lesson:
1.   Tell the students to review the Godly Character Traits listed on day 9 in the *Student Book* on their own. Then, have the students silently read the story of David as a boy, either from the book you provided or from the Bible in 1 Samuel 17.

2.   Have students do their best to complete the Biblical Character column on the Godly Character Story Sheet for David on day 9 in the *Student Book.*

3.   Students silently read the assigned pages in the biography for day 9, saving 3 or 4 pages to read aloud to you.

4.   The students meet with you to finish the assignment for day 9. Listen to your students read several pages. Use the Qualities of Good Reading list provided in the Appendix to help you know what to emphasize.

5.   Discuss the following questions with the students as you review what they have already done in the *Student Book* for day 9. Complete the remaining columns in the *Student Book* for day 9.
    a) *How did David's behavior show responsibility, diligence, and initiative?*
       (Possible answers include the following: *Responsibility* by following God's will for David to fight Goliath; *Responsibility* to follow God's calling after Samuel anointed David as a boy; *Diligence* as a shepherd boy in learning to use his sling to protect the sheep; *Initiative* by going to King Saul and asking to fight Goliath.)
    b) *How did the person in your book behave like the Biblical character, David?*
       (List the answers in the *Student Book.*)
    c) *How did the person in your book behave differently from David?* (List the answers in the *Student Book.*)
    d) *Which trait was shown least often by the book character?* (Explain in the *Student Book.*)

Independent   **Level 6/7/8**

Focus: Godly Character Traits - Biblical Comparisons

Preparation:
1.   The students need a Bible for today's lesson.

Lesson:
1.   The students complete the activities in the *Student Book* and read the assigned pages for day 9 on their own.

2.   The directions instruct the students to come and show you the completed Godly Character Story page. (Examples of the traits in Ruth might include the following: *Responsibility* in staying with Naomi; *Diligence* in gleaning and threshing all day with few breaks; *Initiative* to ask permission to glean in Boaz' field; *Cautiousness* in speaking to Boaz and by obeying advice to glean only in his field for her own safety.)

Teacher Directed / Independent   **Level 2/3**

Focus: Comprehension Check - Questions and Answers

Lesson:
1. Review the questions the students wrote on day 6 in the *Student Book*. Students will answer these questions on their own after reading the assigned pages today.

2. Listen to your students read part of the assigned pages out loud to you. Use the Reading Strategies list and the Qualities of Good Reading list provided in the Appendix to help you know what to emphasize.

3. The students finish the assigned reading and complete the previous assignment from day 6 on their own. The directions instruct the students to come and show you the completed assignment.

Independent   **Level 4/5**

Focus: Comprehension Check - Questions and Answers

Lesson:
1. Tell the students to review the questions written on day 6 in the *Student Book*. The students will be answering these questions on their own after reading the assigned pages for day 10.

2. You may choose to have the students leave 3-4 pages to read aloud to you. The directions instruct the students to come and show you the completed work.

Independent   **Level 6/7/8**

Focus: Comprehension Check - Questions and Answers

Lesson:
1. The students complete the activities in the *Student Book* and read the assigned pages for day 10 on their own.

2. The directions instruct the students to come and show you the completed work. You will be checking the completion of the Questions and Answers assignment from day 6.

Teacher Directed   **All Levels Together**

Focus: Prereading Activity - Information Web

Preparation:
1.   If students are beginning new books today, make sure to have the number of pages to be read each day calculated and have those books ready to hand out. (See the *Getting Started* section, item #7, in the back of this guide for details.)

2.   If students are <u>not</u> beginning new books today, they use the books they are currently reading for today's activities.

Lesson:
1.   Say, *Today we will be doing a prereading activity to help you think about the next book you will be reading or the next part of the book you will be reading.*

2.   Give students a little time to look at the cover, read the synopsis, and quickly page through the book.

3.   Discuss the following questions with the students:
        a) *What is one thing you know about the person in this biography?*
        b) *How do you know that about this person?*
        c) *What is one question you would like to have answered about this person?*
        d) *What made you think of that question?*

4.   Tell the students that today they will be writing what they know about the person in the biography and also any questions they have about this person.

5.   Have students open the *Student Book* to the Information Web on day 11.

6.   Students write what is known about the main character in the center of the web. This part of the web shows information students know without looking in the book. In the outer circles of the web, students write the questions they have about this person. Students should get ideas for this part of the web by looking through the book.

7.   Help students update their *Assigned Reading Calendar* for days 11-15.

8.   Have students read the assigned pages for day 11 on their own.

Teacher Directed   **Level 2/3**

Focus: Story Discussion and Optional Phonics <u>or</u> Vocabulary Work

Preparation:
1.   You may choose to have students at this level review phonics <u>or</u> complete a vocabulary assignment. Use your own program for the phonics review. Refer to the Appendix for a reproducible vocabulary assignment. The lesson on this day is much shorter to compensate for the additional time you may spend on phonics or on vocabulary work.

Lesson:
1.   Optional phonics or vocabulary work

2.   Listen to your students read the assigned pages out loud to you. Use the Reading Strategies list and the Qualities of Good Reading list provided in the Appendix to help you know what to emphasize.

3.   Discuss the following questions with your students:
   a) *When did the story take place?*
   b) *What do you think is going to happen next? Explain.*

Independent / Teacher Directed   **Level 4/5**

Focus: Story Element Instruction - Character Relationships

Lesson:
1.   Tell the students to read the assigned pages on their own, leaving 3-4 pages to read aloud to you.

2.   Listen to your students read several pages. Use the Qualities of Good Reading list provided in the Appendix to help you know what to emphasize.

3.   Work with the students to complete Relationships on day 12 in the *Student Book*. In the middle, write the name of the main person from the biography. Write the names of four other people from the biography in the outer circles. On each arrow list words that describe how the person at the base of the arrow feels about the person at the tip of the arrow. You may want to write the answers on a marker board as you discuss them, so the students can copy them. Then, the students can concentrate on the discussion.

4.	Discuss the following questions with your students:
	a) *Where and when does the story take place?*
	b) *Does this story remind you of any other story? Explain.*
	c) *What do you think is going to happen next? What clues help you predict what will happen next?*

Independent   Level 6/7/8

Focus: Vocabulary Builder - Prediction Practice

Preparation:
1.	Have a dictionary available.

Lesson:
1.	The students complete the activities in the *Student Book* and read the assigned pages for day 12 on their own.

2.	The directions instruct students to come and show you the completed Prediction Practice vocabulary assignment.

Teacher Directed   **Level 2/3**

Focus: Story Element Instruction - Character Connections

Lesson:

1.   Listen to your students read the assigned pages out loud to you. Use the Reading Strategies list and the Qualities of Good Reading list provided in the Appendix to help you know what to emphasize.

2.   Work with the students to complete Connections on day 13 in the *Student Book.* Write or draw the main person from the biography in the center. Write or draw five other people from the biography in the outer spots. On the lines between the center and the outer spots, write the main person's relationship to each listed person. (example: brother, father, friend). You may want to write the answers on a marker board as you discuss them, so the students can copy them. Then, the students can concentrate on the discussion, rather than on spelling and capitalization.

3.   Discuss the following questions with your students:
      a) *What feelings have you had while reading this biography? Why have you felt that way?*
      b) *What is the most exciting or strangest thing that has happened?*

Independent   **Level 4/5**

Focus: Story Element Extension - Character Problem Solver

Lesson:

1.   Tell the students to read the assigned pages for day 13 on their own.

2.   Tell them to complete Problem Solver on day 13 in their *Student Book* when they finish reading.

3.   The directions instruct students to come and show you the completed assignment.

Teacher Directed / Independent   **Level 6/7/8**

Focus: Story Element Discussion - Character Associations

Lesson:

1.   The students read the assigned pages for day 13 on their own.

2.	The students meet with you to discuss the following questions:
	a) *How does the writer create the atmosphere of the setting?*
	b) *Does the mood of the story change? Explain.*
	c) *What conflicts has this character experienced?*
	d) *How did the conflict affect the main character and the other characters in the story?*
	e) *What relationships does this main character have with the other characters in the story?*

3.	Introduce Associations in the *Student Book* for day 13. Have the students work to complete it on their own.

4.	The directions instruct students to come and show you the completed assignment.

Teacher Directed   **Level 2/3**

Focus: Godly Character Traits - Personal Assessment

Preparation:
1.   You will need an index card or note card for each of your students today.

Lesson:
1.   Review the following definitions and scripture passages:
   a) *Responsibility is being accountable to God and to others as you carry out your duties or obligations in a faithful way.*
   b) *Key Scripture verse: Each one should use whatever gift he has received to serve others, faithfully administering God's grace in its various forms. 1 Peter 4:10*
   c) *Diligence is continuing to work at something without giving up.*
   d) *Key Scripture verse: Let us not become weary in doing good, for at the proper time we will reap a harvest if we do not give up. Galations 6:9*

2.   Listen to your students read the assigned pages for day 14 out loud to you.

3.   Discuss the following questions with the students:
   a) *Which trait was shown less often by the book character, responsibility or diligence? Explain.*
   b) *Choose the trait that is harder for you to show, responsibility or diligence. Explain.*

4.   Hand out one index card to each student. Have the students write the trait they chose and 3 ways to work on showing the trait more often in their own lives.

5.   On the other side of the card, have the students draw themselves portraying this trait. The students may also write the matching Bible verse if you choose for them to do so.

6.   Have the students post their cards in a place where they will see them often.

Independent / Teacher Directed   **Level 4/5**

Focus: Godly Character Traits - Personal Assessment

Preparation:
1.   You will need an index card or note card for each of your students today.

Biography - Day 14

Lesson:

1. Tell the students to review the Godly Character Traits listed on day 9 in the *Student Book* on their own.

2. Have the students silently read the assigned pages in the biography for day 14, saving 3-4 pages to read aloud to you.

3. Meet with the students to finish the assignment for day 14.

4. Listen to your students read 3-4 pages. Use the Qualities of Good Reading list provided in the Appendix to help you know what to emphasize.

5. Discuss the following questions with the students:
    a) *Refer to day 9 in the Student Book. Choose the trait that is the hardest for you to show - responsibility, diligence, or initiative. Explain.*
    b) *Look at the Bible verse on day 9 in the Student Book for the trait you chose. How does the behavior of your book characters compare to this verse? Explain.*
    c) *What ways can you demonstrate the verse you chose in your own life?*

6. Hand out one index card to each student. Have students list actions they will take to help them live according to the verse they chose.

7. On the other side of the card, have the students divide the card into 3-4 sections, by drawing vertical lines. Instruct the students to break the chosen verse into sections and draw a quick picture or symbol to stand for each section of the verse. When the students look at the pictures, it should remind them of each part of the verse.

8. The Bible verse may be written on the bottom or on the back of the card if you choose to have the students do so.

9. Have the students post their cards in a place where they will see them often.

Independent   **Level 6/7/8**

Focus: Godly Character Traits - Personal Assessment

Preparation:
1. The students each need an index card or note card for today.

Unit 1

Lesson:

1. The students complete the activities in the *Student Book* and read the assigned pages for day 14 on their own.

2. The directions instruct the students to come and show you the completed assignment for day 14, including the completed index card or note card for posting.

Teacher Directed   **All Levels Together**

Preparation:

1.   Choose which **one** of the following project options you would like your students to complete as a culminating project for this genre. Each option is explained in detail on the pages that follow. For ease in planning, you should choose the same option for each of the students.
   a) **Option 1:** You may choose a character based project, which focuses on the Godly character trait for this genre. The directions for these projects are more general. The project does not involve any of the books from the unit. It does include a final reflection form.
   b) **Option 2:** You may choose a book based project, which is an individual project that is tailored to the student's individual level. Students will choose one of the books they read for this genre to use for the project. In order to choose this option, you must purchase *Book Projects to Send Home* by Lori Sanders and Linda Kimble for your particular students' levels. There is one book for each of the three levels. The project directions are very detailed and include a final reflection for each project.
   c) **Option 3:** Your final option is to choose a group project, which requires two or more students working together. This project is based on one common person the students all know and agree to interview.

2.   Have the directions for the project copied for each student. Make sure to read over the directions for the project option you chose in order to know what supplies you will need to have available for the projects.

3.   The plans allow 5 work days for the projects to be completed. This time allotment includes the planning and any presenting of the projects. The plans assume that the students will use only their normal amount of reading time to complete the projects.

Lesson:

1.   Say, *Today we will be starting our culminating project for biographies. You will have 5 days, counting today, to work on your project. Your projects are due at the end of that time on _____. (give due date)*

2.   Introduce the project you have chosen for this unit. Go through the directions and make sure students have a copy of the directions, so they can work as independently as possible. Show them where the needed supplies can be found.

3.   Then, have students read the assigned pages for day 15 to finish reading the biographies. Students may begin the project after the reading is complete.

Focus: <u>Godly Character Trait Project</u>   <u>Responsible Goals</u>

Project Notes:

1.   Teach students responsibility through the use of individual goals.

2.   Reproduce the two-page Responsible Goals Planning Form that is included in this guide. Review the definitions and key verses for the traits your students studied. Have students give examples of ways each trait can be shown.

3.   For <u>each</u> trait that was studied, the students need to make one individual goal. Goals may be based on a task that needs improvement or on a new task that you would like a student to begin performing. Tasks need to be clear and need to be performed daily.

4.   Students in level 2/3 will write 2 individual goals, one for the trait *responsibility* and one for the trait *diligence.*

5.   Students in level 4/5 will write 3 individual goals; one for the trait *responsibility,* one for the trait *diligence,* and one for the trait *initiative.*

6.   Students in level 6/7/8 will write 4 individual goals; one for the trait *responsibility,* one for the trait *diligence,* one for the trait *initiative,* and one for the trait *cautiousness.*

7.   Each student needs a container such as a can or a box. The students will track their goal progress by receiving "counters" to put in their containers each time their tasks are done correctly. Counters may be any item such as pennies, buttons, or pasta shells.

8.   You must work with the students to assign a counter value to their goals. The value you assign to each goal represents the number of "counters" the student receives for performing the task listed in the goal. Each time the task is performed correctly the student may put the number of counters assigned to that goal in their container. You may want to set one time each day to check goals.

9.   Students will track their goals for 5 days. Help each student choose a final count to reach by day 5. Make sure the count is attainable for the 5 day period. Reproduce the Responsible Goals Daily Count sheet included in this guide for each student. These half-sheets need to be posted for students to record the number of counters in their container each day.

10.   On day 19, students tally their final count. You may choose whether or not to reward students who reach their goal. Reproduce the reflection form included in this guide for each student to complete.

Responsible Goals Planning Form

Name: _____

Definitions:

RESPONSIBILITY is being accountable to God and to others as you carry out your duties or obligations in a faithful way.

DILIGENCE is continuing to work at something without giving up.

INITIATIVE is noticing something that needs to be done and taking care of it without being asked.

CAUTIOUSNESS is being watchful for evil, alert to danger, and careful in your approach to each situation.

Key Verses:

RESPONSIBILITY - Each one should use whatever gift he has received to serve others, faithfully administering God's grace in its various forms. 1 Peter 4:10

DILIGENCE - Let us not become weary in doing good, for at the proper time we will reap a harvest if we do not give up. Galations 6:9

INITIATIVE - Dear children, let us not love with words or tongue but with actions and truth. 1 John 3:18

CAUTIOUSNESS - Test everything. Hold on to the good. Avoid every kind of evil. 1 Thessalonians 5:21,22

Directions:

1. Circle the traits listed above that you studied in this unit. Your teacher will tell you which traits to circle, if you are unsure.

2. For each trait you circled, you need to make one individual goal. Goals may be based on a task that needs improvement or on a new task that you would like to begin performing. Tasks need to be clear and need to be performed daily.

3. Write your goals on the next page.

4. Your teacher will help you assign a *counter value* to each goal. Each time the task is performed correctly you may put the number of counters assigned to that goal in a container.

5. Your teacher will help you choose a *final count* to reach at the end of 5 days.

6. You will keep a record of your counters on the Daily Count Sheet.

Note: This planning form is continued on the next page.

Unit 1

Responsible Goals Planning Form
(continued)

Remember: You only need to complete the parts of the planning form that match the traits you circled on the previous page.

My individual goal for *responsibility* is_____

_____.

The value of this goal is _____ counters.

My individual goal for *diligence* is_____

_____.

The value of this goal is _____ counters.

My individual goal for *initiative* is_____

_____.

The value of this goal is _____ counters.

My individual goal for *cautiousness* is_____

_____.

The value of this goal is _____ counters.

My final count goal is _____ counters.

Show the teacher this page when you are finished.

Responsible Goals
Daily Count

Name: _____

Day 1	Day 2	Day 3	Day 4	Day 5
Number of Counters	Number of Counters	Number of Counters	Number of Counters	Number of Counters
_____	_____	_____	_____	_____

Final Goal: _____ counters

--- CUT --

Responsible Goals
Daily Count

Name: _____

Day 1	Day 2	Day 3	Day 4	Day 5
Number of Counters	Number of Counters	Number of Counters	Number of Counters	Number of Counters
_____	_____	_____	_____	_____

Final Goal: _____ counters

Focus: Book Based Project　　　　　　　**Individual Projects by Level**

Project Notes:

1.　This is an individual project tailored to the students' individual levels.

2.　In order to choose this option, you must purchase *Book Projects to Send Home* by Lori Sanders and Linda Kimble (McGraw-Hill, 2004) for your particular students' levels. There is one project book for each of the 3 levels. The books include detailed reproducible directions, work schedules, and reflection forms.

3.　The students each need to choose **one** book from those that **were read in this genre**. That book is the basis for the project.

4.　The project titles, corresponding page numbers, and levels in the *Book Projects to Send Home* books are listed below.

Use Grade 2 of *Book Projects to Send Home*　　　　　　**Level 2/3**

Project Title: Patchwork of Facts　　　　　　　Page Numbers: 31-34

Preparation:

1.　Read the project description box and the materials to provide section on p. 31. The rest of the items on p. 31 are <u>optional</u> ideas to use if you enjoy teaching through themes.

2.　Copy pp. 32-34 for your students. Save p. 34 for the students to complete on day 19 as a reflection on their project. This is listed in the plans for day 19.

3.　The sharing your patchwork of facts section on p. 32 will not be done at home.

Use Grade 4 of *Book Projects to Send Home*　　　　　　**Level 4/5**

Project Title: Three for Three　　　　　　　Page Numbers: 39-42

Preparation:

1.　Read the project description box and the materials to provide section on p. 39. The rest of the items on p. 39 are <u>optional</u> ideas to use if you enjoy teaching through themes.

2.　Copy pp. 40-42 and 47 for your students. Save p. 47 for the students to complete on day 19 as a reflection on their project. This is listed in the plans for day 19.

3.   Instruct students to think of the schedule on p. 41 as steps to complete, rather than a time frame for each part of the project. The students will be working solely on completing the projects for 5 reading days, instead of doing them gradually for 4 weeks as the project book suggests.

4.   The students have already completed the project requirements listed under week 1 in the schedule on p. 41. They will not need to choose another book to read.

5.   The presentation guidelines listed on p. 41 will not be used at home, unless you choose to do so.

Use Grade 5 of *Book Projects to Send Home*   Level 6/7/8

Note: Although these projects are listed for grade 5, they are very challenging to complete which makes them appropriate for level 6/7/8.

Project Title: It's in the News   Page Numbers: 23-26

Preparation:
1.   Read the project description box and the materials to provide section on p. 23. The rest of the items on p. 23 are optional ideas to use if you enjoy teaching through themes.

2.   Copy pp. 24-26 and 47 for your students. You may want to remove the "Dear Fifth Grader" greeting on p. 24. Save p. 47 for the students to complete on day 19 as a reflection on their projects. This is listed in the plans for day 19.

3.   Instruct students to think of the schedule on p. 25 as steps to complete, rather than a time frame for each part of the project. The students will be working solely on completing the projects for 5 reading days, instead of doing them gradually for 4 weeks as the project book suggests.

4.   The students have already completed the project requirements listed under week 1 on the schedule on p. 25. They will not need to choose another book to read.

5.   The presentation guidelines listed on p. 25 will not be used at home, except for the newscast portion.

Focus: Group Project   **Interview**

Project Notes:

1.   In order to choose this option, you must have two or more students (unless you are willing to do part of the project with your student).

2.   The group chooses **one** real-life person to interview. It must be someone the students have access to and can meet in person. If a personal meeting is not possible, students may do the interview on the telephone or by e-mail. A reproducible form is included in this guide for planning the interview.

3.   Group members decide when they will all be together to interview the person. Contact the person to set up the interview. Choose the earliest date possible, or choose another person to interview if the person is unable to meet with you soon. It is best if the interview is done in one meeting, rather than each group member contacting the person individually.

4.   The group decides on 3 categories of questions to ask the person.

5.   Each group member must be responsible for writing at least one question. All 3 categories should be utilized for the interview.

6.   During the interview, group members should take notes on the answers to their questions. You may require older students to take notes on the entire interview. Tape recording the interview is an option you may want to consider.

7.   After the interview, group members must plan a way to share what was learned at the interview. Remember: All parts of the project must be completed in 5 days. Possible ideas for sharing what was learned include the following:
      a) acting out the person's answers
      b) making a group poster of the questions and answers
      c) role-playing a news report about the person
      d) drawing a picture to go with each question and answer

8.   On day 19, students present the interview project.   Reproduce the reflection form included in this guide for each student to complete.

Interview Planning Sheet

Name:_____

Person to be interviewed: _____

Date of the interview (as soon as possible): _____

3 categories of questions for the interview: 1. _____

2. _____ 3. _____

Question(s) I plan to ask this person and the category of the question:

_____

_____

_____

_____

(Meet to make sure group members' questions are not the same and that all
3 categories are included in the interview.)

Answers to the questions: _____

_____

_____

_____

_____

(Continue on another sheet of paper if necessary.)

Group plan for presenting the information gained through the interview: _____

_____

_____

Independent / Teacher Directed   **All Levels**

Focus: Project Work

Preparation:
1.   For details, read the directions for the project option you chose.

Lesson:
1.   Check students' progress to make sure each student understands what to do and is on schedule to finish by day 19.

2.   Meet with students as a group, if this is needed.

Independent / Teacher Directed   **All Levels**

Focus: Project Completion

Preparation:
1.   For details, read the directions for the project option you chose.

2.   Have the reflection forms copied for each student to match the project option you chose.

Lesson:
1.   Briefly check students' progress. Students should finish their projects today.

2.   Have students share their projects with each other or with you.

3.   Hand out the reflection form that matches the project option you chose. Have the students complete the reflection and show you.

4.   You are ready to choose the next genre your students will study. Look ahead to prepare the kickoff for the upcoming genre.

Responsible Goals Reflection

1. On my goals, I felt that I did a good job of _____

_____.

2. I think that I could have done a better job of_____

_____.

3. If I could do the goals project again, I would _____

_____

_____.

4. From working on my goals these past 5 days, I learned_____

_____

_____.

5. My favorite part of the goals project was _____

_____

_____.

_____   _____
        Signature of student   Date

Interview Reflection

1. On the interview project, I felt that I did a good job of _____

_____.

2. I think that I could have done a better job of_____

_____.

3. If I could do the interview project again, I would _____

_____

_____.

4. From the interview project, I learned _____

_____

_____

_____.

_____   _____
Signature of student   Date

Adventure

GENRE: ADVENTURE

Definition:

    Suspenseful stories filled with action and excitement.

Common Characteristics:

1. Has characters that may be realistic or fantastical.
2. Contains characters who are faced with a difficult task to accomplish.
3. Has a conflict that may include good versus evil.
4. Requires characters to show courage and take risks.
5. May include a setting that focuses on an unfamiliar "world" or place.

Story Element Emphasis: Problem or Conflict

Definition:

    The issues the characters must face as the pressures in the story continue to mount. Conflicts may be character against character, character against nature, character against society, or character against himself.

Godly Character Trait Emphasis: Fear of the Lord

Definition:

    Revering the Lord and his commands and believing the Lord can turn harm into good for those who trust in him.

Subqualities:

1. respect for authority
2. standing against peer pressure
3. deliberation

Teacher Directed   **All Levels Together**

Focus: Genre Kickoff

Preparation:

1.   The goal of the kickoff is to introduce students of all ages to the upcoming genre in a fun and entertaining manner.

2.   Decide how much time you want to spend on the kickoff. You can spend one normal reading class period, several hours, or even a whole day. After the kickoff, you begin with day 1 in the teacher's plans.

3.   Read through the list of ideas below and choose those that interest you for this genre's kickoff. You are welcome to add your own ideas that fit within this genre. Refer to the cover page for a definition and common characteristics for each genre. Introduce the name and definition of the genre to begin the kickoff.

Possible Kickoff Ideas:

1.   Plan a treasure hunt for the students. Either write numbered clues for the students to follow or draw a treasure map on a cut up paper bag. Have a "treasure" that fits with the adventure genre at the end of the hunt. For example, have the treasure be adventure books that the students will be reading or golden-colored pencils.

2.   Create a grab bag of various objects. Students reach in and grab 3 objects. They must tell a short adventure story that contains the 3 items they grabbed. It is helpful for you to discuss the adventure genre and model this activity first.

3.   Read a short adventure story out loud. Have the students imitate or pantomime the actions of the main character.

4.   Create a scavenger hunt for the students. The directions might instruct the students to return with some of the following items: an object that has to do with travel, something from another country, a map of some sort, something to keep your head dry, an object to hold drinking water, a place to write your thoughts, something to write with, an item that is special to you, shoes that are good for walking, something to protect you from wind and rain, and something to carry all of your items.

5.   Play a board game that involves action, suspense, and risk like *You Sunk My Battleship* or *Risk.*

6.   Create a *Choose Your Own Adventure* scenario as a group. Use large paper and start with a box at the top that contains one setting and a task which leads to 2 possible choices. Have the students help you think of the choices to list. Then, those 2 choices lead to 2 more choices <u>each</u> and so on. Depending on the choices you make, you can have a variety of scenarios. Have some of the scenarios end with completion of the beginning task and have others end with failure to complete the task.

7.   Plan an overall "mission" for the students to complete. <u>Do not</u> tell students anything about the mission. Break the "mission" down into enough parts for each student to have a task. Hand each student one "secret task" in writing in a sealed envelope. Set a time limit to complete the tasks. For example, the "mission" could be a picnic lunch. The tasks could include getting a blanket, making sandwiches, preparing the drinks, preparing any other items to eat, getting the picnic basket, providing the plates, cups, napkins, and silverware, and packing the bug spray. At the end of the time limit, have students look over the items and guess the mission. Then, complete it!

8.   Give students a torn paper bag or parchment paper. On the paper, have students draw an adventure map of a fictitious place. The map should show a task to accomplish, and include symbols, arrows, and drawings of landmarks.

9.   Make up a place along with its climate, geographical features, what lives there, and any other details that may be important. Do not share any information about the place with the students, except for the name of the place and a mission for the students to accomplish in this place. Tell students to list 5 items to pack for an adventure on _____. Tell students their mission is to _____.

       After students have listed their 5 items, share the information about the place. For example, the average temperature is 40 degrees F., mainly bears and fish live there, it has many mountains, there is plenty of fresh water, and it rains often. Check to see which items each student packed that would help them on this particular adventure.

10.   Give each student a map of the United States or a map of the world. Students should all be using a map of the same place. You need to have your own map as well. Call out map coordinates and have students follow along from place to place. At the end, see who has followed the coordinates correctly and reached the same final destination as you. It is best to start out with only one or two sets of coordinates and add more as students are successful. Younger students can be paired with older students as needed.

Questions to discuss at the end of the kickoff:

1.   What are some characteristics of the adventure genre? (Refer to the definition on the cover page for this genre.)

2.   What did you learn about adventure from today's activities?

3.   Why do adventure stories fit under the fantasy category?

4.   Why do we read adventure stories?

Adventure - Day 1

<u>**Teacher Directed**</u>   <u>**All Levels Together**</u>

Focus: Prereading Activity - Partial Picture Disclosure

Preparation:
1.   Prior to meeting with the students for day 1, follow the directions for *Getting Started* listed in the back of this guide.

2.   Have the first book and one *Assigned Reading Calendar* ready for each student.

3.   You will need to use sticky notes to put on half of the cover or on half of another illustration in the book for each student before today's lesson. Then, students will have to predict what is under the covered half of the illustration.

Lesson:
1.   Say, *Today we will be doing a prereading activity to help you think about the next book you will be reading.*

2.   Give students the first book they will be reading for this genre. It should have half of an illustration covered as noted in the preparation section above.

3.   Discuss the following questions with the students:
      a) *What do you think the other half of the picture will show?*
      b) *Who do you think you will see?*
      c) *Which colors do you think you will notice?*
      d) *What animals or plants do you think you might see?*
      e) *What type of place is in the illustration?*
      f) *What do you think is happening in the picture?*

4.   Have students remove one sticky note at a time. As they remove each note, have them revise any previous guesses as more of the picture is revealed.

5.   When the entire illustration has been revealed, discuss the following questions:
      a) *After looking at the whole picture, what do you know about the story?*
      b) *What clues do you notice in the picture that show this is an adventure story?*

6.   Read the synopsis and quickly page through through the book.

7.   Have students open their *Student Books* to the *Assigned Reading Calendar* for this genre. Help each student fill in the page numbers to be read for days 1-5. Have students read the assigned pages for day 1 on their own.

Teacher Directed **Level 2/3**

Focus: Story Discussion and Optional Phonics <u>or</u> Vocabulary Work

Preparation:
1. You may choose to have students at this level review phonics <u>or</u> complete a vocabulary assignment. Use your own program for the phonics review. Refer to the Appendix for a reproducible vocabulary assignment. The lesson on this day is much shorter to compensate for the additional time you may spend on phonics or on vocabulary work.

Lesson:
1. Optional phonics or vocabulary work

2. Listen to your students read the assigned pages out loud to you. Use the Reading Strategies list and the Qualities of Good Reading list provided in the Appendix to help you know what to emphasize.

3. Discuss the following questions with your students:
   a) *Are the characters realistic or make-believe? How do you know?*
   b) *Who do you know that is similar to the characters in the story? Explain.*
   c) *Would you like to live in the setting of this story? Why, or why not?*
   d) *What do you like and dislike about the setting of the story?*

Independent / Teacher Directed **Level 4/5**

Focus: Story Element Instruction - Conflict Response

Lesson:
1. Tell the students to read the assigned pages on their own, leaving 3-4 pages to read aloud to you.

2. Listen to your students read several pages. Use the Qualities of Good Reading list provided in the Appendix to help you know what to emphasize.

3. Work with the students to complete Conflict Response on day 2 in the *Student Book*. Write the conflict or problem in the middle. List the names of 4 important characters in the outer circles. Then, write each character's response to the conflict on the line connecting the character's name to the center circle. You may want to write answers on a marker board as you discuss them, so the students can copy them. Then, the students can concentrate on the discussion, rather than on spelling and capitalization.

4. Discuss the following questions with your students:
   a) *How is this place similar to our world?*
   b) *How is it different from our world?*

Independent   **Level 6/7/8**

Focus: Vocabulary Builder - Word Works

Preparation:
1. Have a dictionary and a thesaurus available.

Lesson:
1. The students complete the activities in the *Student Book* and read the assigned pages for day 2 on their own.

2. The directions instruct students to come and show you the completed Word Works vocabulary assignment.

Teacher Directed   **Level 2/3**

Focus: Story Element Instruction - Problem / Solution Story Map

Lesson:
1.   Listen to your students read the assigned pages out loud to you. Use the Reading Strategies list and the Qualities of Good Reading list provided in the Appendix to help you know what to emphasize.

2.   Work with the students to complete the Story Map on day 3 in the *Student Book*. You may want to write the answers on a marker board as you discuss them, so the students can copy them. Then, the students can concentrate on the discussion rather than on spelling and capitalization.

Independent   **Level 4/5**

Focus: Story Element Extension - Problem Comparison

Lesson:
1.   Tell the students to read the assigned pages for day 3 on their own.

2.   Tell them to complete the Problem Comparison on day 3 in their *Student Book* when they finish reading.

3.   The directions instruct students to come and show you the completed assignment.

Teacher Directed / Independent   **Level 6/7/8**

Focus: Story Element Discussion - Conflict Summary

Lesson:
1.   The students read the assigned pages for day 3 on their own.

2.   Say, *There are 4 types of conflict that happen in stories. We will discuss each type today.*

3.   Say, *The first type is character against character or person against person.* (For example, this could be a disagreement between two people with differing viewpoints.) Discuss the following questions with the students:
      a) *What is an example of this type of conflict from your life?*
      b) *Have you noticed this type of conflict in the book you are reading? Explain.*

4. Say, *The second type is character against nature or person against nature.* (For example, this could be an encounter you had with a storm or a natural disaster.) Discuss the following questions with the students:
    a) *What is an example of this type of conflict from your life?*
    b) *Have you noticed this type of conflict in the book you are reading? Explain.*

5. Say, *The third type is character against society or person against society.* (For example, this could be any belief system or opinion you hold that conflicts with the majority opinion.) Discuss the following questions with the students:
    a) *What is an example of this type of conflict from your life?*
    b) *Have you noticed this type of conflict in the book you are reading? Explain.*

6. Say, *The fourth type is character or person against himself.* (For example, this could be an internal conflict as you are torn between two choices. It could also be a struggle against a personal weakness you are trying to overcome.) Discuss the following questions with the students:
    a) *What is an example of this type of conflict from your life?*
    b) *Have you noticed this type of conflict in the book you are reading? Explain.*
    c) *If you could tell the characters one thing, what would you tell them?*

7. Introduce the Conflict Summary in the *Student Book* under day 3.

8. Have the students finish day 3 on their own.

9. The directions instruct students to come and show you the completed assignment.

Teacher Directed   **Level 2/3**

Focus: Godly Character Traits - Examples

Preparation:
1.   Think of examples you can share from your own life for each of the following traits: *fear of the Lord* and *respect for authority.* (Definitions are listed in the lesson below.)

Lesson:
1.   Introduce the following definition and scripture passage for *fear of the Lord:*
        a) *Fear of the Lord* is revering the Lord and his commands, and believing the Lord can turn harm into good for those who trust in him.
        b) *Key Scripture verse:* It is the Lord your God you must follow, and him you must revere. Keep his commands and obey him; serve him and hold fast to him. Deuteronomy 13:4

2.   Share an example of *fear of the Lord* from your own life.

3.   Help the students think of an example of *fear of the Lord* from their own lives.

4.   Introduce the following definition and scripture passage for *respect for authority:*
        a) *Respect for authority* is making sure your words and your actions honor those who are responsible for you.
        b) *Key Scripture verse:* Listen to advice and accept instruction, and in the end you will be wise. Many are the plans in a man's heart, but it is the Lord's purpose that prevails. Proverbs 19:20,21

5.   Repeat steps 2 and 3 for the trait *respect for authority.*

6.   Instruct your students to search for examples of *fear of the Lord* and *respect for authority* as they read part or all of the assigned pages out loud to you. Use the Reading Strategies list and the Qualities of Good Reading list provided in the Appendix to help you know what to emphasize.

7.   Discuss the following questions with your students:
        a) *How do the characters show fear of the Lord? Or respect for authority?*
        b) *Did the characters show the opposite traits of fear of man or rebelliousness? Explain.*
        c) *What could the characters do differently to show more fear of the Lord or respect for authority?*

Independent / Teacher Directed   **Level 4/5**

Focus: Godly Character Traits - Examples

Lesson:

1.   Tell the students to read and complete the Godly Character Sheet on day 4 in the *Student Book* on their own.

2.   The students also silently read the assigned pages for day 4, leaving 3-4 pages to read aloud to you.

3.   The students should come and show you when both are completed.

4.   Review the Godly Character Sheet on day 4 in the *Student Book*, so both the students and you will know what traits you are searching for in the adventure book. *(fear of the Lord, respect for authority,* and *standing against peer pressure)*

5.   Listen to your students read 3-4 pages aloud. Use the Qualities of Good Reading list provided in the Appendix to help you know what to emphasize.

6.   Discuss the following questions with the students:
        a) *How did the characters show fear of the Lord?*
        b) *How did the characters show respect for authority?*
        c) *How did the characters show standing against peer pressure?*
        d) *Did the characters show the opposite traits of fear of man? Or rebelliousness? Or following the crowd? Explain.*
        e) *What might Jesus have done differently if He had been a character in the book?*

Independent   **Level 6/7/8**

Focus: Godly Character Traits - Examples

Lesson:

1.   The students complete the activities in the *Student Book* and read the assigned pages for day 4 on their own.

2.   The directions instruct students to come and show you the completed Godly Character page.

Teacher Directed / Independent   **Level 2/3**

Focus: Comprehension Check - Bits and Pieces

Lesson:

1.   Go over the directions for Bits and Pieces on day 5 in the *Student Book*. Students complete this assignment alone after reading the assigned pages.

2.   Listen to your students read part of the assigned pages out loud to you. Use the Reading Strategies list and the Qualities of Good Reading list provided in the Appendix to help you know what to emphasize.

3.   The students finish the assigned reading and complete Bits and Pieces on their own. The directions instruct the students to come and show you the completed assignment.

Independent   **Level 4/5**

Focus: Comprehension Check - Bookmark

Preparation:

1.   Have tag board or heavier paper cut like a blank bookmark for this level's assignment.

Lesson:

1.   Tell the students to complete the Bookmark on day 5 in the *Student Book* on their own.

2.   The students also read the assigned pages for day 5 on their own. You may choose to have the students leave 3-4 pages to read aloud to you.

3.   The directions instruct the students to come and show you the completed assignment.

Independent   **Level 6/7/8**

Focus: Comprehension Check - Book Cover

Preparation:

1.   Cut tag board or regular paper in the size of a blank book cover.

Lesson:

1. The students complete the activities in the *Student Book* and read the assigned pages for day 5 on their own.

2. The directions instruct students to come and show you the completed Book Cover.

Teacher Directed   **All Levels Together**

Focus: Prereading Activity - Prediction Pick

Preparation:
1.   If students are beginning new books today, make sure to have the number of pages to be read each day calculated and have those books ready to hand out. (See the *Getting Started* section, item #7, in the back of this guide for details.)

2.   If students are <u>not</u> beginning new books today, they use the books they are currently reading for today's activities.

Lesson:
1.   Say, *Today we will be doing a prereading activity to help you think about the next book you will be reading or the next part of the book you will be reading.*

2.   Give students a little time to look at the cover, read the synopsis, and quickly page through the book.

3.   Say, *Today we will be looking for important words in our books.*

4.   Discuss the following questions with the students:
       a) *How do we decide if a word is important or not?* (if we see it often in the story; if it names a character, place, mood, or problem)
       b) *What kinds of words would not be important?* (words that do not have much meaning by themselves, like *and, I ,* or, *what*)
       c) *What are some important words in your book?* (Have students share their ideas. Guide the students to see that words that are important should have meaning on their own and should give a clue to the story.)

5.   Have students open their *Student Books* to the Prediction Pick on day 6. The students will be listing important words from their books. Then, they will categorize the words by guessing their meaning in the story.

6.   Students should come and show you the completed assignment.

7.   Help students update their *Assigned Reading Calendar* for days 6-10.

8.   Have students read the assigned pages for day 6 on their own.

Teacher Directed   **Level 2/3**

Focus: Story Discussion and Optional Phonics <u>or</u> Vocabulary Work

Preparation:

1.   You may choose to have students at this level review phonics <u>or</u> complete a vocabulary assignment. Use your own program for the phonics review. Refer to the Appendix for a reproducible vocabulary assignment. The lesson on this day is much shorter to compensate for the additional time you may spend on phonics or on vocabulary work.

Lesson:

1.   Optional phonics or vocabulary work

2.   Listen to your students read the assigned pages out loud to you. Use the Reading Strategies list and the Qualities of Good Reading list provided in the Appendix to help you know what to emphasize.

3.   Discuss the following questions with your students:
        a) *How is the place in the book similar to our world?*
        b) *How is it different from our world?*
        c) *Does this story remind you of any other story? If so, what is it and why does it remind you of this story?*

Independent / Teacher Directed   **Level 4/5**

Focus: Story Element Instruction - Problem and Solution

Lesson:

1.   Tell the students to read the assigned pages on their own, leaving 3-4 pages to read aloud to you.

2.   Listen to your students read several pages. Use the Qualities of Good Reading list provided in the Appendix to help you know what to emphasize.

3.   Work with the students to complete What Would I Do on day 7 in the *Student Book.* You may want to write the ideas on a marker board as you discuss them, so the students can copy them. Then, the students can concentrate on the discussion rather than on spelling and capitalization.

4.   Discuss the following questions with your students:
      a) *Which characters would be good influences? Explain.*
      b) *Which characters would be bad influences? Explain.*

Independent   ## Level 6/7/8

Focus: Vocabulary Builder - Word Works

Preparation:
1.   Have a dictionary and a thesaurus available.

Lesson:
1.   The students complete the activities in the *Student Book* and read the assigned pages for day 7 on their own.

2.   The directions instruct the students to come and show you the completed Word Works vocabulary assignment.

Teacher Directed / Independent   **Level 2/3**

Focus: Story Element Instruction - Problem and Solution

Lesson:
1.   Listen to your students read the assigned pages out loud to you. Use the Reading Strategies list and the Qualities of Good Reading list provided in the Appendix to help you know what to emphasize.

2.   Discuss the following questions with the students:
        a) *What is the biggest problem in the story?*
        b) *What are some ways you can think of to solve the problem?*
        c) *What advice would you give the main character about how to solve the problem?*

3.   Assign the students Simple Suggestions on day 8 in the *Student Book* to complete on their own. The students should draw the solution they already discussed with you.

4.   The directions instruct the students to come and show you the completed assignment.

Independent   **Level 4/5**

Focus: Story Element Extension - Simple Suggestions

Lesson:
1.   Tell the students to read the assigned pages for day 8 on their own.

2.   Tell them to complete Simple Suggestions on day 8 in their *Student Book* when they finish reading.

3.   The directions instruct the students to come and show you the completed assignment.

Teacher Directed / Independent   **Level 6/7/8**

Focus: Story Element Discussion - Conflict and Resolution

Lesson:
1.   The students read the assigned pages for day 8 on their own.

Unit 2

2.   The students meet with you to discuss the following questions:
     a) *Would you like to live in the setting of the story? Why, or why not?*
     b) *How would your life be different if you did live in the setting of the story?*
     c) *What were the four types of conflict that we discussed on day 3?* (Remind
        the students if needed: character against character, character against
        nature, character against society, and character against himself.)
     d) *What is one of the main conflicts in the story right now?*
     e) *Which of the 4 types of conflict is the main conflict in the story?*
     f) *What are some possible solutions to the conflict?*
     g) *How would you decide what would be the best solution to the conflict?*

3.   Introduce Solution Search on day 8 in the *Student Book*. Make sure the
     students understand what to do. Then, have the students work on their own.

4.   The directions instruct the students to come and show you the completed
     assignment.

Teacher Directed   **Level 2/3**

Focus: Godly Character Traits - Biblical Comparisons

Preparation:
1.   Find a short children's book of the Bible story about Jonah and the big fish. Otherwise, you need to read the story directly from the Bible in Jonah chapters 1-3.

Lesson:
1.   Review the following definitions and scripture passages:
   a) *Fear of the Lord is revering the Lord and his commands, and believing the Lord can turn harm into good for those who trust in him.*
   b) *Key Scripture verse: It is the Lord your God you must follow, and him you must revere. Keep his commands and obey him; serve him and hold fast to him. Deuteronomy 13:4*
   c) *Respect for authority is making sure your words and your actions honor those who are responsible for you.*
   d) *Key Scripture verse: Listen to advice and accept instruction, and in the end you will be wise. Many are the plans in a man's heart, but it is the Lord's purpose that prevails. Proverbs 19:20,21*

2.   Read the children's book, or the Bible passage Jonah chapters 1-3, about Jonah and the big fish. Instruct your students to listen for examples of *fear of the Lord* and *respect for authority* in the story being read.

3.   Discuss the following question with your students:
   a) *How did Jonah's actions show fear of the Lord and respect for authority?*

4.   Record the students' responses in the *Student Book* on day 9 under the Biblical Character column. (Possible answers include the following: *Fear of the Lord* by telling the men on the boat that he was running from the Lord, and they should throw him overboard to stop the storm; *Respect for authority* in Jonah's prayer to the Lord when he was inside the fish; *Fear of the Lord* to do what God asked Jonah to do, even though Jonah didn't really want to do it.)

5.   Listen to your students read the assigned pages for day 9 out loud to you. Remind the students to be searching for examples of *fear of the Lord* and *respect for authority.*

6.   Using the questions listed on the next page, compare Jonah with the main character in the adventure novel. Record the responses on day 9 in the *Student Book* under the Book Character column.

a) *How does the character in your book show fear of the Lord and respect for authority?*

b) *What would the Biblical character, Jonah, do differently from the character in your book?*

Independent / Teacher Directed   **Level 4/5**

Focus: Godly Character Traits - Biblical Comparison

Preparation:

1.   Find a short children's book of the Bible story about Elijah and the prophets of Baal. Otherwise, the students read the passage directly from the Bible in 1 Kings 18:16-45.

Lesson:

1.   Tell the students to review the Godly Character Traits listed on day 9 in the *Student Book* on their own. Then, have the students silently read the story of Elijah and the prophets of Baal, either from the book you provided or from the Bible in 1 Kings 18:16-45.

2.   Have students do their best to complete the Biblical Character column on the Godly Character Story Sheet for Elijah on day 9 in the *Student Book.*

3.   Students silently read the assigned pages in the adventure book for day 9, saving 3 or 4 pages to read aloud to you.

4.   The students meet with you to finish the assignment for day 9. Listen to your students read several pages. Use the Qualities of Good Reading list provided in the Appendix to help you know what to emphasize.

5.   Discuss the following questions with the students as you review what they have already done in the *Student Book* for day 9. Complete the remaining columns in the *Student Book* for day 9.

a) *How did Elijah 's behavior show fear of the Lord, respect for authority, or standing against peer pressure?* (Possible answers include the following: *Fear of the Lord* when Elijah told King Ahab that he and his family had made trouble for Israel by following the Baals; *Fear of the Lord* when Elijah told the people of Israel that they needed to follow the one true God; *Respect for authority* in the way Elijah spoke to God when he asked God to show the people that he was God in Israel; *Standing against peer pressure* by being one of the only prophets of God left in Israel, while there were 450 prophets of Baal and 400 prophets of Asherah.)

b) *How did the person in your book behave like the Biblical character, Elijah?* (List the answers in the *Student Book*.)

c) *How did the person in your book behave differently from Elijah?* (List the answers in the *Student Book*.)

d) *Which trait was shown least often by the book character?* (Explain in the *Student Book*.)

Independent   Level 6/7/8

Focus: Godly Character Traits - Biblical Comparison

Preparation:

1.   The students need a Bible for today's lesson.

Lesson:

1.   The students complete the activities in the *Student Book* and read the assigned pages for day 9 on their own.

2.   The directions instruct the students to come and show you the completed Godly Character Story page. (Possible examples of the traits in Nehemiah include the following: *Fear of the Lord* by praying to the Lord about the enemies and knowing the Lord could see all that was happening; *Respect for authority* by the laborers listening to Nehemiah; *Standing against peer pressure* by not quitting the rebuilding of the wall, even though their enemies were attacking them; *Deliberation* in planning for half of the men to work on the wall while the other half fought; *Deliberation* to come up with a plan of blowing the trumpet to unite the workers when needed).

Teacher Directed   <u>**All Levels Together**</u>

Focus: Comprehension Check - Listen Up

Lesson:

1. Say, *When you read an adventure book, the author makes sure to have suspenseful parts in the story that leave you wondering what will happen next. Today you will be choosing parts of your book to share that you think are very suspenseful.*

2. Have the students complete the Listen Up planning form for day 10 in the *Student Book.*

3. Have each student share the parts they chose with the group.

4. Allow group members to ask questions after the person has shared about the book.

5. When all students have finished sharing, have students read the assigned pages in their adventure book for day 10 on their own.

Adventure - Day 11

Focus: Prereading Activity - Object Riddle

Preparation:
1. If students are beginning new books today, make sure to have the number of pages to be read each day calculated and have those books ready to hand out. (See the *Getting Started* section, item #7, in the back of this guide for details.)

2. If students are not beginning new books today, they use the books they are currently reading for today's activities.

Lesson:
1. Say, *Today we will be doing a prereading activity to help you think about the next book you will be reading or the next part of the book you will be reading. As we are prereading today, we will be searching for one object that seems to be very important to the story. Watch for an item that is mentioned in your book repeatedly.*

2. Say, *Do not share what the object is with the rest of the group. We will be writing a riddle about your chosen object for the group to guess later.*

3. Discuss the following questions with the students:
    a) *Take time to look carefully at the cover. What kind of place is shown? What characters do you notice? What is happening in the picture?*
    b) *Read the synopsis of the book. What important names or places are mentioned? Do you notice any objects from the cover that are mentioned in the synopsis too?* (Reminder: Keep the object a secret from the group.)
    c) *Page through your book and look for important words. Remember, important words are words that give clues to the story, even when the word stands alone.* (Have students share several important words from their books.)
    d) *Pay careful attention to any words that you see again and again. Are any of these words the same object that you noticed on the cover or in the synopsis?* (Reminder: Keep the object a secret from the rest of the group.)

4. Have students open their *Student Book* to the Object Riddle on day 11. Follow the directions to complete the Object Riddle.

5. When the students are done, they take turns sharing their riddles with the rest of the group. Group members try to guess the objects from the riddles.

6. Help students update their *Assigned Reading Calendar* for days 11-15. Have students read the assigned pages for day 11 on their own.

Teacher Directed   **Level 2/3**

Focus: Story Discussion and Optional Phonics <u>or</u> Vocabulary Work

Preparation:
1.   You may choose to have students at this level review phonics <u>or</u> complete a vocabulary assignment. Use your own program for the phonics review. Refer to the Appendix for a reproducible vocabulary assignment. The lesson on this day is much shorter to compensate for the additional time you may spend on phonics or on vocabulary work.

Lesson:
1.   Optional phonics or vocabulary work

2.   Listen to your students read the assigned pages out loud to you. Use the Reading Strategies list and the Qualities of Good Reading list provided in the Appendix to help you know what to emphasize.

3.   Discuss the following questions with your students:
         a) *Is the setting in the story realistic? Why, or why not?*
         b) *If you could tell the characters one thing to help them, what would you tell them?*
         c) *What moods does the book make you feel? Why does it make you feel that way?*

Independent / Teacher Directed   **Level 4/5**

Focus: Story Element Instruction - Conflict

Preparation:
1.   Be ready to share a real example from your own life to illustrate each of the 4 types of conflict: person against person, person against nature, person against society, and person against himself.

Lesson:
1.   Tell the students to read the assigned pages alone, leaving 3-4 pages to read aloud to you.

2.   Listen to your students read several pages. Use the Qualities of Good Reading list provided in the Appendix to help you know what to emphasize.

3. Discuss the following questions with the students:
   a) *Would you like to live in the setting from your story? Why, or why not?*
   b) *What changes would you make to the setting if you had your choice?*

4. Say, *There are 4 types of conflict that happen in stories. We will discuss each type today.*

5. Say, *The first type is character against character or person against person.*
   Give the students an example of this type of conflict from your own life. (For example, this could be a disagreement between two people with differing viewpoints.) Discuss the following questions with the students:
   a) *What is an example of this type of conflict from your life?*
   b) *Have you noticed this type of conflict in the book you are reading? Explain.*

6. Say, *The second type is character against nature or person against nature.*
   Give the students an example of this type of conflict from your own life. (For example, this could be an encounter you had with a storm or a natural disaster.) Discuss the following questions with the students:
   a) *What is an example of this type of conflict from your life?*
   b) *Have you noticed this type of conflict in the book you are reading? Explain.*

7. Say, *The third type is character against society or person against society.*
   Give the students an example of this type of conflict from your own life. (For example, this could be any belief system or opinion you hold that conflicts with the majority opinion.) Discuss the following questions with the students:
   a) *What is an example of this type of conflict from your life?*
   b) *Have you noticed this type of conflict in the book you are reading? Explain.*

8. Say, *The fourth type is character or person against himself* . Give the students an example of this type of conflict from your own life. (For example, this could be an internal struggle as you are torn between two choices. It could also be a fight to overcome a personal weakness.) Discuss the following questions with the students:
   a) *What is an example of this type of conflict from your life?*
   b) *Have you noticed this type of conflict in the book you are reading? Explain.*

Independent   **Level 6/7/8**

Focus: Vocabulary Builder - Word Works

Preparation:
1. Have a dictionary and a thesaurus available.

Unit 2

Lesson :

1. The students complete the activities in the *Student Book* and read the assigned pages for day 12 on their own.

2. The directions instruct the students to come and show you the completed Word Works vocabulary assignment.

Teacher Directed   **Level 2/3**

Focus: Story Element Instruction - Problem and Solution

Lesson:

1. Listen to your students read part or all of the assigned pages out loud to you. Use the Reading Strategies list and the Qualities of Good Reading list provided in the Appendix to help you know what to emphasize.

2. Work with the students to complete Story Problems on day 13 in the *Student Book.* You may want to write the answers on a marker board as you discuss them, so the students can copy them. Then, the students can concentrate on the discussion rather than on spelling and capitalization.

Independent   **Level 4/5**

Focus: Story Element Extension - Conflict Questions

Lesson:

1. Tell the students to read the assigned pages for day 13 on their own.

2. Tell them to complete the Conflict Questions on day 13 in their *Student Books* when they finish reading.

3. The directions instruct the students to come and show you the completed assignment.

Teacher Directed / Independent   **Level 6/7/8**

Focus: Story Element Discussion - Conflict and Resolution

Lesson:

1. The students read the assigned pages for day 13 on their own.

2. The students meet with you to discuss the following questions:
   a) *What kind of relationship do the characters have in the story? Explain.*
   b) *How could the conflict or problem be solved more easily?*

3. Have students open their *Student Books* to day 13. Work with the students to complete Rising Action.

Teacher Directed   **Level 2/3**

Focus: Godly Character Traits - Personal Assessment

Preparation:
1.   You will need an index card or note card for each of your students today.

Lesson:
1.   Review the following definitions and scripture passages:
   a) _Fear of the Lord_ is revering the Lord and his commands, and believing the Lord can turn harm into good for those who trust in him.
   b) _Key Scripture verse_: It is the Lord your God you must follow, and him you must revere. Keep his commands and obey him; serve him and hold fast to him. Deuteronomy 13:4
   c) _Respect for authority_ is making sure your words and your actions honor those who are responsible for you.
   d) _Key Scripture verse:_ Listen to advice and accept instruction, and in the end you will be wise. Many are the plans in a man's heart, but it is the Lord's purpose that prevails. Proverbs 19:20,21

2.   Listen to your students read the assigned pages for day 14 out loud to you.

3.   Discuss the following questions with the students:
   a) _Which trait was shown less often by the book character, fear of the Lord or respect for authority? Explain._
   b) _Choose the trait that is harder for you to show, fear of the Lord or respect for authority. Explain._

4.   Hand out one index card to each student. Have the students write the trait they chose and 3 ways to work on showing the trait more often in their own lives.

5.   On the other side of the card, have the students draw themselves portraying this trait. The students may also write the matching Bible verse if you choose for them to do so.

6.   Have the students post their cards in a place where they will see them often.

Independent / Teacher Directed   **Level 4/5**

Focus: Godly Character Traits - Personal Assessment

Preparation:

1.   You will need an index card or note card for each of your students today.

Lesson:

1.   Tell the students to review the Godly Character Traits listed on day 9 in the
        Student Book on their own.

2.   Have the students read the assigned pages in the novel for day 14, saving
        3-4 pages to read aloud to you.

3.   Meet with the students to finish the assignment for day 14.

4.   Listen to your students read 3-4 pages. Use the Qualities of Good Reading list
        provided in the Appendix to help you know what to emphasize.

5.   Discuss the following questions with the students:
        a) *Refer to day 9 in the Student Book. Choose the trait that is the hardest for
           you to show - fear of the Lord, respect for authority, or standing against peer
           pressure. Explain.*
        b) *Look at the Bible verse on day 9 in the Student Book for the trait you chose.
           How does the behavior of the characters in your book compare to this verse?
           Explain.*
        c) *What ways can you demonstrate the verse you chose in your own life?*

6.   Hand out one index card to each student. Have students list actions they will
        take to help them live according to the verse they chose.

7.   On the other side of the card, have the students divide the card into 3-4
        sections, by drawing vertical lines. Instruct the students to break the chosen
        verse into sections and draw a quick picture or symbol to stand for each section
        of the verse. When the students look at the pictures, it should remind them of
        each part of the verse.

8.   The Bible verse may be written on the bottom or on the back of the card if you
        choose to have the students do so.

9.   Have the students post their cards in a place where they will see them often.

Independent   <u>**Level 6/7/8**</u>

Focus: Godly Character Traits - Personal Assessment

Preparation:
1.   The students each need an index card or note card for today.

Lesson:
1.   The students complete the activities in the *Student Book* and read the assigned pages for day 14 on their own.

2.   The directions instruct the students to come and show you the completed assignment for day 14, including the completed index card or note card for posting.

Teacher Directed   **All Levels Together**

Preparation:

1.   Choose which **one** of the following project options you would like your students to complete as a culminating project for this genre. Each option is explained in detail on the pages that follow. For ease in planning, you should choose the same option for each of the students.

   a) **Option 1:** You may choose a character based project, which focuses on the Godly character trait for this genre. The directions for these projects are more general. The project does not involve any of the books from the unit. It does include a final reflection form.

   b) **Option 2:** You may choose a book based project, which is an individual project that is tailored to the student's individual level. Students will choose one of the books they read for this genre to use for the project. In order to choose this option, you must purchase *Book Projects to Send Home* by Lori Sanders and Linda Kimble for your particular students' levels. There is one book for each of the three levels. The project directions are very detailed and include a final reflection for each project.

   c) **Option 3:** Your final option is to choose a group project, which requires two or more students working together. This project is based on a common book the students have all read or had read aloud to them. The **one** book the project is based upon should fit into the genre studied in this unit.

2.   Have the directions for the project copied for each student. Make sure to read the directions for the project option you chose in order to know what supplies you will need to have available for the projects.

3.   The plans allow 5 work days for the projects to be completed. This time allotment includes the planning and any presenting of the projects. The plans assume that the students will use only their normal amount of reading time to complete the projects.

Lesson:

1.   Say, *Today we will be starting our culminating project for adventure. You will have 5 days, counting today, to work on your project. Your projects are due at the end of that time on _____. (give due date)*

2.   Introduce the project you have chosen for this unit. Go through the directions and make sure students have a copy of the directions, so they can work as independently as possible. Show them where the needed supplies are located.

3.   Then, have students read the assigned pages for day 15 to finish the adventure stories. Students may begin the project after the reading is complete.

Focus: <u>Godly Character Trait Project</u>   <u>Watch It Log</u>

Project Notes:

1.   Teach fear of the Lord through the use of a daily "Watch It" log.

2.   Reproduce the log pages that follow these instructions in this guide. Each student will only need the log pages which match the traits that particular student studied in this unit. You need to staple each student's log pages into a booklet. You may choose whether students need to make a cover for their log.

3.   Meet as a group and hand out the log pages. Tell students they will be making a "Watch It" Log to keep watch over their behavior for each of the traits they studied in this unit. For the next 5 days, students will log at least one positive behavior and one negative behavior for each trait in <u>their</u> log. You will model how to make a log entry during today's discussion.

4.   Refer to the definitions and key verses printed on the log pages. As a group, review the definition and key verse for *fear of the Lord.* Have students give examples of times they have shown *fear of the Lord* and times they have <u>not</u> shown *fear of the Lord.*

5.   Have each student record today's date and write his own recent example on the *fear of the Lord* page of the log. Mark positive behaviors with a "+" and negative behaviors with a "-".

6.   As a group, review the definition and key verse for *respect for authority.* Have students give examples of times they have shown *respect for authority* and times they have <u>not</u> shown *respect for authority.*

7.   Have each student record today's date and write his own recent example on the *respect for authority* page of the log. Positive behaviors are marked with a "+" and negative behaviors are marked with a "-".

8.   If you have students in level 4/5 or in level 6/7/8, continue the pattern of reviewing, sharing, and logging for the traits *standing against peer pressure* and *deliberation.*

9.   Have students keep the "Watch It" log for 5 days.   Each day, students must list at least one positive and one negative behavior for each trait in their log. Behaviors should have taken place after the previous day's entry.

10.   On day 19, students share part of their "Watch It" Logs as a group. Reproduce the reflection form included in this guide for each student to complete.

Watch It Log
Trait: Fear of the Lord

Name:_____

Definition:
FEAR OF THE LORD is revering the Lord and his commands, and believing the Lord can turn harm into good for those who trust in him.

Key Verse:
FEAR OF THE LORD - It is the Lord your God you must follow, and him you must revere. Keep his commands and obey him; serve him and hold fast to him. Deuteronomy 13:4

Directions: Each day, list at least one positive <u>and</u> one negative behavior for *fear of the Lord* on this page in your log. Behaviors should have taken place after your last entry in the log.

<u>Date</u>	<u>+ / -</u>	<u>Description of Behavior</u>
_____	____	_____
_____	____	_____
_____	____	_____
_____	____	_____
_____	____	_____
_____	____	_____
_____	____	_____
_____	____	_____
_____	____	_____
_____	____	_____
_____	____	_____

Show the teacher your log each day.

Watch It Log
Trait: Respect for Authority

Name:_____

Definition:
RESPECT FOR AUTHORITY is making sure your words and your actions honor those who are responsible for you.

Key Verse:
RESPECT FOR AUTHORITY - Listen to advice and accept instruction, and in the end you will be wise. Many are the plans in a man's heart, but it is the Lord's purpose that prevails. Proverbs 19:20,21

Directions: Each day, list at least one positive and one negative behavior for *respect for authority* on this page in your log. Behaviors should have taken place after your last entry in the log.

Date	+ / -	Description of Behavior
_____	____	_____
_____	____	_____
_____	____	_____
_____	____	_____
_____	____	_____
_____	____	_____
_____	____	_____
_____	____	_____
_____	____	_____
_____	____	_____
_____	____	_____

Show the teacher your log each day.

Watch It Log
Trait: Standing Against Peer Pressure

Name:_____

Definition:
STANDING AGAINST PEER PRESSURE is making decisions based on what you believe, instead of following what others say and do.

Key Verse:
STANDING AGAINST PEER PRESSURE - Each one should test his own actions. Then he can take pride in himself, without comparing himself to somebody else, for each one should carry his own load.
Galations 6:4

Directions: Each day, list at least one positive <u>and</u> one negative behavior for *standing against peer pressure* on this page in your log. Behaviors should have taken place after your last entry in the log.

<u>Date</u>	<u>+ / -</u>	<u>Description of Behavior</u>
_____	____	_____
_____	____	_____
_____	____	_____
_____	____	_____
_____	____	_____
_____	____	_____
_____	____	_____
_____	____	_____
_____	____	_____
_____	____	_____

Show the teacher your log each day.

Watch It Log
Trait: Deliberation

Name:_____

Definition:
DELIBERATION is giving careful thought or consideration to your options before deciding what to do.

Key Verse:
DELIBERATION - Let us examine our ways and test them, and let us return to the Lord. Lamentations 3:40,41

Directions: Each day, list at least one positive <u>and</u> one negative behavior for *deliberation* on this page in your log. Behaviors should have taken place after your last entry in the log.

<u>Date</u>	<u>+ / -</u>	<u>Description of Behavior</u>
_____	____	_____
_____	____	_____
_____	____	_____
_____	____	_____
_____	____	_____
_____	____	_____
_____	____	_____
_____	____	_____
_____	____	_____
_____	____	_____
_____	____	_____
_____	____	_____

Show the teacher your log each day.

Focus: <u>Book Based Project</u>   **Individual Projects by Level**

Project Notes:

1.   This is an individual project tailored to the students' individual levels.

2.   In order to choose this option, you must purchase *Book Projects to Send Home* by Lori Sanders and Linda Kimble (McGraw-Hill, 2004) for your particular students' levels. There is one project book for each of the 3 levels. The books include detailed reproducible directions, work schedules, and reflection forms.

3.   The students each need to choose **one** book from those that **were read in this genre**. That book is the basis for the project.

4.   The project titles, corresponding page numbers, and levels in the *Book Projects to Send Home* books are listed below.

<u>Use Grade 2 of *Book Projects to Send Home*</u>   **Level 2/3**

Project Title: Adventure Thank-You Note   Page Numbers: 43-46

Preparation:

1.   Read the project description box and the materials to provide section on p. 43. The rest of the items on p. 43 are <u>optional</u> ideas to use if you enjoy teaching through themes.

2.   Copy pages 44-46 for your students. Save p. 46 for the students to complete on day 19 as a reflection on their project. This is listed in the plans for day 19.

3.   The sharing your thank-you adventure note section on p. 44 will be done differently at home.

<u>Use Grade 4 of *Book Projects to Send Home*</u>   **Level 4/5**

Note: If you are opposed to movies, you will want to skip this project.

Project Title: Made for the Movies   Page Numbers: 43-46

Preparation:

1.   Read the project description box, the materials to provide section, and the tips to introduce section on p. 43. The rest of the items on p. 43 are <u>optional</u> ideas to use if you enjoy teaching through themes.

2.   Copy pages 44-47 for your students. Save p. 47 for the students to complete on day 19 as a reflection on their project. This is listed in the plans for day 19.

3.   Instruct students to think of the schedule on p. 45 as steps to complete, rather than a time frame for each part of the project.   The students will be working solely on completing the projects for 5 reading days, instead of doing them gradually for 4 weeks as the project book suggests.

4.   The students have already completed the project requirements listed under week 1 in the schedule on p. 45. They will not need to choose another book to read.

Use Grade 5 of _Book Projects to Send Home_   **Level 6/7/8**

Note: Although these projects are listed for grade 5, they are very challenging to complete which makes them appropriate for level 6/7/8.

Project Title: Far-Out Travel Brochure   Page Numbers: 43-46

Preparation:
1.   Read the project description box and the materials to provide section on p. 43. The rest of the items on p. 43 are <u>optional</u> ideas to use if you enjoy teaching through themes.

2.   Copy pages 44-47 for your students. You may want to remove the "Dear Fifth Grader" greeting on p. 44. If you are opposed to television, you will want to modify step 6 on p. 45. Save p. 47 for the students to complete on day 19 as a reflection on their projects. This is listed in the plans for day 19.

3.   Instruct students to think of the schedule on p. 45 as steps to complete, rather than a time frame for each part of the project. The students will be working solely on completing the projects for 5 reading days, instead of doing them gradually for 4 weeks as the project book suggests.

4.   The students have already completed the project requirements listed under week 1 on the schedule on p. 45. They will not need to choose another book to read.

5.   If you are opposed to television, you will want to change the presentation guidelines on p. 45.

Adventure - Day 15 - **Option 3**

Focus: Group Project   **Book Bar Graph**

Project Notes:

1.   In order to choose this option, you must have two or more students (unless you are willing to do part of the project with your student).

2.   This project is based on **one** common book the students have all read or had read aloud to them. The book the project is based upon should fit into the genre studied in this unit.

3.   Reproduce the planning sheet for the Bar Graph included in this guide for each student. On day 15, the group meets and lists 5 or more main events from the adventure book on the planning form. The events should cover the most important parts of the story and be listed in the order that they occurred in the book.

4.   Group members divide the events by assigning at least one event to each group member. Save the reproducible planning forms to use again on days 18 and 19.

5.   On index cards or on paper cut to approximately 3" x 5" each, students need to draw pictures and write several sentences to explain the events they were assigned.

6.   On day 18, students meet as a group to rate the level of suspense for each chosen event. The most suspenseful event is rated a 10. All other events are rated in reference to the most suspenseful event. The group may not completely agree on the rating, but a consensus needs to be reached for the next step in the project. Ratings should be written on the planning form.

7.   Group members who are finished with their pictures and descriptions work to make a bar graph on a large piece of paper or poster board. Directions for the graph are included on the reproducible planning form from day 15.

8.   On day 19, students glue their pictures on the poster in the order that the events occurred from *1-5* or more, in the book. Each event is also matched with the suspense rating from *1-10* on the left side of the poster.

9.   Once the cards are glued on the poster, students should draw and color a bar from the bottom of each event card to the baseline of the bar graph. The bars will show the rising and falling levels of suspense in the story.

10.   On day 19, students share the Bar Graph project. Reproduce the reflection form included in this guide for each student to complete.

Unit 2

Bar Graph Planning Sheet

Name: _____

List the 5 main events in the order they occurred in the book. (If your group chooses more than 5 events, list the rest on the back of this sheet.)

1._____

2._____

3._____

4._____

5._____

I have been assigned to draw a picture and write a description for event number(s)

_____.

On day 18, meet as a group to assign suspense ratings from 1-10 for each of the 5 main events. (If your group chose more than 5 events, list the rest on the back of this sheet.)

Event 1: _____   Event 2: _____   Event 3: _____

Event 4: _____   Event 5: _____

Group members who are finished with their pictures and descriptions follow the directions below to make a graph on a large piece of paper or poster board.
1. Along the left-hand vertical side of the poster, number from *0-10*. Make sure *0* is at the bottom and 10 is at the top.
2. Along the bottom of the poster, number from 1 to 5 or more going across, depending on the number of events that were drawn. Space the numbers far enough apart to have room to glue one event above each number.

On day 19, glue the cards on the poster in the order they occurred in the book. Each event will also be matched with the suspense rating from *1-10* on the left side of the poster. Draw and color a bar from the bottom of each card to the baseline of the graph.

Adventure - Days 16-18

Independent / Teacher Directed   **All Levels**

Focus: Project Work

Preparation:
1.   For details, read the directions for the project option you chose.

Lesson:
1.   Check students' progress to make sure each student understands what to do and is on schedule to finish by day 19.

2.   Meet with students as a group, if this is needed.

Adventure - Day 19

Independent / Teacher Directed   **All Levels**

Focus: Project Completion

Preparation:
1.   For details, read the directions for the project option you chose.

2.   Have the reflection forms copied for each student to match the project option you chose.

Lesson:
1.   Briefly check students' progress. Students should finish their projects today.

2.   Have students share their projects with each other or with you.

3.   Hand out the reflection form that matches the project option you chose. Have the students complete the reflection and show you.

4.   You are ready to choose the next genre your students will study. Look ahead to prepare the kickoff for the upcoming genre.

Watch It Log Reflection

1. On my Watch It Log, I noticed I did a good job of_____

_____.

2. I noticed I had a hard time with_____

_____.

3. What is one thing that surprised you about your log? _____

_____

_____.

4. What should you do differently when you are making decisions about your actions?

_____

_____

_____.

_____   _____
Signature of student   Date

Unit 2

Bar Graph Reflection

1. On the Bar Graph project, I think that I did a good job of _____

    _____

    _____.

2. I think that I could have done a better job of _____

    _____

    _____.

3. I found out that adventure stories have_____

    _____

    _____.

4. From the Bar Graph project, I learned_____

    _____

    _____

    _____.

5. If a had a chance to do this project again, I would_____

    _____

    _____.

_____   _____
       Signature of student   Date

Historical Fiction

GENRE: HISTORICAL FICTION

Definition:
    The realistic portrayal of an actual place during a time period from
    the past.

Common Characteristics:
    1. Mixes true incidents with fictional incidents.
    2. Describes settings, experiences, and characters clearly.
    3. Has either fictional or true characters that act in a realistic manner.
    4. Includes a conflict or problem that is suitable for the historic
       period.

Story Element Emphasis: Setting

Definition:
    The place where the story happens.

Godly Character Trait Emphasis: Faith

Definition:
    Having a strong belief that stands firm in the face of opposition.

Subqualities:
    1. perseverance
    2. courage
    3. optimism

Teacher Directed   **All Levels Together**

Focus: Genre Kickoff

Preparation:

1. The goal of the kickoff is to introduce students of all ages to the upcoming genre in a fun and entertaining manner.

2. Decide how much time you want to spend on the kickoff. You can spend one normal reading class period, several hours, or even a whole day. After the kickoff, you begin with day 1 in the teacher's plans.

3. Read through the list of ideas below and choose those that interest you for this genre's kickoff. You are welcome to add your own ideas that fit within this genre. Refer to the cover page for a definition and common characteristics for each genre. Introduce the name and definition of the genre to begin the kickoff.

Possible Kickoff Ideas:

1. Act out several true, historic events with or without props. Use real names of actual people and places, but do not give students a script to follow. Instead, give students a general overview of the event and allow them to add their own ideas and actions.

2. Choose a time period in history and a real, historical place that is familiar to the students. Have students decide as a group on two or three characters and a problem that is appropriate for the time period. Develop a short profile for each character. Sit in a circle and orally tell a story about the characters and the problem by taking turns adding one sentence at a time to the story. Students need to be encouraged to describe places and events in the story clearly.

3. Provide a variety of books with pictures of different historical time periods. Have students draw a picture that represents a time period they find interesting. Then, have students add a set number of items to their picture that do not belong in the time period they selected. Trade pictures and see if someone else can identify the items that don't belong.

4. Choose a specific historical time period to recreate. Students can dress the part, play games from that time period, cook period dishes, have school in a manner similar to that time, sing or play music from that time period, or create crafts that represent the period.

5. Visit or take part in a historical reenactment of some kind. For example, students could visit or participate in a reenactment of a battle, gunfight, pioneer days, old-time western town, or Native American dancing.

6.   Visit a historical home that has been redone to represent a certain time period or take a historical homes walking tour.

7.   Choose pictures from different time periods in history. Post a list of time periods that the pictures could represent. Have students guess which time period each picture is showing.

8.   Listen to a historical fiction book on tape or view an appropriate historical fiction video. For example, students could listen to or view *Beethoven Lives Upstairs* by the Classical Kids or *Anne of Green Gables* by Lucy Maud Montgomery.

9.   Guide students to choose a time and place they would like to be able to visit. It is helpful to have books available that show various time periods. Students need to understand this is a actual place and time, not an imaginary place. Have students picture themselves in the time period and describe the following things on paper: the landscape, the activities people are doing, the sounds they hear, the way they are dressed, and the things they find surprising.

Questions to discuss at the end of the kickoff:
1.   What is historical fiction? (Refer to the definition on the cover page for this genre.)

2.   What was historically accurate, and what was fictional in the activities we did today?

3.   Can the characters and places in a historical fiction book be true? (Yes, but the dialogue and some of the events in a historical fiction book are not true.)

4.   Why do we read historical fiction books?

Teacher Directed   **All Levels Together**

Focus: Prereading Activity - Book Examination

Preparation:
1.   Prior to meeting with the students for day 1, follow the directions for *Getting Started* listed in the back of this guide.

2.   Have the first book and one *Assigned Reading Calendar* ready for each student.

Lesson:
1.   Say, *Today we will be doing a prereading activity to help you think about the next book you will be reading.*

2.   Give students the first book they will be reading for this genre.

3.   Discuss the following questions with your students:
        a) *Find the dedication in your book. What can you learn about the book from reading the dedication?*
        b) *Read the title of the book. What hints does the title give you about the book?*
        c) *Look carefully at the cover illustration. What clues to the story do you see?*
        d) *Find the synopsis of the book. What characters, settings, and problems are mentioned?*
        e) *Do you see any reviews, recommendations or awards listed for the book? What can you learn from reading those?*
        f) *What predictions can you make about the book after reviewing the items we just discussed?*
        g) *What makes your book historical fiction?*

4.   Have students open their *Student Books* to the *Assigned Reading Calendar* for this genre. Help each student fill in the page numbers to be read for days 1-5.

5.   Have students read the assigned pages for day 1 on their own.

Teacher Directed   **Level 2/3**

Focus: Story Discussion and Optional Phonics <u>or</u> Vocabulary Work

Preparation:
1.   You may choose to have students at this level review phonics <u>or</u> complete a vocabulary assignment. Use your own program for the phonics review. Refer to the Appendix for a reproducible vocabulary assignment. The lesson on this day is much shorter to compensate for the additional time you may spend on phonics or on vocabulary work.

Lesson:
1.   Optional phonics or vocabulary work

2.   Listen to your students read the assigned pages out loud to you. Use the Reading Strategies list and the Qualities of Good Reading list provided in the Appendix to help you know what to emphasize.

3.   Discuss the following questions with your students:
         a) *Who are the main characters?*
         b) *Where does the story take place? How can you see this is a realistic place?*
         c) *What problems do you predict may happen? Explain.*

Independent / Teacher Directed   **Level 4/5**

Focus: Story Element Instruction - Setting

Lesson:
1.   Tell the students to read the assigned pages on their own, leaving 3-4 pages to read aloud to you.

2.   Listen to your students read several pages. Use the Qualities of Good Reading list provided in the Appendix to help you know what to emphasize.

3.   Work with the students to complete Picture Words for day 2 in the *Student Book*. Help the students skim through their historical fiction book to find words and phrases that describe the setting. Have students write the words and phrases in the *Student Book.* You may want to write answers on a marker board as you discuss them, so the students can copy them. Then, the students can concentrate on the discussion rather than on spelling and capitalization.

4.   Discuss the following questions with your students:
      a) *Who are the main characters in the story? How could you describe them?*
      b) *What is the problem or conflict in the story?*

Independent   **Level 6/7/8**

Focus: Vocabulary Builder - Synonym Search

Preparation:
1.   Have a dictionary and a thesaurus available.

Lesson:
1.   The students complete the activities in the *Student Book* and read the assigned pages for day 2 on their own.

2.   The directions instruct students to come and show you the completed Synonym Search vocabulary assignment.

Teacher Directed / Independent   **Level 2/3**

Focus: Story Element Instruction - A Scenic Picture

Lesson:
1.   Listen to your students read part or all of the assigned pages out loud to you.
      Use the Reading Strategies list and the Qualities of Good Reading list provided
      in the Appendix to help you know what to emphasize.

2.   Discuss the following questions with the students:
      a) *What things do the characters do that you think are right?*
      b) *What things do the characters do that you think are wrong?*
      c) *Do you know anyone like the characters in the story? Explain.*

3.   Go over the directions for A Scenic Picture on day 3 in the *Student Book*.
      Make sure the students know what to do. Then, have them finish on their own.

Independent   **Level 4/5**

Focus: Story Element Extension - Detailed Scenery

Lesson:
1.   Tell the students to read the assigned pages for day 3 on their own.

2.   Tell them to complete the Detailed Scenery on day 3 in their *Student Book*
      when they finish reading.

3.   The directions instruct students to come and show you the completed
      assignment.

Teacher Directed / Independent   **Level 6/7/8**

Focus: Story Element Discussion - Setting Moods

Lesson:
1.   The students read the assigned pages for day 3 on their own.

2.   The students meet with you to discuss the following questions:
      a) *Who are the main characters in the story?*
      b) *Do you like or dislike them? Why?*
      c) *Tell me about the historical time period of the book and the places that are
         mentioned.*

3.   Introduce the Setting Moods in the *Student Book* for day 3.

4.   Have the students work to complete day 3 in the *Student Book* on their own.

5.   The directions instruct students to come and show you the completed assignment.

Teacher Directed   **Level 2/3**

Focus: Godly Character Traits - Examples

Preparation:
1.   Think of examples you can share from your own life for each of the following traits: *faith* and *perseverance*. (Definitions are listed in the lesson below.)

Lesson:
1.   Introduce the following definition and scripture passage for *faith:*
        a) <u>*Faith*</u> *is having a strong belief that stands firm in the face of opposition.*
        b) <u>*Key Scripture verse:*</u> *So we fix our eyes not on what is seen, but on what is unseen. For what is seen is temporary, but what is unseen is eternal.*
        2 Corinthians 4:18

2.   Share an example of *faith* from your own life.

3.   Help students think of an example of *faith* from their own lives.

4.   Introduce the following definition and scripture passage for *perseverance*:
        a) <u>*Perseverance*</u> *is continuing to work toward a goal despite obstacles or difficulties.*
        b) <u>*Key Scripture verse:*</u> *You need to persevere so that when you have done the will of God, you will receive what he has promised. Hebrews 10:36*

5.   Repeat steps 2 and 3 for the trait *perseverance*.

6.   Instruct your students to search for examples of *faith* and *perseverance* as they read part or all of the assigned pages out loud to you. Use the Reading Strategies list and the Qualities of Good Reading list provided in the Appendix to help you know what to emphasize.

7.   Discuss the following questions with your students:
        a) *How do the characters show faith? Or perseverance?*
        b) *Did the characters show the opposite traits of unbelief or giving up? Explain.*
        c) *What could the characters do differently to show more faith or perseverance?*

Independent / Teacher Directed   **Level 4/5**

Focus: Godly Character Traits - Examples

Lesson:
1.   Tell the students to read and complete the Godly Character Sheet on day 4 in the *Student Book* on their own.

2.   Have the students silently read the assigned pages for day 4, leaving 3-4 pages to read aloud to you.

3.   The students should come and show you when both are completed.

4.   Review the Godly Character Sheet on day 4 in the *Student Book*, so the students and you will know what traits you are searching for in the story. *(faith, perseverance, and courage)*

5.   Listen to your students read 3-4 pages aloud. Use the Qualities of Good Reading list provided in the Appendix to help you know what to emphasize.

6.   Discuss the following questions with the students:
      a) *How did the characters show faith?*
      b) *How did the characters show perseverance?*
      c) *How did the characters show courage?*
      d) *Did the characters show the opposite traits of unbelief? Or giving up? Or cowardice? Explain.*
      e) *What might Jesus have done differently if He had been the character in the book?*

Independent   **Level 6/7/8**

Focus: Godly Character Traits - Examples

Lesson:
1.   The students complete the activities in the *Student Book* and read the assigned pages for day 4 on their own.

2.   The directions instruct the students to come and show you the completed Godly Character page.

Teacher Directed / Independent   **Level 2/3**

Focus: Comprehension Check - Book Boxes

Lesson:
1.   Go over the directions for Book Boxes on day 5 in the *Student Book*. Students complete this assignment alone after reading the assigned pages.

2.   Listen to your students read part of the assigned pages out loud to you. Use the Reading Strategies list and the Qualities of Good Reading list provided in the Appendix to help you know what to emphasize.

3.   The students finish the assigned reading and complete Book Boxes on their own. The directions instruct students to come and show you the completed assignment.

Independent   **Level 4/5**

Focus: Comprehension Check - Story Sections

Lesson:
1.   Tell the students to complete the Story Sections on day 5 in the *Student Book* on their own.

2.   The students silently read the assigned pages for day 5 on their own. You may choose to have the students leave 3-4 pages to read aloud to you.

3.   The students are instructed to come and show you when both are assignments are complete.

Independent   **Level 6/7/8**

Focus: Comprehension Check - Significant Events

Lesson:
1.   The students complete the activities in the *Student Book* and read the assigned pages for day 5 on their own.

2.   The directions instruct students to come and show you the completed Significant Events assignment.

Teacher Directed   **All Levels Together**

Focus: Prereading Activity - Prereading Map

Preparation:

1.   If students are beginning new books today, make sure to have the number of pages to be read each day calculated and have those books ready to hand out. (See the *Getting Started* section, item #7, in the back of this guide for details.)

2.   If students are <u>not</u> beginning new books today, they use the books they are currently reading for today's activities.

Lesson:

1.   Say, *Today we will be doing a prereading activity to help you think about the next book you will be reading or the next part of the book you will be reading.*

2.   Give students a little time to look at the cover, read the synopsis, and quickly page through the book.

3.   Have students open their *Student Books* to the Prereading Map on day 6. As you discuss the following questions, students should write their answers to the first questions in the squares. The answers to the second questions should be written on the lines by the squares.
   a) *What is the historical time period of your novel? What do you know about that time period?*
   b) *Who are the main characters in your novel? Do you notice anything about them from looking through your book?*
   c) *What places are important in this novel? Do you know anything about these places?*
   d) *What seems to be the problem or conflict in this story? What do you know about this kind of problem?*
   e) *What might be some possible solutions to the problem or conflict in the novel? Which solution would you choose?*

4.   Help students update the *Assigned Reading Calendar* for days 6-10.

5.   Have students read the assigned pages for day 6 on their own.

Teacher Directed   **Level 2/3**

Focus: Story Discussion and Optional Phonics <u>or</u> Vocabulary Work

Preparation:
1.   You may choose to have students at this level review phonics <u>or</u> complete a vocabulary assignment. Use your own program for the phonics review. Refer to the Appendix for a reproducible vocabulary assignment. The lesson on this day is much shorter to compensate for the additional time you may spend on phonics or on vocabulary work.

Lesson:
1.   Optional phonics or vocabulary work

2.   Listen to your students read the assigned pages out loud to you. Use the Reading Strategies list and the Qualities of Good Reading list provided in the Appendix to help you know what to emphasize.

3.   Discuss the following questions with your students:
        a) *Choose one character. Why is this character important in the story?*
        b) *Does this story remind you of any other story? Explain.*
        c) *Describe the setting of this story.*

Independent / Teacher Directed   **Level 4/5**

Focus: Story Element Instruction - Comparing Actual Places

Lesson:
1.   Tell the students to read the assigned pages on their own, leaving 3-4 pages to read aloud to you.

2.   Listen to your students read several pages. Use the Qualities of Good Reading list provided in the Appendix to help you know what to emphasize.

3.   Work with the students to complete Actual Places on day 7 in the *Student Book.* The students will be comparing their surroundings and the time period they live in, to the setting and time period of the book. You may want to write the answers on a marker board as you discuss them, so the students can copy them. Then, the students can concentrate on the discussion rather than on spelling and capitalization.

4.   Discuss the following questions with your students:
        a) *Do you like or dislike the main characters? Explain.*
        b) *Does the mood of the story change? If so, how?*

Independent   **Level 6/7/8**

Focus: Vocabulary Builder - Synonym Search

Preparation:
1.   Have a dictionary and a thesaurus available.

Lesson:
1.   The students complete the activities in the *Student Book* and read the assigned
        pages for day 7 on their own.

2.   The directions instruct students to come and show you the completed
        Synonym Search vocabulary assignment.

Teacher Directed / Independent   **Level 2/3**

Focus: Story Element Instruction - Setting Map

Lesson:
1.   Listen to your students read the assigned pages out loud to you. Use the Reading Strategies list and the Qualities of Good Reading list provided in the Appendix to help you know what to emphasize.

2.   Discuss the following questions with the students:
        a) *What possible solutions can you think of for solving the problem in the story?*
        b) *What is the most exciting part?*

3.   Assign students the Setting Map on day 8 in the *Student Book* to complete on their own. Unless they choose to, the students do not have to color.

4.   The directions instruct the students to come and show you the completed assignment.

Independent   **Level 4/5**

Focus: Story Element Extension - Scenic Outlines

Lesson:
1.   Tell the students to read the assigned pages for day 8 on their own.

2.   Tell them to complete Scenic Outlines on day 8 in their *Student Book* when they finish reading.

3.   The directions instruct students to come and show you the completed assignment.

Teacher Directed / Independent   **Level 6/7/8**

Focus: Story Element Discussion - Setting Poem

Lesson:
1.   The students read the assigned pages for day 8 on their own.

2.   The students meet with you to discuss the following questions:
        a) *What do you remember most about the story?*
        b) *What are some causes and effects in the story?*
        c) *What place do you know of that is similar to a place in the story? Explain.*

3.	Introduce the Setting Poem on day 8 in the *Student Book*. Make sure the students understand what to do. Then, have the students work on their own.

4.	The directions instruct students to come and show you the completed assignment.

Teacher Directed   **Level 2/3**

Focus: Godly Character Traits - Biblical Comparisons

Preparation:
1.   Find a short children's book of the Bible story about Noah. Otherwise, you will
        need to read the story directly from the Bible in Genesis chapters 6-9.

Lesson:
1.   Review the following definitions and scripture passages:
        a) _Faith_ is having a strong belief that stands firm in the face of opposition.
        b) _Key Scripture verse:_ So we fix our eyes not on what is seen, but on what is
           unseen. For what is seen is temporary, but what is unseen is eternal.
           2 Corinthians 4:18
        c) _Perseverance_ is continuing to work toward a goal despite obstacles or
           difficulties.
        d) _Key Scripture verse:_ You need to persevere so that when you have done the
           will of God, you will receive what he has promised. Hebrews 10:36

2.   Read the children's book, or the Bible passage Genesis 6-9, about Noah.
        Instruct your students to listen for examples of _faith_ and _perseverance_ in the
        story being read.

3.   Discuss the following question with your students:
        a) _How did Noah's actions show faith and perseverance?_

4.   Record the students' responses in the _Student Book_ on day 9 under the Biblical
        Character column. (Possible answers include the following: _Faith_ by believing
        in God and what He commanded Noah to do, even though Noah could not see
        God; _Perseverance_ to build an ark of huge proportions even though the rest of
        mankind did not believe in what Noah and his family were doing.)

5.   Listen to your students read the assigned pages for day 9 out loud to you.
        Remind the students to be searching for examples of _faith_ and _perseverance_.

6.   Using the questions listed below, compare Noah with the main character in the
        historical fiction book. Record the responses on day 9 in the _Student Book_
        under the Book Character column.
        a) _How do the character's actions in your book show faith and perseverance?_
        b) _What would the Biblical character, Noah, do differently from the character in
           your book?_

Unit 3

Independent / Teacher Directed   **Level 4/5**

Focus: Godly Character Traits - Biblical Comparisons

Preparation:
1. Find a short children's book of the Bible story about Esther. Otherwise, the students read the story directly from the Bible in Esther chapters 2-8.

Lesson:
1. Tell the students to review the Godly Character Traits listed on day 9 in the *Student Book* on their own. Then, have the students read the story of Esther, silently, either from the book you provided or from the Bible in Esther chapters 2-8.

2. Have students do their best to complete the Biblical Character column on the Godly Character Story Sheet for Esther on day 9 in the *Student Book.*

3. Students silently read the assigned pages in the historical fiction novel for day 9, saving 3 or 4 pages to read aloud to you.

4. Students meet with you to finish the assignment for day 9. Listen to your students read several pages. Use the Qualities of Good Reading list provided in the Appendix to help you know what to emphasize.

5. Discuss the following questions with the students as you review what they have already done in the *Student Book* for day 9. Complete the remaining columns in the *Student Book* for day 9.
   a) *How did Esther show faith, perseverance, and courage?* (Possible answers include the following: *Faith* in not revealing that she was a Jew until the time was right, as Mordecai had instructed her; *Faith* in trusting God's perfect timing in the events in her life; *Perseverance* by inviting the king to two banquets and later asking him to make a new order that would protect, rather than harm, the Jewish people; *Courage* to go to see King Xerxes, even though she had not been invited and could have been killed; *Courage* to reveal Haman's plot against her people.)
   b) *How did the person in your book behave like the Biblical character, Esther?* (List the answers in the *Student Book.*)
   c) *How did the person in your book behave differently from Esther?* (List the answers in the *Student Book.*)
   d) *Which trait was shown least often by the book character?* (Explain in the *Student Book.*)

Independent   **Level 6/7/8**

Focus: Godly Character Traits - Biblical Comparisons

Preparation:
1.   The students need a Bible for today's lesson.

Lesson:
1.   The students complete the activities in the *Student Book* and read the assigned pages for day 9 on their own.

2.   The directions instruct the students to come and show you the completed Godly Character Story page. (Examples of the traits in Joshua might include the following: *Faith* that God would deliver Jericho into the Israelites' hands; *Perseverance* by marching around the wall of Jericho for seven days as the Lord commanded; *Courage* to cross the Jordan and to travel into the land of the Canaanites; *Optimism* that the Lord would help the Israelites conquer the Promised Land.)

Teacher Directed   **All Levels Together**

Focus: Comprehension Check - Vivid Scenes

Lesson:

1. Say, *As you read, the text paints a scene in your imagination. Today you will be sharing parts from your book that you think paint a vivid scene for the reader.*

2. Have the students complete the Vivid Scenes planning form on day 10 in the *Student Book* .

3. Have each student share the parts they chose with the group.

4. Allow group members to ask questions after the person has shared about the book.

5. When all students have finished sharing, have students read the assigned pages in their historical fiction books for day 10 on their own.

Teacher Directed   **All Levels Together**

Focus: Prereading Activity - Important Illustration

Preparation:
1.   If students are beginning new books today, make sure to have the number of pages to be read each day calculated and have those books ready to hand out. (See the *Getting Started* section, item #7, in the back of this guide for details.)

2.   If students are <u>not</u> beginning new books today, they use the books they are currently reading for today's activities.

3.   Choose 1 illustration from the book the students are about to read at each level.

4.   For students <u>not</u> beginning a new book today, choose an illustration they have not come to in the book. If there are no illustrations, use the cover's illustration.

Lesson:
1.   Say, *Today we will be doing a prereading activity to help you think about the next book you will be reading or the next part of the book you will be reading.*

2.   Have the students look at the illustration you have chosen for them.

3.   Discuss the following questions with the students:
       a) *What is the setting of this illustration?*
       b) *How can you guess the historical time period of this picture? Explain.*
       c) *What can you learn about the characters from the illustration?*
       d) *What activities are the characters performing?*
       e) *Which clues are you using to help you make those predictions?*
       f) *What is the mood or overall feeling in the picture? Explain.*
       g) *How does reading the title help you learn about the story?*

4.   Have students read the synopsis of the book. Even if students are <u>not</u> starting a new book, have them read the synopsis again to discover any new clues about the story.

5.   Ask students to share one thing they are excited to learn as they read the story.

6.   Help students update the *Assigned Reading Calendar* for days 11-15.

7.   Have students read the assigned pages for day 11 on their own.

<u>Teacher Directed</u>   **<u>Level 2/3</u>**

Focus: Story Discussion and Optional Phonics <u>or</u> Vocabulary Work

Preparation:
1.   You may choose to have students at this level review phonics <u>or</u> complete a
        vocabulary assignment. Use your own program for the phonics review. Refer to
        the Appendix for a reproducible vocabulary assignment. The lesson on this day
        is much shorter to compensate for the additional time you may spend on
        phonics or on vocabulary work.

Lesson:
1.   Optional phonics or vocabulary work

2.   Listen to your students read the assigned pages out loud to you. Use the
        Reading Strategies list and the Qualities of Good Reading list provided in the
        Appendix to help you know what to emphasize.

3.   Discuss the following questions with your students:
        a) *Do you like the main characters? Why, or why not?*
        b) *Could the problems in the story have been avoided? If so, how?*
        c) *Have you ever been to a place like the one in the book? Explain.*

<u>Independent / Teacher Directed</u>   **<u>Level 4/5</u>**

Focus: Story Element Instruction - Eventful Settings

Lesson:
1.   Tell the students to read the assigned pages on their own, leaving 3-4 pages to
        read aloud to you.

2.   Listen to your students read several pages. Use the Qualities of Good Reading
        list provided in the Appendix to help you know what to emphasize.

3.   Work with the students to complete Eventful Settings on day 12 in the *Student
        Book*. You may want to write the answers on a marker board as you discuss
        them, so the students can copy them. Then, the students can concentrate on
        the discussion, rather than on spelling and capitalization.

4.   Discuss the following questions with your students:
        a) *What do you think is going to happen next?*
        b) *What clues help you predict what will happen?*

Independent   **Level 6/7/8**

Focus: Vocabulary Builder - Synonym Search

Preparation:
1.   Have a dictionary and a thesaurus available.

Lesson :
1.   The students complete the activities in the *Student Book* and read the assigned
        pages for day 12 on their own.

2.   The directions instruct the students to come and show you the completed
        Synonym Search vocabulary assignment.

Teacher Directed   **Level 2/3**

Focus: Story Element Instruction - Setting Response

Lesson:

1.   Listen to your students read part or all of the assigned pages out loud to you. Use the Reading Strategies list and the Qualities of Good Reading list provided in the Appendix to help you know what to emphasize.

2.   Discuss the following questions with your students:
       a) *Do any of the characters change during the story? If so, how?*
       b) *What is the author trying to tell you in this book?*

3.   Introduce Setting Response on day 13 in the *Student Book.* Make sure the students understand what to do. Then, have them complete the assignment on their own.

4.   The directions instruct the students to come and show you the completed assignment.

Independent   **Level 4/5**

Focus: Story Element Extension - Setting Analysis

Lesson:

1.   Tell the students to read the assigned pages for day 13 on their own.

2.   Tell them to complete Setting Analysis for day 13 in their *Student Book* when they finish reading.

3.   The directions instruct students to come and show you the completed assignment.

Teacher Directed / Independent   **Level 6/7/8**

Focus: Story Element Discussion - Evaluating the Setting

Lesson:

1.   The students read the assigned pages for day 13 on their own.

2.   The students meet with you to discuss the following questions:
       a) *Are people really like these characters? If so, how?*
       b) *Does the mood of the story change? Explain.*
       c) *Does this story remind you of another story? If so, what is it?*   Unit 3

3.   Introduce Evaluating the Setting in the *Student Book* under day 13. Have the students work to complete it on their own.

4.   The directions instruct the students to come and show you the completed assignment.

Teacher Directed   **Level 2/3**

Focus: Godly Character Traits - Personal Assessment

Preparation:
1.   You need an index card or note card for each of your students today.

Lesson:
1.   Review the following definitions and scripture passages:
        a) _Faith_ is having a strong belief that stands firm in the face of opposition.
        b) _Key Scripture verse:_ So we fix our eyes not on what is seen, but on what is
           unseen. For what is seen is temporary, but what is unseen is eternal.
           2 Corinthians 4:18
        c) _Perseverance_ is continuing to work toward a goal despite obstacles or
           difficulties.
        d) _Key Scripture verse:_ You need to persevere so that when you have done the
           will of God, you will receive what he has promised. Hebrews 10:36

2.   Listen to your students read the assigned pages for day 14 out loud to you.

3.   Discuss the following questions with the students:
        a) _Which trait was shown less often by the book character, faith or
           perseverance? Explain._
        b) _Choose the trait that is harder for you to show, faith or perseverance.
           Explain._

4.   Hand out an index card to each student. Have the students write the trait they
        chose and 3 ways to work on showing the trait more often in their own lives.

5.   On the other side of the card, have the students draw themselves portraying this
        trait. The students may also write the matching Bible verse if you choose for
        them to do so.

6.   Have the students post the card in a place where they will see it often.

Independent / Teacher Directed   **Level 4/5**

Focus: Godly Character Traits - Personal Assessment

Preparation:
1.   You need an index card or note card for each of your students today.

Lesson:

1.   Tell the students to review the Godly Character Traits listed on day 9 in the *Student Book* on their own.

2.   Students silently read the assigned pages in the historical fiction book for day 14, saving 3-4 pages to read aloud to you.

3.   The students meet with you to finish the assignment for day 14.

4.   Listen to your students read 3-4 pages. Use the Qualities of Good Reading list provided in the Appendix to help you know what to emphasize.

5.   Discuss the following questions with the students:
       a) *Refer to day 9 in the Student Book. Choose the trait that is the hardest for you to show - faith, perseverance, or courage. Explain.*
       b) *Look at the Bible verse on day 9 in the Student Book for the trait you chose. How does the behavior of your book characters compare to this verse? Explain.*
       c) *What ways can you demonstrate the verse you chose in your own life?*

6.   Hand out an index card to each student. Have students list actions they will take to help them live according to the verse they chose.

7.   On the other side of the card, have the students divide the card into 3-4 sections, by drawing vertical lines. Instruct the students to break the chosen verse into sections and draw a quick picture or symbol to stand for each section of the verse. When the students look at the pictures, it should remind them of each part of the verse.

8.   The Bible verse may be written on the bottom or on the back of the card if you choose to have the students do so.

9.   Have the students post the card in a place where they will see if often.

Independent   **Level 6/7/8**

Focus: Godly Character Traits - Personal Assessment

Preparation:
1.   Each student needs an index card or note card for today.

Lesson:

1. The students complete the activities in the *Student Book* and read the assigned pages for day 14 on their own.

2. The directions instruct the students to come and show you the completed assignment for day 14, including the completed index card or note card for posting.

<u>**Teacher Directed**</u>   <u>**All Levels Together**</u>

Preparation:
1.   Choose which **one** of the following project options you would like your students to complete as a culminating project for this genre. Each option is explained in detail on the pages that follow. For ease in planning, you should choose the same option for each of the students.
   a) <u>**Option 1:**</u> You may choose a character based project, which focuses on the Godly character trait for this genre. The directions for these projects are more general. The project does not involve any of the books from the unit. It does include a final reflection form.
   b) <u>**Option 2:**</u> You may choose a book based project, which is an individual project that is tailored to the student's individual level. Students will choose one of the books they read for this genre to use for the project. In order to choose this option, you must purchase *Book Projects to Send Home* by Lori Sanders and Linda Kimble for your particular students' levels. There is one book for each of the three levels. The project directions are very detailed and include a final reflection for each project.
   c) <u>**Option 3:**</u> Your final option is to choose a group project, which requires two or more students working together. This project is based on a common book the students have all read or had read aloud to them. The **one** book the project is based upon <u>should fit into the genre studied in this unit.</u>

2.   Have the directions for the project copied for each student. Make sure to read over the directions for the project option you chose in order to know what supplies you will need to have available for the projects.

3.   The plans allow 5 work days for the projects to be completed. This time allotment includes the planning and any presenting of the projects. <u>The plans assume that the students will use only their normal amount of reading time to complete the projects.</u>

Lesson:
1.   Say, *Today we will be starting our culminating project for historical fiction. You will have 5 days, counting today, to work on your project. Your projects are due at the end of that time on _____. (give due date)*

2.   Introduce the project you have chosen for this unit. Go through the directions and make sure students have a copy of the directions, so they can work as independently as possible. Show them where the needed supplies are located.

3.   Then, have students read the assigned pages for day 15 to finish the historical fiction novels. Students may begin the project after the reading is complete.

Unit 3

Focus: <u>Godly Character Trait Project</u>   **Faith Encouragement Cards**

Project Notes:

1.   Teach students to encourage others through the use of faith encouragement cards. The cards will need to be completed by day 19.

2.   Reproduce the Encouragement Card planning form included in this guide for each student. Review the definitions and key verses of the traits that your students studied in this unit. You will not use all of the definitions if you do not have students in all three of the levels.

3.   Have each student think of at least one person they know who is experiencing hardship or difficulty in life at this time.

4.   Discuss with students which trait on the planning sheet that person needs most right now.

5.   Students will make a faith encouragement card for the person they selected. Show students a variety of examples of cards you have purchased or received. Discuss the following questions with the students:
a) Which things do you notice that the cards have in common?
b) Which cards do you like the best? Why?
c) What types of lettering do you notice on the cards?
d) Do all of the cards contain pictures?
e) How are the cards decorated?

6.   Help students complete the Faith Encouragement Card Planning Form. You may want to consider having students use special parchment paper or card stock to make their cards. Each card needs to include the following things:
a) the Bible verse for the trait you matched to the person
b) a colorful design
c) a personal note or poetic saying
d) the student's signature

7.   Students will also make an index card that has the key verse written on it to send with the encouragement card. The index card should be the size of a driver's license. The index card is meant for the person to carry in a wallet or to post as a daily source of encouragement.

8.   If students have time, they may make another faith encouragement card for a different person.

9.   On day 19, mail the faith encouragement cards. Reproduce the reflection form included in this guide for each student to complete.

Faith Encouragement Card Planning Form

Name: _____

Definitions:

FAITH is having a strong belief that stands firm in the face of opposition.

PERSEVERANCE is continuing to work toward a goal despite obstacles or difficulties.

COURAGE is bravely facing a difficult or dangerous situation by taking action based on your belief.

OPTIMISM is deciding to take a hopeful or positive view of things.

Key Verses:

FAITH - So we fix our eyes not on what is seen, but on what is unseen. For what is seen is temporary, but what is unseen is eternal. 2 Corinthians 4:18

PERSEVERANCE - You need to persevere so that when you have done the will of God, you will receive what he has promised. Hebrews 10:36

COURAGE - For who is God besides the Lord? And who is the Rock except our God? It is God who arms me with strength and makes my way perfect. Psalms 18:31,32

OPTIMISM - And we know that in all things God works for the good of those who love him, who have been called according to his purpose. Romans 8:28

List the name of the person who will receive a faith encouragement card from you:

_____

(front)	(inside)

Using the diagram of the card at the left, "map" the spots where you will place each the following items:
a) the Bible verse for the trait
b) a colorful design
c) a personal note or poetic saying
d) your signature

You will also make an index card with the key verse written on it. Explain that it is meant for the person to carry in a wallet or to post as a daily source of encouragement.

Focus: <u>Book Based Project</u>   **Individual Projects by Level**

Project Notes:

1.   This is an individual project tailored to the students' individual levels.

2.   In order to choose this option, you must purchase *Book Projects to Send Home* by Lori Sanders and Linda Kimble (McGraw-Hill, 2004) for your particular students' levels. There is one project book for each of the 3 levels. The books include detailed reproducible directions, work schedules, and reflection forms.

3.   The students will each need to choose **one** book from those that **were read in this genre**. That book is the basis for the project.

4.   The project titles, corresponding page numbers, and levels in the *Book Projects to Send Home* books are listed below.

<u>Use Grade 2 of *Book Projects to Send Home*</u>   **Level 2/3**

Project Title: Face-to-Face Character Mask   Page Numbers: 19-22

Preparation:

1.   Read the project description box and the materials to provide section on p. 19. The rest of the items on p. 19 are <u>optional</u> ideas to use if you enjoy teaching through themes.

2.   Copy pp. 20-22 for your students. Save p. 22 for the students to complete on day 19 as a reflection on their projects. This is listed in the plans for day 19.

3.   Note: Taking photographs of the role-playing is a good idea for portfolios.

<u>Use Grade 4 of *Book Projects to Send Home*</u>   **Level 4/5**

Project Title: Scraps of the Past   Page Numbers: 35-38

Preparation:

1.   Read the project description box, the materials to provide section, and the tips to introduce section on p. 35. The rest of the items on p. 35 are <u>optional</u> ideas to use if you enjoy teaching through themes.

2.   Copy pp. 36-38 and 47 for your students. Save p. 47 for the students to complete on day 19 as a reflection on their projects. This is listed in the plans for day 19.

3. Instruct students to think of the schedule on p. 37 as steps to complete, rather than a time frame for each part of the project. The students will be working solely on completing the projects for 5 reading days, instead of doing them gradually for 4 weeks as the project book suggests.

4. The students have already completed the project requirements listed under week 1 in the schedule on p. 37. They will not need to choose another book to read.

5. The presentation guidelines listed on p. 37 explain how the scrapbook projects will be shared.

Use Grade 5 of *Book Projects to Send Home*   Level 6/7/8

Note: Although these projects are listed for grade 5, they are very challenging to complete which makes them appropriate for level 6/7/8.

Project Title: Fiction Friend   Page Numbers: 11-14

Preparation:

1. Read the project description box and the materials to provide section on p. 11. The rest of the items on p. 11 are optional ideas to use if you enjoy teaching through themes.

2. Copy pp. 12-14 and 47 for your students. You may want to remove the "Dear Fifth Grader" greeting on p. 12. Save p. 47 for the students to complete on day 19 as a reflection on their projects. This is listed in the plans for day 19.

3. Instruct students to think of the schedule on p. 13 as steps to complete, rather than a time frame for each part of the project. The students will be working solely on completing the projects for 5 reading days, instead of doing them gradually for 4 weeks as the project book suggests.

4. The students have already completed the project requirements listed under week 1 in the schedule on p. 13. They will not need to choose another book to read.

5. The presentation guidelines listed on p. 13 explain how the "Fiction Friend" projects will be shared.

Unit 3

Focus: Group Project   **Character Role Play**

Project Notes:

1. In order to choose this option, you must have two or more students (unless you are willing to do part of the project with your student).

2. This project is based on **one** common book the students have all read or had read aloud to them. The book the project is based upon should fit into the genre studied in this unit.

3. Students will participate in a character role play.

4. Each student chooses 1 character from the historical fiction book to role play. Students may choose the same character.

5. Reproduce the planning form included in this guide for each student to complete in preparation for the role play.

6. The group meets to decide which activities will be part of the role play. Remember that the project should be completed in 5 days. Possible suggestions for role play activities include the following:
    a) recreating a social event that represents the historic period of the novel
    b) playing games from the historic period of the novel
    c) oral reading favorite parts of the novel as a group
    d) acting out short scenes from the novel
    e) demonstrating talents that reflect each character's personality

7. Students gather any needed costumes.

8. Students practice the quotes from the book that they selected for their character to say.

9. Group members are responsible for gathering any needed materials and for planning the role play activities.

10. Students will perform their Character Role Play on day 19. Characters should have their planning forms with them when they come to the role play. This will remind them of any quotes they need to say and any information they need to share about their character.

11. On day 19, reproduce the reflection form included in this guide for each student to complete.

Character Role Play Planning Sheet

Name: _____

Book Title: _____

Which character do you plan to role play?_____

Meet as a group to plan the role play activities. Write your plan below:

_____

_____

_____

_____

What will your costume include?_____

_____

What items will you carry as part of your costume? _____

What things does your character often do that are unique? _____

_____

Which quotes from the book will you choose for your character to say?_____

_____

_____

_____

What information will you share about your character? _____

_____

_____

_____

Independent / Teacher Directed   **All Levels**

Focus: Project Work

Preparation:
1.   For details, read the project option you chose.

Lesson:
1.   Check students' progress to make sure each student understands what to do and is on schedule to finish by day 19.

2.   Meet with students as a group, if this is needed.

Independent / Teacher Directed   **All Levels**

Focus: Project Completion

Preparation:
1.   For details, read the project option you chose.

2.   Have the reflection forms copied for each student to match the project option you chose.

Lesson:
1.   Briefly check students' progress. Students should finish their projects today.

2.   Have students share their projects with each other or with you.

3.   Hand out the reflection form that matches the project option you chose. Have the students complete the reflection and show you.

4.   You are ready to choose the next genre your students will study. Look ahead to prepare the kickoff for the upcoming genre.

Faith Encouragement Card Reflection

1. On my encouragement card, I felt that I did a good job of_____

_____.

2. I think that I could have done a better job of_____

_____.

3. If I could make another faith encouragement card, I would _____

_____

_____.

4. This project helped teach me about faith by_____

_____

_____.

_____   _____
Signature of student   Date

Character Role Play Reflection

1. During the character role play, I felt that I did a good job of _____

_____.

2. I think that I could have done a better job of_____

_____.

3. If I could do the character role play again, I would _____

_____

_____.

4. From the character role play, I learned_____

_____

_____

_____.

5. My favorite part of this project was_____

_____

_____.

_____   _____
Signature of student   Date

Fantasy

GENRE: FANTASY

Definition:
A fictional story that is not limited by reality.

Common Characteristics:
1. Includes the subcategories of animal fantasy, science fiction, and adventure stories.
2. Focuses on the courageous ideas and actions of ordinary characters.
3. Emphasizes decisions resulting in consequences.
4. Points out the need to be watchful for wickedness and to seek the truth.

Story Element Emphasis: Mood

Definition:
The feeling, sensation, or state of mind created by a story.

Godly Character Trait Emphasis: Brotherly Love

Definition:
Sincerely caring for others regardless of the circumstance.

Subqualities:
1. compassion
2. tolerance
3. patience

Teacher Directed   **All Levels Together**

Focus: Genre Kickoff

Preparation:

1.   The goal of the kickoff is to introduce students of all ages to the upcoming genre in a fun and entertaining manner.

2.   Decide how much time you want to spend on the kickoff. You can spend one normal reading class period, several hours, or even a whole day. After the kickoff, you begin with day 1 in the teacher's plans.

3.   Read through the list of ideas below and choose those that interest you for this genre's kickoff. You are welcome to add your own ideas that fit within this genre. Refer to the cover page for a definition and common characteristics for each genre. Introduce the name and definition of the genre to begin the kickoff.

Possible Kickoff Ideas:

1.   Role play one or more scenes from an animal fantasy, such as any of the *Frog and Toad* stories by Arnold Lobel. Afterwards, list the things that make it an animal fantasy.

2.   Have students dress up and act out courageous deeds such as knights fighting with swords, frontiersman fending off bears, or soldiers doing battle. The students need to add something fantastical to the act. Instruct other students in the audience to guess what is happening.

3.   Assign one character, setting, and problem to each student; such as Clara Cow lives at Willow Farm and cannot get her calf to say, *Moo.* The student needs to draw a fantastical invention this character could use to help solve the problem.

4.   Cut out magazine ads and pictures that demonstrate evil corrupting the truth in our society. Show the ads to students one at a time and discuss how the truth has been twisted in each ad. Explain that in some fantasy books, the forces of evil try to get away with twisting the truth as well.

5.   Allow students to choose one of their stuffed animals, dolls, or toys and pretend it has come to life. Have students make a list on paper of ideas for possible adventures the toy might have. You may want to read the book *Corduroy* by Don Freeman as an example of the adventures of a stuffed bear. Ask students to choose one adventure off their list to have the "toy" describe to the group. Take turns having the "toys" share their adventures.

6.   Play a fantasy board game, such as *Chutes and Ladders* or *Candyland.* Discuss what makes the game fanciful.

Unit 4

7. Choose several fantasy and several reality sentences to read to the students. Mix the sentences up and read one sentence at a time to the students. Instruct students to listen to each sentence and respond one of the following ways:
    a) For a fantasy sentence, students slap their knee and say, *Ha! Ha!*
    b) For a realistic sentence, students hold their hands up to their eyes like binoculars and say, *I saw it.*

8. Have a fanciful Olympics where each student makes up a fanciful event, such as dolphin riding, thunder catching, or star jumping. Students make or find props to act out the event they imagined. The rest of the group can cheer for the child acting out the event. At the end of the Olympics, award students with a medal or sticker for showing a "creative imagination".

9. List ordinary items and have students change them into something fanciful. For example, the ordinary item *dog* might turn into the fanciful item *talking dog who loves to read*. Cut index cards in half and instruct students to write the ordinary and fanciful items on the cards. Each card should have only one item written on it. Turn all the cards face down and play *Concentration*. The goal is to turn over an ordinary item and its matching fanciful item in order to keep those two cards and take another turn. The game may be played alone or in a group.

10. Have students write a fantasy sentence and trade with another student. Have that student rewrite the fantasy sentence as a realistic sentence. For example, the fantasy sentence "The blue frog talked to his brother" could be rewritten as the realistic sentence "The green frog croaked to another frog." Continue writing and trading sentences for additional practice.

11. Tape up a very large piece of paper. Provide markers, colored pencils, crayons, and paint. Instruct students to work together to create a fanciful mural or scene. You may want to read the book *Cloudy with a Chance of Meatballs* by Judi Barrett, which shows the town of Chewandswallow receiving weather in the form of various foods.

Questions to discuss at the end of the kickoff:
1. What are some characteristics of the fantasy genre? (Refer to the definition on the cover page for this genre.)

2. What did you learn about fantasies from today's activities?

3. What common characteristics do fantasies have?

4. Why do we read fantasy books?

Teacher Directed

Focus: Prereading Activity - Helpful Hints

Preparation:

1.   Prior to meeting with the students for day 1, follow the directions for *Getting Started* listed in the back of this guide.

2.   Have the first book and one *Assigned Reading Calendar* ready for each student.

Lesson:

1.   Say, *Today we will be doing a prereading activity to help you think about the next book you will be reading.*

2.   Give students the first book they will be reading for this genre.

3.   Have students open their *Student Books* to day 1, Helpful Hints. They will be following along in their *Student Books* and writing answers to the questions listed below as you discuss them.
      a) *Who is the author? Have you read anything else by this author? If so, what?*
      b) *What clues to the story are given in the title?*
      c) *What interesting details do you notice on the cover?*

4.   Say, *Quickly page through the book. Choose three pages to read to yourself. The pages should be from different places in the book. List the important information you discovered after reading each page.*

5.   Have students share some of the important information they discovered.

6.   Say, *Read the synopsis of the book.*

7.   Discuss the following questions with the students:
      a) *What did you learn from reading the synopsis of the book?*
      b) *What questions do you have about the story?*
      c) *What makes this book a fantasy?*

8.   Have students open their *Student Books* to the *Assigned Reading Calendar* for this genre. Help each student fill in the page numbers to be read for days 1-5.

9.   Have students read the assigned pages for day 1 on their own.

Teacher Directed   **Level 2/3**

Focus: Story Discussion and Optional Phonics <u>or</u> Vocabulary Work

Preparation:
1.   You may choose to have students at this level review phonics <u>or</u> complete a vocabulary assignment. Use your own program for the phonics review. Refer to the Appendix for a reproducible vocabulary assignment. The lesson on this day is much shorter to compensate for the additional time you may spend on phonics or on vocabulary work.

Lesson:
1.   Optional phonics or vocabulary work

2.   Listen to your students read the assigned pages out loud to you. Use the Reading Strategies list and the Qualities of Good Reading list provided in the Appendix to help you know what to emphasize.

3.   Discuss the following questions with your students:
        a) *What makes this story a fantasy?* (Have the students give examples of things from the book that could not happen in real life.)
        b) *Choose 1 character from the story. Why do you think this character is important to the story?*
        c) *What feelings do you have as you read this story? Explain.*

Independent / Teacher Directed   **Level 4/5**

Focus: Story Element Instruction - Mood Search

Lesson:
1.   Tell the students to read the assigned pages on their own, leaving 3-4 pages to read aloud to you.

2.   Listen to your students read several pages. Use the Qualities of Good Reading list provided in the Appendix to help you know what to emphasize.

3.   Work with the students to complete the Mood Search on day 2 in the *Student Book*. Discuss the meaning of each mood. Show students how to use the chapter titles, pictures, synopsis, and anything already read in the book to guess the moods in the book. You may want to write answers on a marker board as you discuss them, so the students can copy them. Then, the students can concentrate on the discussion rather than on spelling and capitalization.

Independent   <u>**Level 6/7/8**</u>

Focus: Vocabulary Builder - Word Draw

Preparation:
1.   Have a dictionary available.

Lesson:
1.   The students complete the activities in the *Student Book* and read the assigned
       pages for day 4 on their own.

2.   The directions instruct the students to come and show you the completed
       Word Draw vocabulary assignment.

Teacher Directed   **Level 2/3**

Focus: Story Element Instruction - Moods

Lesson:

1.   Listen to your students read part or all of the assigned pages out loud to you. Have students search for examples of exclamation points being used in their books as they read. Use the Reading Strategies list and the Qualities of Good Reading list provided in the Appendix to help you know what to emphasize.

2.   The teacher reads the following sentences out loud. After each sentence, have students name the emotion shown in the sentence.
       a) *I got a new kitten this morning!* (happiness or excitement)
       b) *The wind is blowing really hard outside!* (anxiety or fear)
       c) *I can hardly wait until my birthday!* (excitement or anticipation)
       d) *The puppy chewed on my new shoes!* (disappointment or anger)

3.   Discuss the following questions with your students:
       a) *How does an exclamation point change a sentence?* (It makes the sentence show strong emotions such as happiness, sadness, fear, worry or relief.)
       b) *Read an example from your book of a place where an exclamation point was used. Read the sentence first without emotion and then with emotion.*
       c) *What feeling was the author trying to show you in the sentence you just read? How do you know?* (Guide students to name an emotion that fits with what is happening in the story.)
       d) *What mood does the sentence you read help create in the story?* (Note: An emotion lasts for a moment, while a mood lasts longer and encompasses a larger part of the story.)

4.   Repeat steps *b, c,* and *d* several times, having students use different examples from their books.

5.   Discuss the following questions with your students:
       a) *Why are moods important to a story?* (It makes the reader feel what the characters in the story are feeling.)
       b) *Why should you change your voice when you read a part that has strong feeling?* (Otherwise, the mood is lost, and the story becomes dull.)

Independent   **Level 4/5**

Focus: Story Element Extension - Fantasy Focus

Lesson:

1.   Tell the students to read the assigned pages for day 3 on their own.

2.   Tell them to complete Fantasy Focus on day 3 in their *Student Book* when they finish reading.

3.   The directions instruct the students to come and show you the completed work.

Teacher Directed / Independent   **Level 6/7/8**

Focus: Story Element Discussion - Mood Chart

Lesson:

1.   The students read the assigned pages for day 3 on their own.

2.   The students meet with you to discuss the following questions:
      a) *Who are the main characters in the story?*
      b) *Why are these characters important to the story?*
      c) *What are some of the moods or general feelings that you have noticed in the book?*
      d) *What happened in the story to create those moods?*

3.   Introduce the Mood Chart in the *Student Book* under day 3.

4.   Have the students work to complete the Mood Chart on their own.

5.   The directions instruct the students to come and show you the completed assignment.

Teacher Directed   **Level 2/3**

Focus: Godly Character Traits - Examples

Preparation:
1.   Think of examples you can share from your own life for each of the following traits: *brotherly love* and *compassion*. (Definitions are listed in the lesson below.)

Lesson:
1.   Introduce the following definition and scripture passage for *brotherly love:*
        a) *Brotherly love is sincerely caring for others regardless of the circumstance.*
        b) *Key Scripture verse: And this is my prayer: that your love may abound more and more in knowledge and depth of insight, so that you may be able to discern what is best and may be pure and blameless until the day of Christ. Philippians 1:9*

2.   Share an example of *love* from your own life.

3.   Help the students think of an example of *love* from their own lives.

4.   Introduce the following definition and scripture passage for *compassion*:
        a) *Compassion is feeling the suffering of someone else enough to help them, without expecting something in return.*
        b) *Key Scripture verse: Finally, all of you, live in harmony with one another; be sympathetic, love as brothers, be compassionate and humble. 1 Peter 3:8*

5.   Repeat steps 2 and 3 for the trait *compassion*.

6.   Instruct your students to search for examples of *love* and *compassion* as they read part or all of the assigned pages out loud to you. Use the Reading Strategies list and the Qualities of Good Reading list provided in the Appendix to help you know what to emphasize.

7.   Discuss the following questions with your students:
        a) *How do the characters show love? Or compassion?*
        b) *Did the characters show the opposite traits of hatred or indifference? Explain.*
        c) *What could the characters do differently to be more loving or compassionate?*

Independent / Teacher Directed   **Level 4/5**

Focus: Godly Character Traits - Examples

Lesson:

1.   Tell the students to read and complete the Godly Character Sheet on day 4 in the *Student Book* on their own.

2.   Have the students silently read the assigned pages for day 4, leaving 3-4 pages to read aloud to you.

3.   The students should come and show you when both are completed.

4.   Review the Godly Character Sheet on day 4 in the *Student Book*, so both the students and you know what traits you are searching for in the fantasy book. *(love, compassion,* and *tolerance)*

5.   Listen to your students read 3-4 pages aloud. Use the Qualities of Good Reading list provided in the Appendix to help you know what to emphasize.

6.   Discuss the following questions with the students:
       a) *How did the characters show brotherly love?*
       b) *How did the characters show compassion?*
       c) *How did the characters show tolerance?*
       d) *Did the characters show the opposite traits of hatred? Or indifference? Or intolerance? Explain.*
       e) *What might Jesus have done differently if He had been a character in the book?*

Independent   **Level 6/7/8**

Focus: Godly Character Traits - Examples

Lesson:

1.   The students complete the activities in the *Student Book* and read the assigned pages for day 4 on their own.

2.   The directions instruct the students to come and show you the completed Godly Character page.

Teacher Directed / Independent   **Level 2/3**

Focus: Comprehension Check - Story Retelling

Lesson:
1.   Go over the directions for Story Retelling on day 5 in the *Student Book*. Students complete this assignment on their own after reading the assigned pages.

2.   Listen to your students read part of the assigned pages out loud to you. Use the Reading Strategies list and the Qualities of Good Reading list provided in the Appendix to help you know what to emphasize.

3.   The students finish the assigned reading and complete Story Retelling on their own. The directions instruct the students to come and show you the completed assignment.

Independent   **Level 4/5**

Focus: Comprehension Check - Focus on Emotions

Lesson:
1.   Tell the students to complete Focus on Emotions on day 5 in the *Student Book* on their own.

2.   The students also read the assigned pages for day 5 on their own. You may choose to have the students leave 3-4 pages to read aloud to you.

3.   The directions instruct the students to come and show you the completed assignment.

Independent   **Level 6/7/8**

Focus: Comprehension Check - Emotional Events

Lesson:
1.   The students complete the activities in the *Student Book* and read the assigned pages for day 5 on their own.

2.   The directions instruct the students to come and show you the completed Emotional Events assignment.

Teacher Directed   **All Levels Together**

Focus: Prereading Activity - Setting Sketch

Preparation:
1.   If students are beginning new books today, make sure to have the number of
        pages to be read each day calculated and have those books ready to hand out.
        (See the *Getting Started* section, item #7, in the back of this guide for details.)

2.   If students are <u>not</u> beginning new books today, they use the books they are
        currently reading for today's activities. If you have only one student, you will
        need to do this activity and be the student's partner.

3.   Provide one piece of white drawing paper for each student.

Lesson:
1.   Say, *Today we will be doing a prereading activity to help you think about the
        next book you will be reading or the next part of the book you will be reading.*

2.   Give students a little time to look at the cover, read the synopsis, and quickly
        page through the book.

3.   Discuss the following questions with the students:
        a) *What fantastic or unrealistic things do you notice in the story?*
        b) *Are all of the characters people? If not, why might the author choose the
           characters he did?*
        c) *What conflict or problem do you notice?*

4.   Tell the students to choose one setting or place to describe from their book. The
        students should find a picture of this setting in their books, if at all possible.
        Students <u>should not</u> let other group members see the setting they chose.

5.   Have students open their *Student Book* to Setting Sketch on day 6. They
        should write their answers using the setting they chose. Give students a time
        limit of 10 minutes to complete this part.

6.   When all students have completed the *Student Book*, have them exchange
        books with another group member.   Group members follow the directions to
        draw the setting described in the *Student Book* on white paper. Give the
        students 10 minutes to complete the drawing. The drawing is meant to be a
        quick sketch.

Unit 4

7. After students are done drawing, they return the *Student Book* to the owner. All students compare their drawing to the picture in the book that matches the setting they drew.

8. Discuss the following questions with the students:
   a) *Is the setting in your book realistic? What makes it realistic?*
   b) *Did the setting you drew match the picture in the book?*
   c) *Why did some parts of your picture match the book's picture, while other parts didn't?* (Guide students to understand that words paint a picture in our minds. The more specific the words are, the more exactly the picture in our mind matches what the writer is thinking. This is why word choice is so important.)

9. Help students update their *Assigned Reading Calendar* for days 6-10.

10. Have students read the assigned pages for day 6 on their own.

Teacher Directed   **Level 2/3**

Focus: Story Discussion and Optional Phonics <u>or</u> Vocabulary Work

Preparation:
1.   You may choose to have students at this level review phonics <u>or</u> complete a
        vocabulary assignment. Use your own program for the phonics review. Refer to
        the Appendix for a reproducible vocabulary assignment. The lesson on this day
        is much shorter to compensate for the additional time you may spend on
        phonics or on vocabulary work.

Lesson:
1.   Optional phonics or vocabulary work

2.   Listen to your students read the assigned pages out loud to you. Use the
        Reading Strategies list and the Qualities of Good Reading list provided in the
        Appendix to help you know what to emphasize.

3.   Discuss the following questions with your students:
        a) *If you were a character in this story, what would you like the best about what's
           happening in the story?*
        b) *What would you change? Why would you change this?*
        c) *Who are the main characters in the story?*
        d) *Do you like or dislike each character? Explain.*

Independent / Teacher Directed   **Level 4/5**

Focus: Story Element Instruction - Mood Web

Lesson:
1.   Tell the students to read the assigned pages on their own, leaving 3-4 pages to
        read aloud to you.

2.   Listen to your students read several pages. Use the Qualities of Good Reading
        list provided in the Appendix to help you know what to emphasize.

3.   Work with the students to complete the Mood Web on day 7 in the *Student
        Book.* You may want to write the answers on a marker board as you discuss
        them, so the students can copy them. Then, the students can concentrate on
        the discussion rather than on spelling and capitalization.

4.   Discuss the following question with your students:
     a) *Who do you know that is similar to the main character? Explain.*

Independent   **Level 6/7/8**

Focus: Vocabulary Builder - Word Draw

Preparation:
1.   Have a dictionary available.

Lesson:
1.   The students complete the activities in the *Student Book* and read the assigned
     pages for day 7 on their own.

2.   The directions instruct students to come and show you the completed
     Word Draw vocabulary assignment.

Teacher Directed / Independent   **Level 2/3**

Focus: Story Element Instruction - Mood Map

Lesson:
1.   Listen to your students read the assigned pages out loud to you. Use the Reading Strategies list and the Qualities of Good Reading list provided in the Appendix to help you know what to emphasize.

2.   Discuss the following questions with the students:
      a) *What do you think is going to happen next?*
      b) *What clues help you predict what will happen next?*

3.   Have student open their *Student Books* to day 8. Help the students brainstorm a list of possible moods. Write the moods on the lines provided in the *Student Book* for day 8. (Examples of ideas for moods include the following: mysterious, frightening, gloomy, peaceful, intense, hopeful, exciting, funny, sad, suspenseful, happy, unhappy, lonely, humorous, and thrilling.)

4.   Assign the students the Mood Map on day 8 in the *Student Book.* Do the first two events and moods with the students to make sure they understand what to do.

5.   The directions instruct the students to come and show you the completed assignment.

Independent   **Level 4/5**

Focus: Story Element Extension - Mood Web

Lesson:
1.   Tell the students to read the assigned pages for day 8 on their own.

2.   Tell them to complete the Mood Web on day 8 in their *Student Book* when they finish reading. Students need to use a different character than they used for the web on day 7.

3.   The directions instruct students to come and show you the completed assignment.

Teacher Directed / Independent   **Level 6/7/8**

Focus: Story Element Discussion - Mood Chart

Lesson:

1.   The students read the assigned pages for day 8 on their own.

2.   The students meet with you to discuss the following questions:
      a) *What do you remember most about the story? Why?*
      b) *What types of conflict are in the story - character against character, character against nature, character against society, or character against himself? Explain.*
      c) *Which character reminds you of yourself? Explain.*

3.   Introduce the Mood Chart on day 8 in the *Student Book*. Do the first event together. Then, have the students work on their own.

4.   The directions instruct students to come and show you the completed assignment.

Teacher Directed   **Level 2/3**

Focus: Godly Character Traits - Biblical Comparisons

Preparation:
1.   Find a short children's book of the Bible story about the boy who shared his
        lunch. Otherwise, you will need to read the story directly from the Bible in
        Matthew 14:13-21.

Lesson:
1.   Review the following definitions and scripture passages:
        a) *Brotherly love is sincerely caring for others regardless of the circumstance.*
        b) *Key Scripture verse: And this is my prayer: that your love may abound more*
           and more in knowledge and depth of insight, so that you may be able to
           discern what is best and may be pure and blameless until the day of Christ.
           Philippians 1:9
        c) *Compassion is feeling the suffering of someone else enough to help them,*
           without expecting something in return.
        d) *Key Scripture verse: Finally, all of you, live in harmony with one another; be*
           sympathetic, love as brothers, be compassionate and humble.
           1 Peter 3:8

2.   Read the children's book, or the Bible passage Matthew 14:13-21, about Jesus
        feeding the crowd. Instruct your students to listen for examples of *brotherly love*
        and *compassion* in the story being read.

3.   Discuss the following question with your students:
        a) *How did Jesus and the little boy show brotherly love and compassion?*

4.   Record the students' responses in the *Student Book* on day 9 under the Biblical
        Character column. (Possible answers include the following: *Brotherly love* by
        Jesus wanting to feed the people, rather than send them away as night
        approached; *Brotherly love* by the little boy when he gave his fish and bread to
        Jesus; *Compassion* when Jesus healed the sick, even though He was grieving
        over the death of John the Baptist; *Compassion* when Jesus knew the people
        were hungry, and He fed them.)

5.   Listen to your students read the assigned pages for day 9 out loud to you.
        Remind the students to be searching for examples of *brotherly love* and
        compassion.

6.   Using the questions on the next page, compare Jesus with the main character
        in the fantasy. Record the responses on day 9 in the *Student Book* under the
        Book Character column.

                                                                              Unit 4

a) *How does the character in your book show brotherly love and compassion?*
b) *What would Jesus do differently from the character in your book?*

Independent / Teacher Directed   **Level 4/5**

Focus: Godly Character Traits - Biblical Comparisons

Preparation:
1.   Find a short children's book of the Bible story about the good Samaritan. Otherwise, the students read the story directly from the Bible in Luke 10:25-37.

Lesson:
1.   Tell the students to review the Godly Character Traits listed on day 9 in the *Student Book* on their own. Then, have the students silently read the story of the good Samaritan, either from the book you provided or from the Bible in Luke 10:25-37.

2.   Have students do their best to complete the Biblical Character column on the Godly Character Story Sheet for the Samaritan on day 9 in the *Student Book.*

3.   Students silently read the assigned pages in the fantasy for day 9, saving 3 or 4 pages to read aloud to you.

4.   The students meet with you to finish the assignment for day 9. Listen to your students read several pages. Use the Qualities of Good Reading list provided in the Appendix to help you know what to emphasize.

5.   Discuss the following questions with the students as you review what they have already done in the *Student Book* for day 9. Complete the remaining columns in the *Student Book* for day 9.
      a) *How did the Samaritan's behavior show brotherly love, compassion, and tolerance?* (Possible answers include the following: *Brotherly love* by feeling sorrow for the man who was hurt, even though the man was a Jew; *Compassion* when the Samaritan bandaged the man's wounds and took him to an inn to recover; *Tolerance* by stopping to help the man even though there was deep hatred between the Samaritans and the Jews.)
      b) *How did the person in your book behave like the Biblical character, the Samaritan?* (List the answers in the *Student Book.*)
      c) *How did the person in your book behave differently from the Samaritan?* (List the answers in the *Student Book.*)
      d) *Which trait was shown least often by the book character?* (Explain in the *Student Book.*)

<u>Independent</u>   **<u>Level 6/7/8</u>**

Focus: Godly Character Traits - Biblical Comparisons

Preparation:
1.   The students need a Bible for today's lesson.

Lesson:
1.   The students complete the activities in the *Student Book* and read the assigned pages for day 9 on their own.

2.   The directions instruct the students to come and show you the completed Godly Character Story page. (Examples of the traits in the prodigal son might include the following: *Tolerance* by the father when he gave the younger son his share of the estate, even though the son's request showed arrogant disregard for his father's authority as head of the family; *Patience* as the father waited for the son to learn his lesson and return; *Compassion* as the father welcomed the son home by throwing his arms around him and kissing him, even though the father could have stubbornly refused to forgive the son; *Brotherly love* when the father clothed the son in the best robe and sandals, and had a feast to celebrate the son's return.)

Fantasy - Day 10

Focus: Comprehension Check - Full of Feeling

Lesson:
1.   Say, *Today we will be discussing sentences that show strong emotion.*

2.   The teacher reads the following sentences out loud. After each sentence, students name the emotion shown in the sentence:
    a) *My dog had puppies this morning!* (happiness or excitement)
    b) *The thunder is booming loudly outside!* (anxiety or fear)
    c) *I can hardly wait until Christmas!* (excitement or anticipation)
    d) *My new toy is broken!* (disappointment or anger)

3.   Discuss the following question with your students:
    a) *How does an exclamation point change a sentence?* (It makes the sentence show strong emotion.)

4.   Have students read examples from their books of places where exclamation points were used. Students read the sentences first without emotion and then with emotion. After students share their examples, discuss the following questions:
    a) *What feeling was the author trying to show in the sentence you just read? How do you know?* (Guide students to name an emotion that fits with what is happening in the story at that point.)
    b) *What mood does that sentence help create in the story?* (An emotion lasts for a moment, while a mood lasts longer and encompasses a larger part of the story. Some possible moods include the following: mysterious, frightening, gloomy, peaceful, intense, hopeful, exciting, funny, sad, suspenseful, happy, unhappy, lonely, humorous, and thrilling.)
    c) *Give an example of a time you felt a similar mood in your own life.*

5.   Repeat step 4 several times, having students use different sentences from the book.

6.   Discuss the following questions with your students:
    a) *Why are moods important to a story?* (It makes the reader feel what the characters in the story are feeling.)
    b) *Why should you change your voice when you read a part that has strong feeling?* (Otherwise, the mood is lost and the story becomes dull.)

7.   When all students have finished sharing, have students read the assigned pages in their fantasy book for day 10 on their own.

Unit 4 --

Teacher Directed   **All Levels Together**

Focus: Prereading Activity - Picture Clues

Preparation:

1.   If students are beginning new books today, make sure to have the number of pages to be read each day calculated and have those books ready to hand out. (See the *Getting Started* section, item #7, in the back of this guide for details.)

2.   If students are <u>not</u> beginning new books today, they use the books they are currently reading for today's activities.

Lesson:

1.   Say, *Today we will be doing a prereading activity to help you think about the next book you will be reading or the next part of the book you will be reading.*

2.   Students read the title of their book and inspect the cover. Discuss the following questions with the students:
      a) *What clues does the reading the title give us about the story?*
      b) *What guesses can you make about the characters, settings, or problems from looking at the cover of the book?*

3.   Have students page through all the pictures in the book. Students should examine each picture for clues to the story. Students may share their observations as they are looking through their books. Ask students the following question:
      a) *How do the pictures help you predict what will happen in the story?*

4.   Have students read the synopsis of the story. Ask students the following question:
      a) *What have you learned about the characters, settings and problems after reading the synopsis?*

5.   Instruct students to compare this story to any other fantasy stories that are similar. Emphasize the similarities among fantasy stories, such as the following: The subcategories include animal fantasy, science fiction, and adventure stories. The stories often focus on the courageous ideas and actions of ordinary characters. Fantasies point out the need to be watchful for wickedness and to seek the truth, emphasize decisions resulting in consequences, and are not limited by reality.

6.   Help students update their *Assigned Reading Calendar* for days 11-15. Have students read the assigned pages for day 11 on their own.

Teacher Directed   **Level 2/3**

Focus: Story Discussion and Optional Phonics <u>or</u> Vocabulary Work

Preparation:
1.   You may choose to have students at this level review phonics <u>or</u> complete a vocabulary assignment. Use your own program for the phonics review. Refer to the Appendix for a reproducible vocabulary assignment. The lesson on this day is much shorter to compensate for the additional time you may spend on phonics or on vocabulary work.

Lesson:
1.   Optional phonics or vocabulary work

2.   Listen to your students read the assigned pages out loud to you. Use the Reading Strategies list and the Qualities of Good Reading list provided in the Appendix to help you know what to emphasize.

3.   Discuss the following questions with your students:
        a) *What other story is similar to this story? Explain.*
        b) *What is the problem in this story?*
        c) *How do you suggest the characters solve the problem? Why?*

Independent / Teacher Directed   **Level 4/5**

Focus: Story Element Instruction - Story Moods

Lesson:
1.   Tell the students to read the assigned pages on their own, leaving 3-4 pages to read aloud to you.

2.   Listen to your students read several pages. Use the Qualities of Good Reading list provided in the Appendix to help you know what to emphasize.

3.   Discuss the following questions with your students:
        a) *How can you determine the mood of the story?*
        b) *What is the main conflict or problem in the story?*

4.   Work with the students to complete the Story Moods on day 12 in the *Student Book.* You may want to write the answers on a marker board as you discuss them, so the students can copy them. Then, the students can concentrate on the discussion rather than on spelling and capitalization.

5.   Discuss the following questions with your students:
    a) *How do you think the main conflict or problem will be solved?*
    b) *What would you do to solve the conflict or problem?*

Independent   **Level 6/7/8**

Focus: Vocabulary Builder - Word Draw

Preparation:
1.   Have a dictionary available.

Lesson:
1.   The students complete the activities in the *Student Book* and read the assigned pages for day 12 on their own.

2.   The directions instruct students to come and show you the completed Word Draw vocabulary assignment.

Teacher Directed   **Level 2/3**

Focus: Story Element Instruction - Intense Events

Lesson:
1.   Listen to your students read part or all of the assigned pages out loud to you. Use the Reading Strategies list and the Qualities of Good Reading list provided in the Appendix to help you know what to emphasize.

2.   Work with the students to complete Intense Events on day 13 in the *Student Book.* You may want to write the answers on a marker board as you discuss them, so the students can copy them. Then, the students can concentrate on the discussion rather than on spelling and capitalization.

3.   Discuss the following questions with your students:
        a) *What other moods are in this story? When did they happen?*
        b) *What do you like or dislike about the setting?*

Independent   **Level 4/5**

Focus: Story Element Extension - Story Moods

Lesson:
1.   Tell the students to read the assigned pages for day 13 on their own.

2.   Tell them to complete the Story Moods on day 13 in their *Student Book* when they finish reading. Make sure students add events to continue in sequence from where they ended on day 12.

3.   The directions instruct students to come and show you the completed assignment.

Teacher Directed / Independent   **Level 6/7/8**

Focus: Story Element Discussion - Line Graph

Lesson:
1.   The students read the assigned pages for day 13 on their own.

2.   The students meet with you to discuss the following questions:
        a) *Describe the place in the story.*
        b) *How does the writer create the atmosphere of the setting?*

Unit 4

c) *How do the characters change in the story?*
d) *What are some causes and effects in the story?*

3. Introduce the Line Graph in the *Student Book* for day 13. Make sure students understand the directions. Have the students work on their own to complete it.

4. The directions instruct students to come and show you the completed assignment.

<u>Teacher Directed</u>   **<u>Level 2/3</u>**

Focus: Godly Character Traits - Personal Assessment

Preparation:
1.   You will need an index card or note card for each of your students today.

Lesson:
1.   Review the following definitions and scripture passages:
   a) <u>*Brotherly love*</u> *is sincerely caring for others regardless of the circumstance.*
   b) <u>*Key Scripture verse*</u>*: And this is my prayer: that your love may abound more and more in knowledge and depth of insight, so that you may be able to discern what is best and may be pure and blameless until the day of Christ. Philippians 1:9*
   c) <u>*Compassion*</u> *is feeling the suffering of someone else enough to help them, without expecting something in return.*
   d) <u>*Key Scripture verse:*</u> *Finally, all of you, live in harmony with one another; be sympathetic, love as brothers, be compassionate and humble. 1 Peter 3:8*

2.   Listen to your students read the assigned pages for day 14 out loud to you.

3.   Discuss the following questions with the students:
   a) *Which trait was shown less often by the book character, brotherly love or compassion? Explain.*
   b) *Choose the trait that is harder for you to show, brotherly love or compassion. Explain.*

4.   Hand out one index card to each student. Have the students write the trait they chose and 3 ways to work on showing the trait more often in their own lives.

5.   On the other side of the card, have the students draw themselves portraying this trait. The students may also write the matching Bible verse if you choose for them to do so.

6.   Have the students post their cards in a place where they will see them often.

<u>Independent / Teacher Directed</u>   **<u>Level 4/5</u>**

Focus: Godly Character Traits - Personal Assessment

Preparation:
1.   You will need an index card or note card for each of your students today.

Lesson:
1.   Tell the students to review the Godly Character Traits listed on day 9 in the *Student Book* on their own.

2.   Have the students silently read the assigned pages in their novel for day 14, saving 3-4 pages to read aloud to you.

3.   Meet with the students to finish the assignment for day 14.

4.   Listen to your students read 3-4 pages. Use the Qualities of Good Reading list provided in the Appendix to help you know what to emphasize.

5.   Discuss the following questions with the students:
   a) *Refer to day 9 in the Student Book. Choose the trait that is the hardest for you to show - brotherly love, compassion, or tolerance. Explain.*
   b) *Look at the Bible verse on day 9 in the Student Book for the trait you chose. How does the behavior of your book characters compare to this verse? Explain.*
   c) *What ways can you demonstrate the verse you chose in your own life?*

6.   Hand out one index card to each student. Have students list actions they will take to help them live according to the verse they chose.

7.   On the other side of the card, have the students divide the card into 3-4 sections, by drawing vertical lines. Instruct the students to break the chosen verse into sections and draw a quick picture or symbol to stand for each section of the verse. When the students look at the pictures, it should remind them of each part of the verse.

8.   The Bible verse may be written on the bottom or on the back of the card if you choose to have the students do so.

9.   Have the students post their cards in a place where they will see them often.

Independent   **Level 6/7/8**

Focus: Godly Character Traits - Personal Assessment

Preparation:
1.   The students each need an index card or note card for today.

Lesson:

1.   The students complete the activities in the *Student Book* and read the assigned pages for day 14 on their own.

2.   The directions instruct the students to come and show you the completed assignment for day 14, including the completed index card or note card for posting.

Teacher Directed   **All Levels Together**

Preparation:

1.   Choose which **one** of the following project options you would like your students to complete as a culminating project for this genre. Each option is explained in detail on the pages that follow. For ease in planning, you should choose the same option for each of the students.

   a) **Option 1:** You may choose a character based project, which focuses on the Godly character trait for this genre. The directions for these projects are more general. The project does not involve any of the books from the unit. It does include a final reflection form.

   b) **Option 2:** You may choose a book based project, which is an individual project that is tailored to the student's individual level. Students will choose one of the books they read for this genre to use for the project. In order to choose this option, you must purchase *Book Projects to Send Home* by Lori Sanders and Linda Kimble for your particular students' levels. There is one book for each of the three levels. The project directions are very detailed and include a final reflection for each project.

   c) **Option 3:** Your final option is to choose a group project, which requires two or more students working together. This project is based on a common book the students have all read or had read aloud to them. The **one** book the project is based upon should fit into the genre studied in this unit.

2.   Have the directions for the project copied for each student. Make sure to read over the directions for the project option you chose in order to know what supplies you will need to have available for the projects.

3.   The plans allow 5 work days for the projects to be completed. This time allotment includes the planning and any presenting of the projects. The plans assume that the students will use only their normal amount of reading time to complete the projects.

Lesson:

1.   Say, *Today we will be starting our culminating project for fantasy. You will have 5 days, counting today, to work on your project. Your projects are due at the end of that time on _____. (give due date)*

2.   Introduce the project you have chosen for this unit. Go through the directions and make sure students have a copy of the directions, so they can work as independently as possible. Show them where the needed supplies are located.

3.   Then, have students read the assigned pages for day 15 to finish the fantasy books. Students may begin the project after the reading is complete.

Fantasy - Day 15 - **Option 1**

Focus: <u>**Godly Character Trait Project**</u>   <u>**Family Spirit**</u>

Project Notes:

1.   Have students show brotherly love by working on goals that center around other family members.

2.   Refer to day 4 or day 9 in the texts to review the definitions and key verses your students studied in this unit.

3.   Reproduce the Family Spirit Planning Form included in this guide for each student. Tell students they will each set 2 goals to work on for the next 5 days.

4.   Goal one will focus on *brotherly love.* This goal needs to be something the student will <u>do</u> for another family member. For example, I will cheerfully read books or play blocks or puzzles with John for 30 minutes each day.

5.   Goal 2 will focus on *compassion, tolerance,* or *patience.* This goal needs to be something the student will <u>show</u> to another family member. For example, I will show patience with Rebecca by not getting upset when she plays with my things and doesn't put them away.

6.   Each goal must follow the guidelines listed below:
    a) needs to be something students will do daily
    b) must involve one or more family members
    c) should be specific
    d) cannot be something the students are already doing

7.   Help students write their goals. It is a good idea to try to include as many family members as possible in the goals, so the whole family can be involved.

8.   Reproduce one Family Spirit Daily Goal Chart from this guide for each student. Students will use the half-sheet to keep track of whether or not their goals have been met. You may decide how to have students mark their goals. Some possible ideas include coloring in the boxes, using stickers, or taping an item such as a penny or a small candy to be removed each time the goal is met.

9.   When the goal charts are complete, you will have a family celebration. This should be something you all enjoy doing together. Some possible suggestions include a special meal, outdoor activity, game night, or a musical activity. Students need to help plan and prepare for the family celebration.

10.   On day 19, reproduce the reflection form included in this guide for each student to complete.

Family Spirit Planning Form

Name: _____

Directions: You will write 2 goals that center around other family members. Each goal needs to be something you will do daily, must involve one or more family members, should be specific, and cannot be something you are already doing

Goal 1: Brotherly Love

Note: This goal needs to be something you will <u>do</u> for another family member.

My goal involves the following family member (write his/her name):_____

I will _____

_____

_____

Goal 2 (circle one):   **Compassion**   **Patience**   **Tolerance**

Note: This goal needs to be something you will <u>show</u> another family member.

My goal involves the following family member (write his/her name):_____

I will _____

_____

_____

Family Celebration:

When my goal chart is complete, our family will _____

_____

_____

Show the teacher this page when you are finished.   Unit 4

Family Spirit Daily Goal Chart

Goal 1: Brotherly Love   Name: _____
Goal 2: Compassion, Tolerance, or Patience

Day 1	Day 2	Day 3	Day 4	Day 5
Goal 1	Goal 1	Goal 1	Goal 1	Goal 1
Goal 2	Goal 2	Goal 2	Goal 2	Goal 2

---Cut---

Goal 1: Brotherly Love   Name: _____
Goal 2: Compassion, Tolerance, or Patience

Day 1	Day 2	Day 3	Day 4	Day 5
Goal 1	Goal 1	Goal 1	Goal 1	Goal 1
Goal 2	Goal 2	Goal 2	Goal 2	Goal 2

Focus: <u>Book Based Project</u>   **Individual Projects by Level**

Project Notes:

1.   This is an individual project tailored to the students' individual levels.

2.   In order to choose this option, you must purchase *Book Projects to Send Home* by Lori Sanders and Linda Kimble (McGraw-Hill, 2004) for your particular students' levels. There is one project book for each of the 3 levels. The books include detailed reproducible directions, work schedules, and reflection forms.

3.   The students each need to choose **one** book from those that **were read in this genre**. That book is the basis for the project.

4.   The project titles, corresponding page numbers, and levels in the *Book Projects to Send Home* books are listed below.

Use Grade 2 of *Book Projects to Send Home*   **Level 2/3**

Project Title: Cylinder Sequence Lit Kit   Page Numbers: 11-14

Preparation:

1.   Read the project description box and the materials to provide section on p. 11. The rest of the items on p. 11 are <u>optional</u> ideas to use if you enjoy teaching through themes.

2.   Copy pp. 12-14 for your students. Save p. 14 for the students to complete on day 19 as a reflection on their project. This is listed in the plans for day 19.

3.   The sharing your cylinder sequence lit kit on p. 12 will be presented to your family instead.

Use Grade 4 of *Book Projects to Send Home*   **Level 4/5**

Note: This project will not use a multicultural book, as the directions suggest. Instead, students use one of the fantasy stories they read. The setting and details of that story will be thought of as a different culture for the purposes of this project.

Project Title: Lit Kit Brag Bag   Page Numbers: 19-22

Preparation:

1.   Read the project description box and the materials to provide section on p. 19. The rest of the items on p. 19 are <u>optional</u> ideas to use if you enjoy teaching through themes.

2.   Copy pp. 20-22 and 47 for your students. Save p. 47 for the students to complete on day 19 as a reflection on their project. This is listed in the plans for day 19.

3.   Instruct students to think of the schedule on p. 21 as steps to complete, rather than a time frame for each part of the project.   The students will be working solely on completing the projects for 5 reading days, instead of doing them gradually for 4 weeks as the project book suggests.

4.   The students have already completed the project requirements listed under week 1 in the schedule on p. 21. Remember: We are <u>not</u> using multicultural books for this project. Students will choose one of the fantasy stories they have already read and think of the setting and details of that story as another culture.

<u>Use Grade 5 of *Book Projects to Send Home*</u>   <u>Level 6/7/8</u>

Note: Although these projects are listed for grade 5, they are very challenging to complete which makes them appropriate for level 6/7/8.

Project Title: Lit Kit   Page Numbers: 27-30

Preparation:

1.   Read the project description box and the materials to provide section on p. 27. The rest of the items on p. 27 are <u>optional</u> ideas to use if you enjoy teaching through themes.

2.   Copy pp. 28-30 and 47 for your students. You may want to remove the "Dear Fifth Grader" greeting on p. 28. Save p. 47 for the students to complete on day 19 as a reflection on their projects. This is listed in the plans for day 19.

3.   Instruct students to think of the schedule on p. 29 as steps to complete, rather than a time frame for each part of the project. The students will be working solely on completing the projects for 5 reading days, instead of doing them gradually for 4 weeks as the project book suggests.

4.   The students have already completed the project requirements listed under week 1 on the schedule on p. 29. They will not need to choose another book to read.

5.   The presentation guidelines listed on p. 29 will not include guests when used at home.

Focus: Group Project   **Mural**

Project Notes:
1.   In order to choose this option, you must have two or more students (unless you are willing to do part of the project with your student).

2.   This project is based on **one** common book the students have all read or had read aloud to them. The book the project is based upon should fit into the genre studied in this unit.

3.   Students work together to create a mural about the book as a group. Reproduce the planning form in this guide for each student to complete as the group meets. The planning form needs to be completed on day 15. Remember, the mural must be completed by day 19.

4.   The teacher must decide the size of the mural and the place where it will be hung, prior to the group's planning meeting.

5.   The mural can be drawn on a large piece of tag board, a long roll of paper, or on several smaller sheets of paper placed end to end to resemble a long strip of paper.

6.   On days 16-19, the students follow their planning form to complete the mural. The students should each know their roles in completing the mural.

7.   On day 19, students hang the mural. The students read the planning form out loud to describe the mural to the teacher. Reproduce the reflection form included in this guide for each student to complete.

Mural Planning Sheet

Name:_____

Title of Book:_____

Who are the main characters in the story?_____

What are the important settings in the story?_____

What is the main problem in the story? _____

How is the problem solved? _____

What will be the big idea or focus of the mural?_____

_____

Which events from the book will be part of the mural?_____

_____

_____

_____

_____

Mark the "map of the mural" below to show how the mural will be divided in order to include the events your group selected.

_____

What supplies will you need to create the mural?

_____

What will be your assignment for the mural?_____

_____

Show the teacher this page when you are finished.

Independent / Teacher Directed   **All Levels**

Focus: Project Work

Preparation:
1.   For details, read the directions for the project option you chose.

Lesson:
1.   Check students' progress to make sure each student understands what to do and is on schedule to finish by day 19.

2.   Meet with students as a group, if this is needed.

Independent / Teacher Directed   **All Levels**

Focus: Project Completion

Preparation:
1.   For details, read the directions for the project option you chose.

2.   Have the reflection forms copied for each student to match the project option you chose.

Lesson:
1.   Briefly check students' progress. Students should finish their projects today.

2.   Have students share their projects with each other or with you.

3.   Hand out the reflection form that matches the project option you chose. Have the students complete the reflection and show you.

4.   You are ready to choose the next genre your students will study. Look ahead to prepare the kickoff for the upcoming genre.

Family Spirit Reflection

1. On my goal chart, I felt that I did a good job of _____

_____.

2. I think that I could have done a better job of_____

_____.

3. If I could make a goal chart again, I would _____

_____.

4. I learned the following things about my family by doing this project:_____

_____

_____

_____.

5. The best part of this project is_____

_____.

_____   _____
Signature of student   Date

Mural Reflection

1. On the mural project, I felt that I did a good job of_____

_____.

2. I think that I could have done a better job of_____

_____.

3. If I could do the mural project again, I would _____

_____

_____.

4. From the mural project, I learned_____

_____

_____

_____.

5. My favorite part of the project was _____

_____.

_____   _____
Signature of student   Date

Mystery

GENRE: MYSTERY

Definition:
A story involving a puzzling situation with a problem to be solved.

Common Characteristics:
1. Intertwines the characters' lives through their connection to the mystery.
2. Encourages the reader to search for links between events.
3. Provides clues as hints to help solve the mystery.
4. Presents distractions to divert you from the outcome.
5. Ends with a credible solution to the mystery.

Story Element Emphasis: Prediction and Inference

Definition of Prediction:
Anticipating what will happen next using clues in the story combined with any background knowledge you have.

Definition of Inference:
Pondering details from the story in order to draw conclusions that make sense of what the text implies.

Godly Character Trait Emphasis: Loyalty

Definition:
Showing firm, faithful support even in times of trouble.

Subqualities:
1. fairness
2. discretion
3. discernment

Teacher Directed   **All Levels Together**

Focus: Genre Kickoff

Preparation:
1.   The goal of the kickoff is to introduce students of all ages to the upcoming genre in a fun and entertaining manner.

2.   Decide how much time you want to spend on the kickoff. You can spend one normal reading class period, several hours, or even a whole day. After the kickoff, you begin with day 1 in the teacher's plans.

3.   Read through the list of ideas below and choose those that interest you for this genre's kickoff. You are welcome to add your own ideas that fit within this genre. Refer to the cover page for a definition and common characteristics for each genre. Introduce the name and definition of the genre to begin the kickoff.

Possible Kickoff Ideas:
1.   Read the beginning page of several different mysteries aloud to your students. Go through the common characteristics of a mystery. Have students write their own mysterious beginning of a story. Share the beginnings with the group.

2.   Make a code with symbols for each letter of the alphabet. Have students apply the code by writing various words or sentences. Then, students can make their own codes.

3.   Play a board game that has students solve a mystery, like *Where in the World is Carmen Sandiego?* or *Clue Jr.*

4.   Choose one item and put it in a box or lidded tub. Give clues to the contents of the box. Have students guess what item is in the box. Next, each student thinks of one item to put in the box and writes clues about that item. Students take turns secretly placing their item in the box and reading their clues for others to guess the contents.

5.   Select a set of 3 or 4 objects that have something in common. Then, add one object that does not fit with the criteria used for the other objects. Place the set of objects, including the odd one, on display for the students. Have students try and guess which object is the odd one and explain why. Repeat this activity with several other sets of objects.

       Have students make their own display of similar objects, making sure to include one odd object. A variation would be to have students draw pictures of similar objects, making sure to include one odd object. Students share their displays or pictures with the group. The group tries to guess which object is the odd one.

6.   Read aloud a short mystery story. Have students use a variety of noisemakers to create a mysterious accompaniment to the mystery story. It is helpful to read the story one time without accompaniment, so students can decide where to add sounds. Then, read the story a second time with accompaniment.
Some examples of noisemakers include the following: pots and pans, wooden spoons, aluminum foil, paper crumpling, shaking a salt container, aluminum pie plates with hard macaroni noodles, musical instruments, and any toys that make sounds.

7.   Draw a picture of a scene that shows a variety of mysterious things among ordinary things. Trade pictures and see if someone else can find the mysterious things. For example, you could draw a summer scene at the beach and have someone dressed in a snowsuit, a steaming cup of hot chocolate, a child sledding on the water, and so on. Or, you could draw an ordinary house with a broken window, muddy footprints across the floor, lightning outside the window, and so on.

8.   Read or give the students brain teasers or logic problems to try to solve.

9.   Have a mystery lunch or snack. Create a menu with 3 or more simple courses of mystery foods and eating utensils with made-up names. The names need to have clues to the real food or eating utensil. Students order a set number of items off the menu, one course at a time, not knowing what food they'll get, or if they'll get any silverware to eat the food. Serve courses one at a time to extend the mystery. Keep courses and food simple, so you don't have so much to prepare. See the sample lunch menu listed below:

Real Food or Utensil Name:	Course 1 (choose 2 items):
(peaches)	fuzzy slice
(applesauce)	yellow smoothie
(spoon)	shovel
(water)	clear quencher

	Course 2 (choose 2 items):
(peas)	green spheres
(corn)	rows of ears
(juice)	refreshing squeeze
(fork)	pointy peaks

	Course 3 (choose 2 items):
(ham sandwich)	piggie pie
(hot dog)	puppy in the sun
(soup)	steaming surprise
(spoon)	shallow bowl
(milk)	dairy dream

10. Read a short mystery book aloud. Stop at a crucial point in the mystery. Discuss as a group and list on a large paper or marker board any possible clues. Refer back to the book as needed. List the possible suspects. Have each student write a guess about "who did it" and "why" on a slip of paper. Put the slips of papers in a box. Read the rest of the mystery. Then, share the guesses in the box and see if any were correct. Discuss the guesses that were not correct. Decide if those guesses made sense too. Do not share who made which guess.

Questions to discuss at the end of the kickoff:

1. What is a mystery? (Refer to the definition on the cover page for this genre.)

2. What did you learn about mysteries from today's activities?

3. What are some common characteristics of mysteries?

4. Why do we read mysteries?

Teacher Directed   **All Levels Together**

Focus: Prereading Activity - Important Information

Preparation:
1.   Prior to meeting with the students for day 1, follow the directions for *Getting Started* listed in the back of this guide.

2.   Have the first book and one *Assigned Reading Calendar* ready for each student.

Lesson:
1.   Say, *Today we will be doing a prereading activity to help you think about the next book you will be reading.*

2.   Give students the first book they will be reading for this genre.

3.   Have students briefly look at the cover, read the synopsis, and quickly page through the book.

4.   Have students open their *Student Books* to Important Information on day 1. Tell students they will complete the assignment as you discuss the following questions: (The teacher's notes below tell you when the students need to write in their *Student Books.)*
      a) *How can you tell that the story is a mystery?* (There is a puzzling situation or problem to solve.)
      b) *What is the mystery in your book?*
      c) *Who are some of the characters that seem important to the mystery?* (Students list the names of these characters in their *Student Books* under the *People* column.)
      d) *What are some of the places in the book?* (Students list the names of these places in their *Student Books* under the *Places* column.)
      e) *What clues or important items do you notice from looking at the pictures and reading the synopsis?* (Students list the names of these things in their *Student Books* under the *Clues or Items* column.)
      f) *What is one possible solution to the mystery?*

5.   The directions instruct the students to come and show you the completed assignment.

6.   Have students open their *Student Books* to the *Assigned Reading Calendar* for this genre. Help each student fill in the page numbers to be read for days 1-5. Have students read the assigned pages for day 1 on their own.

Teacher Directed   **Level 2/3**

Focus: Story Discussion and Optional Phonics <u>or</u> Vocabulary Work

Preparation:
1.   You may choose to have students at this level review phonics <u>or</u> complete a vocabulary assignment. Use your own program for the phonics review. Refer to the Appendix for a reproducible vocabulary assignment. The lesson on this day is much shorter to compensate for the additional time you may spend on phonics or on vocabulary work.

Lesson:
1.   Optional phonics or vocabulary work

2.   Listen to your students read the assigned pages out loud to you. Use the Reading Strategies list and the Qualities of Good Reading list provided in the Appendix to help you know what to emphasize.

3.   Discuss the following questions with your students:
      a) *Who are the main characters in the story?*
      b) *What does each character have to do with the problem that needs to be solved?*
      c) *Have you ever been to a place like the one in the book? If so, describe it.*
      d) *What do you think is going to happen next? Why?*

Independent / Teacher Directed   **Level 4/5**

Focus: Story Element Instruction - Prediction Journal

Lesson:
1.   Tell the students to read <u>one third</u> of the assigned pages on their own.

2.   Tell students to open their *Student Books* to the Prediction Journal on day 2. Have students do the first section of the assignment on their own. Students are asked to summarize the important details or evidence from the story.

3.   Meet with the students. Introduce the following definition for prediction: *Anticipating what will happen next using clues in the story combined with any background knowledge you might have.* Have students write a prediction in their *Student Books* about what they think will happen next in the mystery.

4.   Listen to the students read the <u>next third</u> of the assigned pages out loud.

5.   Ask students to review the prediction they wrote in their *Student Books*. Discuss how their prediction compares to what really took place in the story.

6.   Ask students to share the important details or evidence they learned in the second section of the story. They should write these facts in their *Student Books*. You may want to write answers on a marker board as you discuss them, so the students can copy them. Then, the students can concentrate on the discussion rather than on spelling and capitalization.

7.   Have students write a prediction in their *Student Books* about what they think will happen next.

8.   Listen to the students read the <u>last third</u> of the assigned pages out loud.

9.   Ask students to review the prediction they wrote in their *Student Books*. Discuss how their prediction compares to what really took place in the story.

10.   Ask students to share the important details or evidence they learned in the third section of the story. They should write these facts in their *Student Books*. You may want to write answers on a marker board as you discuss them, so the students can copy them. Then, the students can concentrate on the discussion rather than on spelling and capitalization.

11.   Guide students to write a prediction in their *Student Books*. The prediction should be about what they think will happen in the mystery when they continue reading on day 3.

<u>Independent</u>   **<u>Level 6/7/8</u>**

Focus: Vocabulary Builder - Clue Finder

Lesson:
1.   The students complete the activities in the *Student Book* and read the assigned pages for day 2 on their own.

2.   The directions instruct students to come and show you the completed Clue Finder vocabulary assignment.

Teacher Directed   **Level 2/3**

Focus: Story Element Instruction - Prediction Practice

Preparation:
1.   You need a large piece of paper or a marker board for the lesson.

Lesson:
1.   Prior to listening to the students read, ask students to share the important facts they have learned in the story. You need to write the students' answers on a marker board or large piece of paper as you discuss them, so the students can refer to them.

2.   Introduce the following definition for prediction: *Anticipating what will happen next using clues in the story combined with any background knowledge you might have.* Have students open their *Student Books* to Prediction Practice on day 3. Have students write a prediction in their *Student Books* about what they think will happen next.

3.   Listen to the students read the <u>first third</u> of the assigned pages out loud.

4.   Ask students to review the prediction they wrote in their *Student Books*. Discuss how their prediction compares to what really took place in the story.

5.   Have students volunteer the important facts they learned in the section of the story they just read. You need to write the students' answers on a marker board or a large piece of paper as you discuss them, so the students can refer to them.

6.   Help students write a prediction in their *Student Books* about what they think will happen next in the mystery.

7.   Listen to the students read the <u>middle third</u> of the assigned pages out loud.

8.   Ask students to review the prediction they wrote in their *Student Books*. Discuss how their prediction compares to what really took place in the story.

9.   Have students volunteer the important facts they learned in the section of the story they just read. You need to write the students' answers on a marker board or large piece of paper as you discuss them, so the students can refer to them.

10.   Have students write a prediction in their *Student Books* about what they think will happen next.

Mystery - Day 3

11.   Listen to the students read the <u>last third</u> of the assigned pages out loud.

12.   Ask students to review the prediction they wrote in their *Student Books.* Discuss how their prediction compares to what really took place in the story.

Independent   **Level 4/5**

Focus: Story Element Extension - Prediction Journal

Lesson:
1.   Help the students divide the assigned reading for day 3 into two equal parts. Instruct the students to follow the directions on day 3 of their *Student Books* after they read the first part of the assigned pages on their own.

2.   The *Student Book* gives students directions for reading the other half of the assigned pages.

3.   The directions instruct students to come and show you the completed assignment.

Teacher Directed / Independent   **Level 6/7/8**

Focus: Story Element Discussion - Prediction Review

Lesson:
1.   The students read the assigned pages for day 3 on their own.

2.   The students meet with you to discuss the following questions:
      a) *How did the author make the setting seem mysterious?*
      b) *How did the author make the characters seem mysterious?*
      c) *In what way is each character involved in the mystery that needs to be solved?*
      d) *What do you think it means to predict?* (Introduce the following definition for prediction: *Anticipating what will happen next using clues from the story and any background knowledge you might have.*)

3.   Introduce the Prediction Review in the *Student Book* under day 3.

4.   Have the students work alone to complete day 3.

5.   The directions instruct students to come and show you the completed assignment.

Unit 5

Teacher Directed   **Level 2/3**

Focus: Godly Character Traits - Examples

Preparation:
1.   Think of examples you can share from your own life for each of the following
      traits: *loyalty* and *fairness.* (Definitions are listed in the lesson below.)

Lesson:
1.   Introduce the following definition and scripture passage for *loyalty:*
      a) *Loyalty is showing firm, faithful support even in times of trouble.*
      b) *Key Scripture verse: A man's wisdom gives him patience; it is to his glory to
         overlook an offense. Proverbs 19:11*

2.   Share an example of *loyalty* from your own life.

3.   Help the students think of an example of *loyalty* from their own lives.

4.   Introduce the following definition and scripture passage for *fairness:*
      a) *Fairness is weighing each choice in order to be just and pleasing to God in
         your decisions.*
      b) *Key Scripture verse: I the Lord search the heart and examine the mind, to
         reward a man according to his conduct, according to what his deeds
         deserve. Jeremiah 17:10*

5.   Repeat steps 2 and 3 for the trait *fairness.*

6.   Instruct your students to search for examples of *loyalty* and *fairness* as they read
      part or all of the assigned pages out loud to you. Use the Reading Strategies
      List and the Qualities of Good Reading list provided in the Appendix to help you
      know what to emphasize.

7.   Discuss the following questions with your students:
      a) *How do the characters show loyalty? Or fairness?*
      b) *Did the characters show the opposite traits of treachery and partiality?
         Explain.*
      c) *What could the characters do differently to be more loyal or fair?*

Independent / Teacher Directed   **Level 4/5**

Focus: Godly Character Traits - Examples

Lesson:
1.   Tell the students to read and complete the Godly Character Sheet on day 4 in the *Student Book* on their own.

2.   The students also need to silently read the assigned pages for day 4, leaving 3-4 pages to read aloud to you.

3.   The students should come and show you when both are completed.

4.   Review the Godly Character Sheet on day 4 in the *Student Book*, so the students and you will know what traits you are searching for in the mystery. *(loyalty, fairness,* and *discretion)*

5.   Listen to your students read 3-4 pages aloud. Use the Qualities of Good Reading list provided in the Appendix to help you know what to emphasize.

6.   Discuss the following questions with the students:
       a) *How did the characters show loyalty?*
       b) *How did the characters show fairness?*
       c) *How did the characters show discretion?*
       d) *Did the characters show the opposite traits of treachery? Or partiality? Or simplemindedness? Explain.*
       e) *What might Jesus have done differently if He had been the character in the book?*

Independent   **Level 6/7/8**

Focus: Godly Character Traits - Examples

Lesson:
1.   The students complete the activities in the *Student Book* and read the assigned pages for day 4 on their own.

2.   The directions instruct students to come and show you the completed Godly Character page.

Teacher Directed / Independent   **Level 2/3**

Focus: Comprehension Check - Artful Artist

Lesson:
1.   Go over the directions for Artful Artist on day 5 in the *Student Book*. Students complete this assignment on their own after reading the assigned pages.

2.   Listen to your students read part of the assigned pages out loud to you. Use the Reading Strategies list and the Qualities of Good Reading list provided in the Appendix to help you know what to emphasize.

3.   The students finish the assigned reading and complete Artful Artist on their own. The directions instruct the students to come and show you the completed assignment.

Independent   **Level 4/5**

Focus: Comprehension Check - It's a Mystery

Lesson:
1.   Tell the students to complete It's a Mystery on day 5 in the *Student Book* on their own.

2.   The students also read the assigned pages for day 5 on their own. You may choose to have the students leave 3-4 pages to read aloud to you.

3.   The directions instruct the students to come and show you the completed assignment.

Independent   **Level 6/7/8**

Focus: Comprehension Check - Mystery Detective

Lesson:
1.   The students complete the activities in the *Student Book* and read the assigned pages for day 5 on their own.

2.   The directions instruct students to come and show you the completed Mystery Detective assignment.

Teacher Directed

All Levels Together

Focus: Prereading Activity - Mystery Item

Preparation:
1.   If students are beginning new books today, make sure to have the number of pages to be read each day calculated and have those books ready to hand out. (See the *Getting Started* section, item #7, in the back of this guide for details.)

2.   If students are <u>not</u> beginning new books today, they use the books they are currently reading for today's activities.

3.   You need one item that symbolizes something important in the story each student is reading. Place each item in a separate container. Do not use transparent containers.

Lesson:
1.   Say, *Today we will be doing a prereading activity to help you think about the next book you will be reading or the next part of the book you will be reading.*

2.   If students are beginning new books, hand the books to those students.

3.   Give each student the container with the item that matches the student's story.

4.   Say, *There is a mystery item in the container I have given you. The item has to do with the mystery book you are reading. Your job is to guess what the item might be.*

5.   Allow the students to shake the container. Instruct students to listen carefully because the sound the item makes should give clues about its size, shape, and weight.

6.   Remind students that the mystery items have to do with the stories they are reading. Give each student time to look at the cover, read the synopsis, and quickly page through the mystery book.

7.   Discuss the following questions with the students:
      a) *What item do you predict is in your mystery container?*
      b) *What clues are you using to make your prediction?*
      c) *What is the mystery in your story?*
      d) *What might the item have to do with the mystery in your story?*

8.   Reveal each item after the students have made their predictions.

9.   Help student update their *Assigned Reading Calendar* for days 6-10.

10.   Have students read the assigned pages for day 6 on their own.

Teacher Directed   **Level 2/3**

Focus: Story Discussion and Optional Phonics <u>or</u> Vocabulary Work

Preparation:
1.   You may choose to have students at this level review phonics <u>or</u> complete a vocabulary assignment. Use your own program for the phonics review. Refer to the Appendix for a reproducible vocabulary assignment. The lesson on this day is much shorter to compensate for the additional time you may spend on phonics or on vocabulary work.

Lesson:
1.   Optional phonics or vocabulary work

2.   Listen to your students read the assigned pages out loud to you. Use the Reading Strategies list and the Qualities of Good Reading list provided in the Appendix to help you know what to emphasize.

3.   Discuss the following questions with your students:
      a) *Describe the setting.*
      b) *Do you like or dislike the main characters? Why?*
      c) *Does this story remind you of any other story? Explain.*

Independent / Teacher Directed   **Level 4/5**

Focus: Story Element Instruction - Prediction Plan

Lesson:
1.   Tell the students to read the assigned pages on their own, leaving 3-4 pages to read aloud to you.

2.   Listen to your students read several pages. Use the Qualities of Good Reading list provided in the Appendix to help you know what to emphasize.

3.   Work with the students to complete Prediction Plan on day 7 in the *Student Book.* You may want to write the answers on a marker board as you discuss them, so the students can copy them. Then, the students can concentrate on the discussion rather than on spelling and capitalization.

Independent

Focus: Vocabulary Builder - Clue Finder

Lesson:

1.   The students complete the activities in the *Student Book* and read the assigned pages for day 7 on their own.

2.   The directions instruct students to come and show you the completed Clue Finder vocabulary assignment.

Teacher Directed   Level 2/3

Focus: Story Element Instruction - Prediction

Lesson:

1.   Listen to your students read the assigned pages out loud to you. Use the Reading Strategies list and the Qualities of Good Reading list provided in the Appendix to help you know what to emphasize.

2.   Ask the students what clues about the mystery they can discover by reading the the title of the story.

3.   Have students look through the pictures in the book. As they study each picture, briefly discuss possible hints the pictures provide about what might happen in the story.

4.   Discuss the following questions with the students:
      a) *What other story have you read that seems similar to this one? Explain.*
      b) *How does what happened in that story help you predict what might happen in this mystery?*

Independent   Level 4/5

Focus: Story Element Extension - What's Next

Lesson:

1.   Tell the students to read the assigned pages for day 8 on their own.

2.   Tell them to complete What's Next on day 8 in their *Student Books* when they finish reading.

3.   The directions instruct students to come and show you the completed assignment.

Teacher Directed / Independent   Level 6/7/8

Focus: Story Element Discussion - Inference Clue Search

Lesson:
1.   The students read the assigned pages for day 8 on their own.

2.	The students meet with you to discuss the following questions:
	a) *How are the main characters alike?*
	b) *How are the main characters different?*
	c) *What hints does the author give that might help you solve the mystery?*

3.	Introduce the following definition for inference: *Pondering details in the story in order to draw conclusions that make sense of what the text implies.*

4.	Discuss the following questions with the students:
	a) *What is the difference between prediction and inference?* (Prediction is anticipating what will happen next using clues in the story and any background knowledge you might have. Inference is pondering details in the story in order to draw conclusions that make sense of what the text implies.)
	b) *What background knowledge from your life could help you to predict how the mystery will be solved?*
	c) *What background knowledge from books you have read could help you to predict how the mystery will be solved?*

5.	Introduce Clue Search on day 8 in the *Student Book*. Make sure the students understand what to do. Then, have the students work on their own.

6.	The directions instruct students to come and show you the completed assignment.

Teacher Directed   **Level 2/3**

Focus: Godly Character Traits - Biblical Comparisons

Preparation:
1.   Find a short children's book of the Bible story about David and his loyalty to
        Saul. Otherwise, you will need to read the story directly from the Bible in 1
        Samuel 24:1-12.

Lesson:
1.   Review the following definitions and scripture passages:
        a) *Loyalty is showing firm, faithful support even in times of trouble.*
        b) *Key Scripture verse: A man's wisdom gives him patience; it is to his glory to
           overlook an offense. Proverbs 19:11*
        c) *Fairness is weighing each choice in order to be just and pleasing to God in
           your decisions.*
        d) *Key Scripture verse: I the Lord search the heart and examine the mind, to
           reward a man according to his conduct, according to what his deeds
           deserve. Jeremiah 17:10*

2.   Read the children's book, or the Bible passage 1 Samuel 24:1-12, about David
        and his loyalty to Saul. Instruct your students to listen for examples of *loyalty*
        and *fairness* in the story being read.

3.   Discuss the following question with your students:
        a) *How did David's actions show loyalty and fairness?*

4.   Record the students' responses in the *Student Book* on day 9 under the Biblical
        Character column. (Possible answers include the following: *Loyalty* by David's
        refusal to kill Saul because he was the Lord's anointed one, even though
        Saul was trying to kill David; *Fairness* by considering the advice of his men, his
        history with Saul, and his responsibility to the Lord before making a decision
        about whether or not to kill Saul.)

5.   Listen to your students read the assigned pages for day 9 out loud to you.
        Remind the students to be searching for examples of *loyalty* and *fairness.*

6.   Using the questions listed below, compare David with the main character in the
        mystery. Record the responses on day 9 in the *Student Book* under the Book
        Character column.
        a) *How does the character in your book show loyalty and fairness?*
        b) *What would the Biblical character, David, do differently from the character in
           your book?*

Independent / Teacher Directed   **Level 4/5**

Focus: Godly Character Traits - Biblical Comparisons

Preparation:
1.   Find a short children's book of the Bible story about Mordecai and Queen Esther and their loyalty to King Xerxes. Otherwise, the students read the passage directly from the Bible in Esther 2:19-23.

Lesson:
1.   Tell the students to review the Godly Character Traits listed on day 9 in the *Student Book* alone. Then, have the students silently read the story of Mordecai and Queen Esther's loyalty to King Xerxes, either in the children's book or directly from the Bible in Esther 2:19-23.

2.   Have students do their best to complete the Biblical Character column on the Godly Character Story Sheet for Mordecai on day 9 in the *Student Book.*

3.   Students silently read the assigned pages in the mystery for day 9, saving 3 or 4 pages to read aloud to you.

4.   The students meet with you to finish the assignment for day 9. Listen to your students read several pages. Use the Qualities of Good Reading list provided in the Appendix to help you know what to emphasize.

5.   Discuss the following questions with the students as you review what they have already done in the *Student Book* for day 9. Complete the remaining columns in the *Student Book* for day 9.
   a) *How did Mordecai's behavior show loyalty, fairness, and discretion?*
     (Possible answers include the following: *Loyalty* by Mordecai having Esther inform King Xerxes of the plot to assassinate him, even though Mordecai's family had been taken captive into Babylon; *Fairness* in having Queen Esther speak to King Xerxes rather than telling the King about the plot himself; *Discretion* by keeping Esther's family background and nationality a secret.)
   b) *How did the person in your book behave like the Biblical character, Mordecai?* (List the answers in the *Student Book.*)
   c) *How did the person in your book behave differently from Mordecai?* (List the answers in the *Student Book.*)
   d) *Which trait was shown least often by the book character?* (Explain in the *Student Book.*)

Independent   **Level 6/7/8**

Focus: Godly Character Traits - Biblical Comparisons

Preparation:
1.   The students need a Bible for today's lesson.

Lesson:
1.   The students complete the activities in the *Student Book* and read the assigned pages for day 9 on their own.

2.   The directions instruct the students to come and show you the completed Godly Character Story page. (Examples of the traits the high priest, Jehoiada, showed might include the following: *Loyalty* to God by having his wife, Jehosheba, steal Joash to keep him from being murdered by Athalilah; *Fairness* in the way he presented Joash as King at the temple on the Sabbath and gave all people, even Athalilah, a chance to respond; *Discretion* when Jehoiada said Athalilah should not be put to death in the temple; *Discernment* when he made the covenant between the Lord, the King, and his people; *Discernment* when the people tore down the temple of Baal and smashed the alters and idols.)

Teacher Directed   **All Levels Together**

Focus: Comprehension Check - Silent Conversation

Lesson:
1.   Say, *Today we will have a silent conversation about your books. Each student will choose 4 questions to ask another student about his/her book. Then, you will trade Student Books and answer someone else's questions.* (Note: If you have only one student, you need to be the student's partner and participate in the assignment.)

2.   Have students open their *Student Books* to day 10, Silent Conversation. Discuss the following questions with the students:
     a) *How do we punctuate a question?* (with a question mark at the end of the sentence)
     b) *How do you decide if a sentence is a question?* (It ends with a question mark, and it asks something.)
     c) *What kinds of words do we find at the beginning of a question?* (asking words - such as *how, where, when, what, who, why)*
     d) *What would be a question you could ask about the mystery?* (Have students share ideas. Guide the students to see that questions should not have one word answers. The questions should require thought on the part of the person answering the question.)
     e) For example, a question asking, *Do you like the story?* does not require much thought. An example of a better question might be, *What do you like about the mystery?*

3.   Have students write four questions to ask another student about their mystery.

4.   Students trade questions and write the answers to someone else's questions.

5.   After answering the questions, have students return the *Student Book* to the person that wrote the questions.

6.   Allow time for students to read the answers to their questions.

7.   Have students read the assigned pages for day 10 on their own.

Teacher Directed   **All Levels Together**

Focus: Prereading Activity - Concentration

Preparation:
1.   If students are beginning new books today, make sure to have the number of
        pages to be read each day calculated and have those books ready to hand out.
        (See the *Getting Started* section, item #7, in the back of this guide for details.)

2.   If students are not beginning new books today, they use the books they are
        currently reading for today's activities.

3.   Choose one important picture from each of the students' mystery books. The
        picture needs to show some of the characters, one of the settings, and part of
        the mystery, if possible. You may need to use the cover, if there are no other
        pictures in the book.

Lesson:
1.   Say, *Today we will be doing a prereading activity to help you think about the
        next book you will be reading or the next part of the book you will be reading.*

2.   Show each student the picture you selected from their mystery book.

3.   Tell students they have 2 minutes to look at the picture and remember as much
        of what they see as possible.

4.   After two minutes, have students put the picture out of sight.

5.   Have students open their *Student Books* to day 11, Concentration. Give
        students a time limit of 5 minutes to write as much information from the picture
        as they can remember.

6.   After 5 minutes, allow students to see the picture again to check and add to their
        answers.

7.   Give the following directions for students to follow in their *Student Books*:
        a) *Circle any details that have to do with the characters in the mystery.*
        b) *Put an "x" by any details that describe the setting in the mystery.*
        c) *Make a check next to any details that are mysterious.*
        d) *Choose the detail that is most important and put a star by it. Share the detail
            you marked. Why do you feel that detail is most important?*
        e) *What is the mystery in your book?*

8.   Give students a little time to look at the cover, read the synopsis, and quickly page through the book.

9.   Help students update their *Assigned Reading Calendar* for days 11-15.

10.   Have students read the assigned pages for day 11 on their own.

Teacher Directed   **Level 2/3**

Focus: Story Discussion and Optional Phonics <u>or</u> Vocabulary Work

Preparation:
1.   You may choose to have students at this level review phonics <u>or</u> complete a vocabulary assignment. Use your own program for the phonics review. Refer to the Appendix for a reproducible vocabulary assignment. The lesson on this day is much shorter to compensate for the additional time you may spend on phonics or on vocabulary work.

Lesson:
1.   Optional phonics or vocabulary work

2.   Listen to your students read the assigned pages out loud to you. Use the Reading Strategies list and the Qualities of Good Reading list provided in the Appendix to help you know what to emphasize.

3.   Discuss the following questions with your students:
        a) *What seems mysterious about the setting?*
        b) *How are the characters reacting to the problem?*
        c) *If you could give the characters advice, what would you tell them?*

Independent / Teacher Directed   **Level 4/5**

Focus: Story Element Instruction - Interesting Inferences

Lesson:
1.   Tell the students to read the assigned pages on their own, leaving 3-4 pages to read aloud to you.

2.   Listen to your students read several pages. Use the Qualities of Good Reading list provided in the Appendix to help you know what to emphasize.

3.   Discuss the following questions with your students:
        a) *Which character is most important to the story? Why?*
        b) *Does this story remind you of any other story? Explain.*
        c) *How does the author make the story seem mysterious?*

4.   Introduce the following definition for *inference: Pondering details in the story in order to draw conclusions that make sense of what the text implies.*

5.   Discuss the following question with the students:
      a) *What is the difference between prediction and inference?* (Prediction is
         anticipating what will happen next using clues from the story combined with
         any background knowledge you might have. Inference is pondering details
         in the story in order to draw conclusions that make sense of what the text
         implies.)

6.   Work with the students to complete Interesting Inferences on day 12 in the
      Student Book. You may want to write the answers on a marker board as you
      discuss them, so the students can copy them. Then, the students can
      concentrate on the discussion rather than on spelling and capitalization.

Independent   **Level 6/7/8**

Focus: Vocabulary Builder - Clue Finder

Lesson:
1.   The students complete the activities in the *Student Book* and read the assigned
      pages for day 12 on their own.

2.   The directions instruct students to come and show you the completed Clue
      Finder vocabulary assignment.

Teacher Directed   **Level 2/3**

Focus: Story Element Instruction - Inference

Lesson:

1.   Listen to your students read the assigned pages out loud to you. Use the Reading Strategies list and the Qualities of Good Reading list provided in the Appendix to help you know what to emphasize.

2.   Introduce two kinds of questions that we ask when we are predicting:
        a) *I found it questions: The answer can be found in the story.*
        b) *Think about it questions: Requires you to use details from the story and your own knowledge to answer the question.*

3.   Tell the students to open their mystery books to an exciting paragraph or part. Your job will be to give examples of the two kinds of questions listed above by using the part the students selected in the mystery.

4.   First, ask a question about something you see written right on that page. For example, *Where did the detective look for his first clue?* Have the students point to the spot on the page where they find the answer and say, *I found it!* Explain that the question was an *I found it question.*

5.   Next, ask a question about something the students will <u>not</u> find right on that page. Make sure it is something the students can make a guess about, based on the information found on the page. For example, *Why do you think the detective looked at the museum for his first clue?* Have the students say, *Hmmm, let me think about it.* Then, have students answer the question. Explain to the students that the question was a *think about it question.*

6.   Ask several more questions using the page the students selected in their mystery. Each time you ask a question, have students either respond *I found it,* or *Hmmm, let me think about it.* Then, students should answer the questions.

7.   Discuss the following questions with your students:
        a) *How did you decide which kind of question I'd asked?*
        b) *What might be one solution to the mystery in your story? What kind of question did I just ask you?*

Independent   **Level 4/5**

Focus: Story Element Extension - Wondering Web

Lesson:
1.   Tell the students to read the assigned pages for day 13 on their own.

2.   Tell them to complete the Wondering Web on day 13 in their *Student Books* when they finish reading.

3.   The directions instruct students to come and show you the completed assignment.

Teacher Directed / Independent   **Level 6/7/8**

Focus: Story Element Discussion - Interesting Inferences

Lesson:
1.   The students read the assigned pages for day 13 on their own.

2.   The students meet with you to discuss the following questions:
         a) *What major events are in the story?*
         b) *How does the mood of the story change?*
         c) *What are some causes and effects in the story?*

3.   Review the following definitions of prediction and inference with the students:
         a) *Prediction is anticipating what will happen next using clues from the story combined with any background knowledge you might have.*
         b) *Inference is pondering details in the story in order to draw conclusions that make sense of what the text implies.*

4.   Discuss the following questions with the students:
         a) *What do you think is going to happen next?*
         b) *What clues from the text and from your background knowledge help you infer what will happen?*

5.   Introduce Interesting Inferences in the *Student Book* under day 13. Have the students work to complete it on their own.

6.   The directions instruct students to come and show you the completed assignment.

<u>Teacher Directed</u>   **<u>Level 2/3</u>**

Focus: Godly Character Traits - Personal Assessment

Preparation:
1.   You will need an index card or note card for each of your students today.

Lesson:
1.   Review the following definitions and scripture passages:
   a) <u>*Loyalty*</u> *is showing firm, faithful support even in times of trouble.*
   b) <u>*Key Scripture verse*</u>: *A man's wisdom gives him patience; it is to his glory to overlook an offense. Proverbs 19:11*
   c) <u>*Fairness*</u> *is weighing each choice in order to be just and pleasing to God in your decisions.*
   d) <u>*Key Scripture verse*</u>: *I the Lord search the heart and examine the mind, to reward a man according to his conduct, according to what his deeds deserve. Jeremiah 17:10*

2.   Listen to your students read the assigned pages for day 14 out loud to you.

3.   Discuss the following questions with the students:
   a) *Which trait was shown less often by the book character, loyalty or fairness? Explain.*
   b) *Choose the trait that is harder for you to show, loyalty or fairness. Explain.*

4.   Hand out one index card to each student. Have the students write the trait they chose and 3 ways to work on showing the trait more often in their own lives.

5.   On the other side of the card, have the students draw themselves portraying this trait. The students may also write the matching Bible verse, if you choose for them to do so.

6.   Have the students post their cards in a place where they will see them often.

<u>Independent / Teacher Directed</u>   **<u>Level 4/5</u>**

Focus: Godly Character Traits - Personal Assessment

Preparation:
1.   You will need an index card or note card for each of your students today.

Lesson:

1.	Tell the students to review the Godly Character Traits listed on day 9 in the *Student Book* on their own.

2.	Have the students silently read the assigned pages in the mystery for day 14, saving 3-4 pages to read aloud to you.

3.	Meet with the students to finish the assignment for day 14.

4.	Listen to your students read 3-4 pages. Use the Qualities of Good Reading list provided in the Appendix to help you know what to emphasize.

5.	Discuss the following questions with the students:
	a) *Refer to day 9 in the Student Book. Choose the trait that is the hardest for you to show, loyalty, fairness, or discretion. Explain.*
	b) *Look at the Bible verse on day 9 in the Student Book for the trait you chose. How does the behavior of the characters in your book compare to this verse? Explain.*
	c) *What ways can you demonstrate the verse you chose in your own life?*

6.	Hand out one index card to each student. Have the students list actions they will take to help them live according to the verse they chose.

7.	On the other side of the card, have the students divide the card into 3-4 sections, by drawing vertical lines. Instruct the students to break the chosen verse into sections and draw a quick picture or symbol to stand for each section of the verse. When the students look at the pictures, it should remind them of each part of the verse.

8.	The Bible verse may be written on the bottom or on the back of the card if you choose to have the students do so.

9.	Have the students post the cards in a place where they will see them often.

Independent   **Level 6/7/8**

Focus: Godly Character Traits - Personal Assessment

Preparation:
1.	The students each need an index card or note card for today.

Lesson:

1. The students complete the activities in the *Student Book* and read the assigned pages for day 14 on their own.

2. The directions instruct the students to come and show you the completed assignment for day 14, including the completed index card or note card for posting.

Teacher Directed   **All Levels Together**

Preparation:
1.   Choose which **one** of the following project options you would like your students to complete as a culminating project for this genre. Each option is explained in detail on the pages that follow. For ease in planning, you should choose the same option for each of the students.
    a) **Option 1:** You may choose a character based project, which focuses on the Godly character trait for this genre. The directions for these projects are more general. The project does not involve any of the books from the unit. It does include a final reflection form.
    b) **Option 2:** You may choose a book based project, which is an individual project that is tailored to the student's individual level. Students will choose one of the books they read for this genre to use for the project. In order to choose this option, you must purchase *Book Projects to Send Home* by Lori Sanders and Linda Kimble for your particular students' levels. There is one book for each of the three levels. The project directions are very detailed and include a final reflection for each project.
    c) **Option 3:** Your final option is to choose a group project, which requires two or more students working together. This project is based on a common book the students have all read or had read aloud to them. The **one** book the project is based upon should fit into the genre studied in this unit.

2.   Have the directions for the project copied for each student. Make sure to read over the directions for the project option you chose in order to know what supplies you will need to have available for the projects.

3.   The plans allow 5 work days for the projects to be completed. This time allotment includes the planning and any presenting of the projects. The plans assume that the students will use only their normal amount of reading time to complete the projects.

Lesson:
1.   Say, *Today we will be starting our culminating project for mysteries. You will have 5 days, counting today, to work on your project. Your projects are due at the end of that time on _____. (give due date)*

2.   Introduce the project you have chosen for this unit. Go through the directions and make sure students have a copy of the directions, so they can work as independently as possible. Show them where the needed supplies are located.

3.   Then, have students read the assigned pages for day 15 to finish the mystery books. Students may begin the project after the reading is complete.

Focus: <u>Godly Character Trait Project</u>   <u>**Loyalty Graph**</u>

Project Notes:

1.   Teach loyalty by graphing daily incidents that fulfill the traits of *loyalty, fairness, discretion,* and *discernment.*

2.   Refer to the definitions and key verses listed on day 4 or day 9 in the texts. Review the meaning of each trait with the students. Ask students to act out situations that would show each trait in action.

3.   Tell students they will be making a bar graph of the times they show these loyalty traits during the next 5 days. Use sticky notes or index cards to write *Day 1, Day 2, Day 3, Day 4,* and *Day 5.* Post the notes or cards in a row on the wall.

4.   Have students try to think of a time since yesterday that they showed one of the loyalty traits. For example, *I showed loyalty to Jill today when I didn't tell Sue how upset I was that Jill broke my pencil.* Students might not be able to think of very many examples.

5.   Write each incident the students share on a separate sticky note or index card. Make sure to include the following things on each note or card:
a) today's date
b) name of the student who showed the trait
c) name of the trait that was shown
d) description of how the trait was shown

6.   Post one note or index card above the other on the wall to create a "bar" above the *Day 1* heading.

7.   Students practice showing the loyalty traits for the next 5 days. Each day have students try to add sticky notes or index cards to the current day's "bar". You may want to set aside one time each day to do this. Make sure each note includes the information listed in number 7.

8.   At the end of 5 days, you should have a bar graph of loyalty incidents. Meet with the students as a group to discuss the following questions:
a) What do you notice about the bars on the graph?
b) How has your behavior towards others changed?
c) Why are the loyalty traits important?
d) How would the world be different if everyone practiced the loyalty traits?

9.   Reproduce the reflection form included in this guide for each student to complete on day 19.

Unit 5

Focus: <u>Book Based Project</u>   **Individual Projects by Level**

Project Notes:

1.   This is an individual project tailored to the students' individual levels.

2.   In order to choose this option, you must purchase *Book Projects to Send Home* by Lori Sanders and Linda Kimble (McGraw-Hill, 2004) for your particular students' levels. There is one project book for each of the 3 levels. The books include detailed reproducible directions, work schedules, and reflection forms.

3.   The students each need to choose **one** book from those that **were read in this genre**. That book is the basis for the project.

4.   The project titles, corresponding page numbers, and levels in the *Book Projects to Send Home* books are listed below.

Use Grade 2 of *Book Projects to Send Home*   **Level 2/3**

Project Title: Detailed Diorama   Page Numbers: 15-18

Preparation:

1.   Read the project description box and the materials to provide section on p. 15. The rest of the items on p. 15 are <u>optional</u> ideas to use if you enjoy teaching through themes.

2.   Copy pp. 16-18 for your students. Save p. 18 for the students to complete on day 19 as a reflection on their project. This is listed in the plans for day 19.

3.   The sharing your detailed diorama section on p. 16 will not be done at home.

Use Grade 4 of *Book Projects to Send Home*   **Level 4/5**

Project Title: Personal Perspective Story Prism   Page Numbers: 27-30

Preparation:

1.   Read the project description box and the materials to provide section on p. 27. The rest of the items on p. 27 are <u>optional</u> ideas to use if you enjoy teaching through themes.

2.   Copy pp. 28-30 and 47 for your students. Save p. 47 for the students to complete on day 19 as a reflection on their project. This is listed in the plans for day 19.

3.   Instruct students to think of the schedule on p. 29 as steps to complete, rather than a time frame for each part of the project.   The students will be working solely on completing the projects for 5 reading days, instead of doing them gradually for 4 weeks as the project book suggests.

4.   The students have already completed the project requirements listed under week 1 in the schedule on p. 29. They will not need to choose another book to read.

5.   The presentation guidelines listed on p. 29 will not be used at home, unless you choose to do so.

Use Grade 5 of *Book Projects to Send Home*   **Level 6/7/8**

Note: Although these projects are listed for grade 5, they are very challenging to complete which makes them appropriate for level 6/7/8.

Project Title: Clue Crew Board Game   Page Numbers: 7-10

Preparation:

1.   Read the project description box, the materials to provide, and the tips to introduce sections on p. 7. The rest of the items on p. 7 are <u>optional</u> ideas to use if you enjoy teaching through themes.

2.   Copy pp. 8-10 and 47 for your students. You may want to remove the "Dear Fifth Grader" greeting on p. 8. Save p. 47 for the students to complete on day 19 as a reflection on their projects. This is listed in the plans for day 19.

3.   Instruct students to think of the schedule on p. 9 as steps to complete, rather than a time frame for each part of the project. The students will be working solely on completing the projects for 5 reading days, instead of doing them gradually for 4 weeks as the project book suggests.

4.   The students have already completed the project requirements listed under week 1 on the schedule on p. 9. They will not need to choose another book to read.

Focus: <u>Group Project</u> <u>Radio Drama</u>

Project Notes:

1.   In order to choose this option, you must have two or more students (unless you are willing to do part of the project with your student).

2.   This project is based on **one** common book the students have all read or had read aloud to them. The book the project is based upon <u>should fit into the genre studied in this unit.</u>

3.   Students will write a radio drama for an exciting scene from the book they read. Explain to students that in a radio drama, acting is done completely with sound. The actors cannot be seen.

4.   The reproducible form in this guide may be copied and used for planning the radio drama project. Encourage students to choose a short scene, so they have time to practice their parts and add sound effects and musical clips.

5.   Each group member needs to have a role in the radio drama. The role can be an acting role, a sound effect role, or a broadcasting role. Group members meet to determine who is responsible for each role.

6.   Students may read their parts directly from the book or from copies of the book pages. All group members need to know which parts of the drama have sound effects, in order to pause for the sound.

7.   Group members must be prepared to share their radio drama on day 19. You may want to tape record the performance, so students can hear their radio drama.

8.   On day 19, students present the radio drama. Reproduce the reflection form included in this guide for each student to complete.

Radio Drama Planning Sheet

Name:_____

Book Title: _____

1. Choose one short, exciting scene from your book to use for the radio drama.

2. List the page numbers for the scene: pp. _____

3. Write the names of the characters in the scene and who will read each role. List the person who will be the director.

   _____

   _____

   _____

4. Who will be the broadcaster? What will that person say to introduce the drama? What will the broadcaster say during the radio drama?

   _____

   _____

   _____

   _____

5. Who will be responsible for the sound effects and musical clips?

   _____

6. What sound effects and musical clips will be included?_____

   _____

   _____

   _____

Independent / Teacher Directed   All Levels

Focus: Project Work

Preparation:
1.   For details, read the directions for the project option you chose.

Lesson:
1.   Check students' progress to make sure each student understands what to do and is on schedule to finish by day 19.

2.   Meet with students as a group, if this is needed.

Independent / Teacher Directed   All Levels

Focus: Project Completion

Preparation:
1.   For details, read the directions for the project option you chose.

2.   Have the reflection forms copied for each student to match the project option you chose.

Lesson:
1.   Briefly check students' progress. Students should finish their projects today.

2.   Have students share their projects with each other or with you.

3.   Hand out the reflection form that matches the project option you chose. Have the students complete the reflection and show you.

4.   You are ready to choose the next genre your students will study. Look ahead to prepare the kickoff for the upcoming genre.

Loyalty Graph Reflection

1. In following the loyalty traits, I felt that I did a good job of _____

_____.

2. I think that I could have done a better job of_____

_____.

3. I noticed the following changes as I practiced the loyalty traits: _____

_____

_____.

4. For the day with the highest bar on the graph, I noticed_____

_____.

5. I think loyalty traits are important because_____

_____

_____.

_____   _____
    Signature of student   Date

Radio Drama Reflection

1. On the radio drama project, I felt that I did a good job of_____

_____.

2. I think that I could have done a better job of_____

_____.

3. If I could do the radio drama again, I would _____

_____

_____.

4. From the radio drama project, I learned_____

_____

_____

_____.

5. My favorite part of the radio drama project was_____

_____

_____.

_____   _____
Signature of student   Date

Folk Tale

GENRE: FOLK TALE

General Definition:
Fables, fairy tales, legends, pourquoi or "why" tales, and trickster tales that have been retold and usually have a lesson or moral. (Definitions for each type of folk tale are on the next page.)

Common Characteristics:
1. Appears in several variations due to being orally retold for generations.
2. Includes fantasy in the tale.
3. Portrays characters as very good or very bad.
4. Includes settings from an indefinite time in the past.
5. Has a lesson or a moral.

Story Element Emphasis: Compare and Contrast

Definition of Compare:
Observing details to note similarities between items.

Definition of Contrast:
Observing details to note differences between items.

Godly Character Trait Emphasis: Virtue

Definition:
Listening to the promptings of the Holy Spirit to do what is right and good so that you may fulfill God's law.

Subqualities:
1. truthfulness
2. kindness
3. self-control

GENRE: FOLK TALE
(continued)

General Definition:
Fables, fairy tales, legends, pourquoi or "why" tales, and trickster tales that have been retold and usually have a lesson or moral.

Definitions of the Types of Folk Tales:

Fables:
Focus on a moral at the end of a short tale and often feature animals acting like humans.

Fairy Tales:
Happen long ago with imaginary characters that have an unusual mission to accomplish. Fanciful or mysterious figures assist the character in completing the mission.

Legends:
Happen in an identifiable time and place with a human hero that has exaggerated characteristics based on an actual, historical person.

Pourquoi Tales:
Use animal characters to explain a natural occurrence, in an imaginary way.

Trickster Tales:
Focus on an animal that loves to trick other animals. The cunning trickster usually triumphs, in part due to a character defect in his prey.

Teacher Directed   <u>**All Levels Together**</u>

Focus: Genre Kickoff

Preparation:

1.   The goal of the kickoff is to introduce students of all ages to the upcoming genre in a fun and entertaining manner.

2.   Decide how much time you want to spend on the kickoff. You can spend one normal reading class period, several hours, or even a whole day. After the kickoff, you begin with day 1 in the teacher's plans.

3.   Read through the list of ideas below and choose those that interest you for this genre's kickoff. You are welcome to add your own ideas that fit within this genre. Refer to the cover page for a definition and common characteristics for each genre. Introduce the name and definition of the genre to begin the kickoff.

Possible Kickoff Ideas:

1.   Listen to a professional storyteller at the library, a bookstore, or at a special event. Discuss the tradition of oral retellings of stories.

2.   Tell a very short folk tale to one child quietly. Have that child quietly retell it to the next child and so on, until it has been retold 3 or more times. Have the last child that hears the folk tale, retell what they heard to the rest of the group. Discuss how retellings often lose some accuracy from the original story. This is the reason there is often more than one version of a tale that has been retold.

3.   Assign each student one lesson or moral. Use *Aesop's Fables* as a resource or any other source that fulfills this purpose. Have each student make up a short story to orally share. This short story should demonstrate a character learning a lesson that fits with the moral the student was assigned.

4.   Perform a dramatization of a folk tale. Use stuffed animals, action figures, or dolls for the characters. Create the scenery from building blocks, boxes, or play sets. Each student needs to have a part. It is necessary to read the story out loud prior to planning the dramatization, so students know what is needed. During the dramatization, read the tale out loud as the students dramatize it.

5.   Introduce the definition for a pourqoi tale. (See the cover page of this genre for the definition.) You may want to read an example of a pourquoi tale to the students. Many Native American stories are pourquoi tales. Have students write a <u>short</u>, silly "why story", or pourquoi tale, and draw a picture to accompany the tale. Some examples include the following: Why do skunks have a white stripe? Why do flowers smell pretty? Why do cats say, *Meow*? Why does snow fall from the sky?   Unit 6

6.   Read one short folk tale and show students the pictures as you read it. Then, have students do a shadow play of the tale on a blank wall. The room needs to be dark and you need a flashlight to shine on the wall. Students use their hands and other small objects to create shadows that portray what is happening in the story. Have students practice making the various shadows. Then, tell the tale along with the shadow play.

7.   Have students participate in the reading of a folk tale. Prior to reading the tale to the group, make signs to tell the students what to do at key parts of the story. Possible signs might include: hurrah!, sigh, clap, boo-hoo, hiss, oh no!, watch out!, ha! ha!

Questions to discuss at the end of the kickoff:
1.   What is a folk tale? (Refer to the definition on the cover page for this genre.)

2.   What did you learn about folk tales from today's activities?

3.   What kinds of folk tales are there?

4.   Which kind of folk tale is your favorite? Explain.

5.   Why do we read folk tales?

Teacher Directed

All Levels Together

Focus: Prereading Activity - All Covered Up

Preparation:
1.   Prior to meeting with the students for day 1, follow the directions for *Getting Started* listed in the back of this guide.

2.   Have the first book and one *Assigned Reading Calendar* ready for each student.

3.   Tape construction paper over the illustration on the cover of each book, so that only the title is visible. Make sure the picture on the cover cannot be seen through the paper at all.

Lesson:
1.   Say, *Today we will be doing a prereading activity to help you think about the next book you will be reading.*

2.   Give students the first book they will be reading for this genre. The title is the only part of the book the students should see.

3.   Discuss the following question with your students:
     a) *What are some things you can predict about your book from reading the title?* (Have students share several predictions. Students may help each other.)

4.   Instruct students to draw their predictions about the book on the construction paper taped to their book covers. Give students a time limit of 10 minutes to draw.

5.   Ask each student to take off the construction paper and view the illustration on the cover.

6.   Discuss the following question with your students:
     a) *Which predictions do you think are correct and which predictions might be incorrect? Explain.*

7.   Have students read the synopsis' of the book and quickly page through it.

8.   Discuss the following questions with your students:
     a) *What would you like to add to or change about your predictions? Explain.*
     b) *Do you think your book is a fairy tale, legend, fable, trickster tale, or pourquoi tale? How can you tell?* (Refer to the folk tale cover page in this teacher's guide to review the definitions for each type of folk tale.)

9.   Have students open their *Student Books* to the *Assigned Reading Calendar* for this genre. Help each student fill in the page numbers to be read for days 1-5.

10. Have students read the assigned pages for day 1 on their own.

Teacher Directed   **Level 2/3**

Focus: Story Discussion and Optional Phonics or Vocabulary Work

Preparation:

1.   You may choose to have students at this level review phonics or complete a vocabulary assignment. Use your own program for the phonics review. Refer to the Appendix for a reproducible vocabulary assignment. The lesson on this day is much shorter to compensate for the additional time you may spend on phonics or on vocabulary work.

Lesson:

1.   Optional phonics or vocabulary work

2.   Listen to your students read the assigned pages out loud to you. Use the Reading Strategies list and the Qualities of Good Reading list provided in the Appendix to help you know what to emphasize.

3.   Discuss the following questions with your students:
       a) *What unrealistic things happen in the story?*
       b) *Describe the problem in the story. Is it a problem that could happen today?*
       c) *Tell me about the setting of the story.*

Independent / Teacher Directed   **Level 4/5**

Focus: Story Element Instruction - Compare and Contrast

Lesson:

1.   Tell the students to read the assigned pages on their own, leaving 3-4 pages to read aloud to you.

2.   Listen to your students read several pages. Use the Qualities of Good Reading list provided in the Appendix to help you know what to emphasize.

3.   Discuss the following questions with your students:
       a) *Which sentences in the story best describe the setting?*
       b) *What is the cause of the problem in the story?*

4.   Introduce the following definitions and terms:
       a) *Compare means observing details to note similarities between items.*
       b) *Contrast means observing details to note differences between items.*

5.   Work with the students to complete the Character Comparison on day 2 in the *Student Book*. List several examples for each part of the diagram. You may want to write answers on a marker board as you discuss them, so the students can copy them. Then, the students can concentrate on the discussion rather than on spelling and capitalization.

Independent   **Level 6/7/8**

Focus: Vocabulary Builder - Categorize It

Preparation:
1.   Have a dictionary available.

Lesson:
1.   The students complete the activities in the *Student Book* and read the assigned pages for day 2 on their own.

2.   The directions instruct students to come and show you the completed Categorize It vocabulary assignment.

Teacher Directed   **Level 2/3**

Focus: Story Element Instruction - Compare and Contrast

Lesson:
1.   Listen to your students read the assigned pages out loud to you. Use the Reading Strategies list and the Qualities of Good Reading list provided in the Appendix to help you know what to emphasize.

2.   Introduce the following definitions and terms:
      a) *Compare means observing details to note similarities between items.*
      b) *Contrast means observing details to note differences between items.*

3.   Work with the students to complete Portraits on day 3 in the *Student Book*. Students often list physical features when they compare themselves with another character. Lead students to compare other traits as well. You may want to write the answers on a marker board as you discuss them, so the students can copy them. Then, the students can concentrate on the discussion rather than on spelling and capitalization.

Independent   **Level 4/5**

Focus: Story Element Extension - Character Adventure

Lesson:
1.   Tell the students to read the assigned pages for day 3 on their own.

2.   Tell them to complete Character Adventure on day 3 in their *Student Books* when they finish reading.

3.   The directions instruct students to come and show you the completed assignment.

Teacher Directed / Independent   **Level 6/7/8**

Focus: Story Element Discussion - Character Compare and Contrast

Lesson:
1.   The students read the assigned pages for day 3 on their own.

2.   Discuss the following questions with the students:
      a) *How can you tell this story is a folk tale?* (See the folk tale cover page for the common characteristics of a folk tale.)
      b) *What is the conflict or problem in the story?*
      c) *What do you think will happen next? What clues help you guess what will happen next?*

3.   Have students open their *Student Books* to day 3, Let's Be Friends. Help students list characters they remember from stories they have read.

4.   Review the list of characters and discuss which characters have the most in common. Choose two characters from the list that could be friends. These two characters cannot be from the same story.

5.   Have the students complete Let's Be Friends in the *Student Book* on their own using the two characters they chose to be friends.

6.   The directions instruct students to come and show you the completed assignment.

Teacher Directed

Focus: Godly Character Traits - Examples

Preparation:
1.   Think of examples you can share from your own life for each of the following traits: *virtue* and *truthfulness.* (Definitions are listed in the lesson below.)

Lesson:
1.   Introduce the following definition and scripture passage for *virtue:*
   a) *Virtue is listening to the promptings of the Holy Spirit to do what is right and good so that you may fulfill God's law.*
   b) *Key Scripture verse: Even a child is known by his actions, by whether his conduct is pure and right. Proverbs 20:11*

2.   Share an example of *virtue* from your own life.

3.   Help the students think of an example of *virtue* from their own lives.

4.   Introduce the following definition and scripture passage for *truthfulness:*
   a) *Truthfulness is being honest without blaming others, without being deceitful, and without making excuses for your behavior.*
   b) *Key Scripture verse: Keep your tongue from evil and your lips from speaking lies. Psalms 34:13*

5.   Repeat steps 2 and 3 for the trait *truthfulness.*

6.   Instruct your students to search for examples of *virtue* and *truthfulness* as they read part or all of the assigned pages out loud to you. Use the Reading Strategies list and the Qualities of Good Reading list provided in the Appendix to help you know what to emphasize.

7.   Discuss the following questions with your students:
   a) *How do the characters show virtue? Or truthfulness?*
   b) *Did the characters show the opposite traits of immorality or dishonesty? Explain.*
   c) *What could the characters do differently to show more virtue or truthfulness?*

Independent / Teacher Directed   **Level 4/5**

Focus: Godly Character Traits - Examples

Lesson:

1.   Tell the students to complete the Godly Character Sheet on day 4 in the *Student Book* on their own.

2.   The students also silently read the assigned pages for day 4, leaving 3-4 pages to read aloud to you.

3.   The students should come and show you when both are completed.

4.   Review the Godly Character Sheet on day 4 in the *Student Book*, so the students and you will know what traits you are searching for in the folk tale. *(virtue, truthfulness,* and *kindness)*

5.   Listen to your students read 3-4 pages aloud. Use the Qualities of Good Reading list provided in the Appendix to help you know what to emphasize.

6.   Discuss the following questions with the students:
      a) *How did the characters show virtue?*
      b) *How did the characters show truthfulness?*
      c) *How did the characters show kindness?*
      d) *Did the characters show the opposite trait of immorality? Or dishonesty? Or rudeness? Explain.*
      e) *What might Jesus have done differently if He had been the character in the book?*

Independent   **Level 6/7/8**

Focus: Godly Character Traits - Examples

Lesson:

1.   The students complete the activities in the *Student Book* and read the assigned pages for day 4 on their own.

2.   The directions instruct students to come and show you the completed Godly Character page.

Teacher Directed / Independent   Level 2/3

Focus: Comprehension Check - Categories

Lesson:

1.   Go over the directions for Categories on day 5 in the *Student Book*. Students complete this assignment alone after reading the assigned pages.

2.   Listen to your students read part of the assigned pages out loud to you. Use the Reading Strategies list and the Qualities of Good Reading list provided in the Appendix to help you know what to emphasize.

3.   Discuss the moral, or the lesson, the story is trying to teach you. Students need to understand the moral for the assignment in the *Student Book*.

4.   The students finish the assigned reading and complete Categories on their own. The directions instruct the students to come and show you the completed assignment.

Independent   Level 4/5

Focus: Comprehension Check - Tell the Tale

Lesson:

1.   Tell the students to complete Tell the Tale on day 5 in the *Student Book* on their own.

2.   Have students silently read the assigned pages for day 5 on their own. You may choose to have the students leave 3-4 pages to read aloud to you.

3.   The directions instruct the students to come and show you the completed assignment.

Independent   Level 6/7/8

Focus: Comprehension Check - Quick Quotes

Lesson:

1.   The students complete the activities in the *Student Book* and read the assigned pages for day 5 on their own.

2.   The directions instruct students to come and show you the completed Quick Quotes assignment.

Folk Tale - Day 6

Focus: Prereading Activity - Object Match

Preparation:
1.   If students are beginning new books today, make sure to have the number of pages to be read each day calculated and have those books ready to hand out. (See the *Getting Started* section, item #7, in the back of this guide for details.)

2.   If students are <u>not</u> beginning new books today, they use the books they are currently reading for today's activities.

3.   Find objects that represent something important in the folk tale each student is reading. You need one or more objects for each story. (Examples: Leaves could represent a forest setting. Cotton could represent a main character who is a bunny.) You might want to write down which objects match each story for your reference during the lesson.

4.   Find objects that <u>do not</u> represent anything in the folk tales the students are reading. These objects are meant to make the students' assignment more thought-provoking.

Lesson:
1.   Say, *Today we will be doing a prereading activity to help you think about the next book you will be reading or the next part of the book you will be reading.*

2.   If students are beginning new books, hand the books to those students.

3.   Set out all of the objects you chose for today's lesson. You must know which objects match each story.

4.   Say, *Some of these objects have to do with the folk tale you are reading. Your job is to decide which objects match your story.*

5.   Discuss each object you set out, so students begin thinking about what the objects could represent. (Examples: A handkerchief could represent the princess in the story crying. Water in a bowl could represent a pond.)

6.   Give students time to look at the cover of their folk tale, read the synopsis, and quickly page through the book.

7.   Have students think which objects could match their folk tales. Students may ask the teacher questions. Give students hints as needed. Set a 15 minute time limit, so students do not become frustrated.

8.   Discuss the following questions with the students:
      a) *Which objects might go with the folk tale you are reading?*
      b) *What do you think the objects represent?*
      b) *What clues are you using to make your prediction?*

9.   Students may make connections to items that you did not intend to match their folk tale. Tell the students that those answers are not wrong. Making connections is the goal of this activity and that is what they did.

10.   Tell students which object you chose for each story. Explain what the objects were meant to represent. Point out the objects that were not meant to match any of the folk tales.

11.   Help students update the *Assigned Reading Calendar* for days 6-10.

12.   Have students read the assigned pages for day 6 on their own.

<u>Teacher Directed</u>   **<u>Level 2/3</u>**

Focus: Story Discussion and Optional Phonics <u>or</u> Vocabulary Work

Preparation:
1.   You may choose to have students at this level review phonics <u>or</u> complete a vocabulary assignment. Use your own program for the phonics review. Refer to the Appendix for a reproducible vocabulary assignment. The lesson on this day is much shorter to compensate for the additional time you may spend on phonics or on vocabulary work.

Lesson:
1.   Optional phonics or vocabulary work

2.   Listen to your students read the assigned pages out loud to you. Use the Reading Strategies list and the Qualities of Good Reading list provided in the Appendix to help you know what to emphasize.

3.   Discuss the following questions with your students:
        a) *What things do the characters do that you think are right?*
        b) *What things do the characters do that you think are wrong?*
        c) *Does the story take place a long time ago, in the future, or is it happening now? Explain.*

<u>Independent / Teacher Directed</u>   **<u>Level 4/5</u>**

Focus: Story Element Instruction - Compare and Contrast

Preparation:
1.   You need a large piece of paper or a marker board to write answers as students share them. Today's assignment is the discussion that takes place between the teacher and the students.

Lesson:
1.   Tell the students to read the assigned pages on their own, leaving 3-4 pages to read aloud to you.

2.   Listen to your students read several pages. Use the Qualities of Good Reading list provided in the Appendix to help you know what to emphasize.

3.   Say, *Today you will think about what the folk tale reminds you of in your own life. You want to list as many comparisons between your life and the folk tale as you can. The comparisons will be listed under the following categories: looks, personality, setting, problem, and events.* (Write the categories on the large piece of paper or on a marker board.)

4.   Give the students an example of a comparison you notice between the students' lives and the story. Write the comparison under the matching category. (Example: You have a good sense of humor just like the rhinoceros in the folk tale. That fits under the *personality* category.)

5.   Have students share their own comparisons and the category that matches the comparison. List a brief version of the comparison under the category. The students do not do any writing.

6.   Say, *Now you will think about how your life is different from the folk tale. You want to list at least one contrast between your life and the folk tale for each of the following categories: looks, personality, setting, problem, or events.*

7.   Have students share their own contrasts and the category that matches the contrast. List a brief version of the contrast under the category. The students do not do any writing.

8.   Discuss the following question with your students:
    a) *Why did we spend time today comparing and contrasting your life with the folk tale you are reading?* (Guide students to understand that books become more meaningful and memorable when you connect them to your own life.)

Independent   **Level 6/7/8**

Focus: Vocabulary Builder - Categorize It

Preparation:
1.   Have a dictionary available.

Lesson:
1.   The students complete the activities in the *Student Book* and read the assigned pages for day 7 on their own.

2.   The directions instruct students to come and show you the completed Categorize It vocabulary assignment.

Teacher Directed   **Level 2/3**

Focus: Story Element Instruction - Compare and Contrast

Preparation:
1.   You need a large piece of paper or a marker board to write answers as students share them.

Lesson:
1.   Listen to your students read the assigned pages out loud to you. Use the Reading Strategies list and the Qualities of Good Reading list provided in the Appendix to help you know what to emphasize.

2.   Discuss the following questions with the students:
      a) *What is the problem in the story?*
      b) *Do you think your book is a fairy tale, legend, fable, trickster tale, or pourquoi tale? How can you tell?* (Refer to the folk tale cover page in this teacher's guide to review the definitions for each type of folk tale.)

3.   Say, *Today you will make connections between the folk tale and your own life. You want to list as many comparisons between your life and the folk tale as you can in the next 5 minutes.*

4.   Give the students an example of a comparison you notice between the students' lives and the story. Write the comparison on the large piece of paper or the marker board. Write *Compare* at the top.

5.   Have students share their own comparisons. Guide students to list comparisons that require more thought, rather than... *We both have two eyes.* List a brief version of the comparisons on the paper or marker board. The students do not do any writing.

6.   Say, *Now you will think about how your life is different from the folk tale. You want to list as many contrasts as you can think of between your life and the folk tale in the next 5 minutes.*

7.   Give the students an example of a contrast you notice between the students' lives and the story. Write the contrast on the large piece of paper or marker board. Write *Contrast* at the top.

8.   Have students share their own contrasts. Guide students to list contrasts that require more thought, rather than... *We have different colored hair.* List a brief version of the contrasts on the paper or the marker board. The students do not do any writing.

9.   Compliment students on the many comparisons and contrasts they made today. Explain that making connections between their lives and the books they are reading, helps them relate to the book in a personal way.

Independent   Level 4/5

Focus: Story Element Extension - Pack Your Bags

Lesson:
1.   Tell the students to read the assigned pages for day 8 on their own.

2.   Tell them to complete Pack Your Bags on day 8 in their *Student Books* when they finish reading.

3.   The directions instruct students to come and show you the completed assignment.

Teacher Directed / Independent   Level 6/7/8

Focus: Story Element Discussion - Compare and Contrast

Lesson:
1.   The students read the assigned pages for day 8 on their own.

2.   The students meet with you to discuss the following questions:
        a) *Do you think your book is a fairy tale, legend, fable, trickster tale, or pourquoi tale? How can you tell?* (Refer to the folk tale cover page in this teacher's guide to review the definitions for each type of folk tale.)
        b) *Does the mood of the story change? Explain.*
        c) *How does the writer create the atmosphere of the setting?*

3.   Review the following definitions and terms:
        a) *Compare means observing details to note similarities between items.*
        b) *Contrast means observing details to note differences between items.*

4.   Introduce Compare and Contrast on day 8 in the *Student Book*. Make sure the students understand what to do. Then, have the students work on their own. The directions instruct students to come and show you the completed assignment.

Folk Tale - Day 9

Teacher Directed   **Level 2/3**

Focus: Godly Character Traits - Biblical Comparisons

Preparation:
1.   Find a short children's book about the Biblical figure John the Baptist. Otherwise, you will need to read about John the Baptist directly from the Bible in John 1:15-34.

Lesson:
1.   Review the following definitions and scripture passages:
   a) _Virtue_ *is listening to the promptings of the Holy Spirit to do what is right and good so that you may fulfill God's law.*
   b) _Key Scripture verse_: *Even a child is known by his actions, by whether his conduct is pure and right. Proverbs 20:11*
   c) _Truthfulness_ *is being honest without blaming others, without being deceitful, and without making excuses for your behavior.*
   d) _Key Scripture verse_: *Keep your tongue from evil and your lips from speaking lies. Psalms 34:13*

2.   Read the children's book, or the Bible passage John 1:15-34, about John the Baptist. Instruct your students to listen for examples of *virtue* and *truthfulness* in the story being read.

3.   Discuss the following question with your students:
   a) *How did John's actions show virtue and truthfulness?*

4.   Record the students' responses in the *Student Book* on day 9 under the Biblical Character column. (Possible answers include the following: *Virtue* as John preached repentance and humbly prepared the way for Jesus; *Virtue* as John lived a life in the desert to be completely focused on his mission from God; *Truthfulness* as John gave his testimony that Jesus is the Son of God in verses 33 and 34; *Truthfulness* as John answered the Pharisees' questions about who he was.)

5.   Listen to your students read the assigned pages for day 9 out loud to you. Remind the students to be searching for examples of *virtue* and *truthfulness*.

6.   Using the questions listed on the next page, compare John the Baptist with the main character in the folk tale. Record the responses on day 9 in the *Student Book* under the Book Character column.

Unit 6

a) *How does the character in your book show virtue and truthfulness?*

b) *What would the Biblical character, John the Baptist, do differently from the character in your book?*

Independent / Teacher Directed   Level 4/5

Focus: Godly Character Traits - Biblical Comparisons

Preparation:

1.   Find a short children's book of the Bible story about Daniel interpreting dreams for King Nebuchadnezzar. Otherwise, the students read the story directly from the Bible in Daniel chapter 4.

Lesson:

1.   Tell the students to review the Godly Character Traits listed on day 9 in the *Student Book* on their own. Then, have the students silently read the story of Daniel and King Nebuchadnezzar, either from the book you provided or from the Bible in Daniel chapter 4.

2.   Students do their best to complete the Biblical Character column on the Godly Character Story Sheet for Daniel on day 9 in the *Student Book.*

3.   Students silently read the assigned pages in the folk tale for day 9, saving 3 or 4 pages to read aloud to you.

4.   The students meet with you to finish the assignment for day 9. Listen to your students read several pages. Use the Qualities of Good Reading list provided in the Appendix to help you know what to emphasize.

5.   Discuss the following questions with the students as you review what they have already done in the *Student Book* for day 9. Complete the remaining columns in the *Student Book* for day 9.

      a) *How did Daniel's behavior show virtue, truthfulness, and kindness?*
        (Possible answers include the following: *Virtue* as Daniel interpreted dreams and served as advisor for the King who had destroyed his nation and taken him into captivity; *Truthfulness* as Daniel told the King the true meaning of the dream, even though he was worried about how it would be received; *Kindness* when Daniel wished the dream was about the King's enemies, rather than about the King; *Kindness* as Daniel pleaded with the King to change his ways during the twelve months God gave the King.)

      b) *How did the character in your book behave like the Biblical character, Daniel?* (List the answers in the *Student Book.*)

c) *How did the character in your book behave differently from Daniel?* (List the answers in the *Student Book*.)

d) *Which trait was shown least often by the book character?* (Explain in the *Student Book*.)

Independent   **Level 6/7/8**

Focus: Godly Character Traits - Biblical Comparisons

Preparation:
1.   The students need a Bible for today's lesson.

Lesson:
1.   The students complete the activities in the *Student Book* and read the assigned pages for day 9 on their own.

2.   The directions instruct the students to come and show you the completed Godly Character Story page. (Examples of the traits Abigail showed could include the following: *Virtue* when she brought food for David's men, after her husband Nabal had refused to do so; *Truthfulness* as Abigail told David that her husband, Nabal, was wicked and foolish; *Kindness* when Abigail took the blame for her husband's actions and begged David to accept her gift as an act of forgiveness; *Self-control* as Abigail waited to tell Nabal what she had done until the timing was right.)

Teacher Directed   **All Levels Together**

Focus: Comprehension Check - Folk Tale Retell

Preparation:
1.   You need 6 index cards and a dark marker for <u>each</u> student today.

Lesson:
1.   Say, *Today you will retell the important parts of your folk tale to the group. You need to complete the planning sheet in your Student Book, so you know what to share.*

2.   Have students open their *Student Books* to day 10, Folk Tale Retell. The students write one or more sentences for each story element listed on the Folk Tale Retell sheet. Give students a time limit of 15 minutes to complete the planning sheet. Guide students to choose the most important details to include for each story element.

3.   Give each student 6 index cards and a dark marker. Have students write each story element listed in the *Student Book* for day 10 on an index card. The story elements are as follows: *characters, setting, problem, solution, mood,* and *theme.*

4.   Say, *Each student will take a turn sharing their Folk Tale Retell sheet with the group. You may share the different parts of your story in any order. <u>Do not</u> read the name of the story element you are sharing - character, setting, problem, solution, mood, or theme. It is the rest of the group members' jobs to decide which part of the story you are sharing and to hold up that card. Stop after each story element to allow group members to make their guess.*

5.   Give students the following examples:
        a) *There is meadow with a pond surrounded by trees. It is a bright, sunny day with birds singing as a gentle breeze blows.*
        b) *Which card would you hold up?* (Students should hold up the card that says setting.)
        c) *The goat wanted a drink of water. He leaned down to get a drink from the well, and he accidentally fell in.*
        d) *Which card would you hold up?* (Students should hold up the card that says problem.)

6.   Allow each student to share the Folk Tale Retell sheet. If your group is large, give students a partner to share with instead of sharing with the whole group.

7.   Have students read the assigned pages in the folk tale for day 10 on their own.

Folk Tale - Day 11

Teacher Directed   **All Levels Together**

Focus: Prereading Activity - Picture Clues

Preparation:
1.   If students are beginning new books today, make sure to have the number of pages to be read each day calculated and have those books ready to hand out. (See the *Getting Started* section, item #7, in the back of this guide for details.)

2.   If students are <u>not</u> beginning new books today, they use the books they are currently reading for today's activities.

Lesson:
1.   Say, *Today we will be doing a prereading activity to help you think about the next book you will be reading or the next part of the book you will be reading.*

2.   Students read the titles of their books and inspect the covers. Discuss the following questions with the students:
      a) *What clues does reading the title give us about the story?*
      b) *What guesses can you make about the characters, settings, or problems from looking at the cover of the book?*

3.   Have students page through all the pictures in the book. Students should examine each picture for clues to the story. Students may share their observations as they are looking through their books.   Ask students the following question:
      a) *How do the pictures help you predict what will happen in the story?*

4.   Have students read the synopsis of the story. Ask students the following question:
      a) *What have you learned about the characters, settings, and problems after reading the synopsis?*

5.   Instruct students to compare this story to any other folk tales that are similar. Emphasize the similarities among folk tales, such as the following: The subcategories include fairy tales, fables, legends, trickster tales, and pourquoi tales. Folk tales appear in several variations due to being orally retold for generations. They include fantasy in the tale. Characters are portrayed as very good or very bad. The setting is from an indefinite time in the past. Often folk tales have a lesson or moral.

Unit 6

6.   Help student update the *Assigned Reading Calendar* for days 11-15.

7.   Have students read the assigned pages for day 11 on their own.

Teacher Directed **Level 2/3**

Focus: Story Discussion and Optional Phonics <u>or</u> Vocabulary Work

Preparation:
1. You may choose to have students at this level review phonics <u>or</u> complete a vocabulary assignment. Use your own program for the phonics review. Refer to the Appendix for a reproducible vocabulary assignment. The lesson on this day is much shorter to compensate for the additional time you may spend on phonics or on vocabulary work.

Lesson:
1. Optional phonics or vocabulary work

2. Listen to your students read the assigned pages out loud to you. Use the Reading Strategies list and the Qualities of Good Reading list provided in the Appendix to help you know what to emphasize.

3. Discuss the following questions with your students:
   a) *Do you like the main character? Why, or why not?*
   b) *Is the setting realistic? Explain.*
   c) *What is the problem in the story?*

Independent / Teacher Directed **Level 4/5**

Focus: Story Element Instruction - Compare and Contrast

Preparation:
1. You need a large piece of paper or a marker board to list ideas today.

Lesson:
1. Tell the students to read the assigned pages on their own, leaving 3-4 pages to read aloud to you.

2. Listen to your students read several pages. Use the Qualities of Good Reading list provided in the Appendix to help you know what to emphasize.

3. Say, *Today we will compare the folk tale you are reading with another story that is similar. What story have you read that reminds you of the folk tale you are reading now?*

4.   Discuss the questions listed below with your students. Write their answers on the marker board or on a large piece of paper, under the appropriate heading of *Compare* or *Contrast.*

a) *When you compare the two folk tales, how are the characters similar?*
b) *When you compare the two folk tales, how are the plots of the story similar?*
c) *When you compare the two folk tales, how are the settings similar?*
d) *As you contrast the two folk tales, which story was more interesting? Why?*
e) *As you contrast the two folk tales, which author made it easier to picture what was happening? How did the author make it easier to picture what was happening?*
f) *As you contrast the two folk tales, which one do you prefer? Explain .*

Independent   **Level   6/7/8**

Focus: Vocabulary Builder - Categorize It

Preparation:
1.   Have a dictionary available.

Lesson:
1.   The students complete the activities in the *Student Book* and read the assigned pages for day 12 on their own.

2.   The directions instruct students to come and show you the completed Categorize It vocabulary assignment.

<u>Teacher Directed / Independent</u>   **<u>Level 2/3</u>**

Focus: Story Element Instruction - Compare and Contrast

Lesson:

1.   Listen to your students read the assigned pages out loud to you. Use the Reading Strategies list and the Qualities of Good Reading list provided in the Appendix to help you know what to emphasize.

2.   Say, *Today you will compare the folk tale you are reading with another story that is similar. What story have you read that reminds you of the folk tale you are reading now?*

3.   Go over the directions for Folk Tale Fun in the *Student Book* on day 13. Help the students write the titles of the two folk tales they are comparing. Have the students complete the rest of the assignment on their own.

<u>Independent</u>   **<u>Level 4/5</u>**

Focus: Story Element Extension - Venn Diagram

Lesson:

1.   Tell the students to read the assigned pages for day 13 on their own.

2.   Tell them to complete the Venn Diagram on day 13 in their *Student Book* when they finish reading.

3.   The directions instruct students to come and show you the completed assignment.

<u>Teacher Directed / Independent</u>   **<u>Level 6/7/8</u>**

Focus: Story Element Discussion - Compare and Contrast

Lesson:

1.   The students read the assigned pages for day 13 on their own.

2.   The students meet with you to discuss the following questions:
       a) *What do you remember most about the story?*
       b) *Why do the characters behave the way they do in the story?*
       c) *Is the setting important in this story? Explain.*
       d) *What story have you read that reminds you of the folk tale you are reading now?* (Tell students they will compare the two folk tales for their assignment.)

Unit 6

3.   Introduce the Venn Diagram in the *Student Book* under day 13. Have the
        students work to complete it on their own.

4.   The directions instruct students to come and show you the completed
        assignment.

Teacher Directed   **Level 2/3**

Focus: Godly Character Traits - Personal Assessment

Preparation:
1.   You will need an index card or note card for each of your students today.

Lesson:
1.   Review the following definitions and scripture passages:
   a) *Virtue is listening to the promptings of the Holy Spirit to do what is right and good so that you may fulfill God's law.*
   b) *Key Scripture verse: Even a child is known by his actions, by whether his conduct is pure and right. Proverbs 20:11*
   c) *Truthfulness is being honest without blaming others, without being deceitful, and without making excuses for your behavior.*
   d) *Key Scripture verse: Keep your tongue from evil and your lips from speaking lies. Psalms 34:13*

2.   Listen to your students read the assigned pages for day 14 out loud to you.

3.   Discuss the following questions with the students:
   a) *Which trait was shown less often by the book character, virtue or truthfulness? Explain.*
   b) *Choose the trait that is harder for you to show, virtue or truthfulness. Explain.*

4.   Hand out one index card to each student. Have the students write the trait they chose and 3 ways to work on showing the trait more often in their own lives.

5.   On the other side of the card, have the students draw themselves portraying this trait. The students may also write the matching Bible verse if you choose for them to do so.

6.   Have the students post their cards in a place where they will see them often.

Independent / Teacher Directed   **Level 4/5**

Focus: Godly Character Traits - Personal Assessment

Preparation:
1.   You will need an index card or note card for each of your students today.

Lesson:

1.   Tell the students to review the Godly Character Traits listed on day 9 in the *Student Book* on their own.

2.   Have the students silently read the assigned pages in the folk tale for day 14, saving 3-4 pages to read aloud to you.

3.   Meet with the students to finish the assignment for day 14.

4.   Listen to your students read 3-4 pages. Use the Qualities of Good Reading list provided in the Appendix to help you know what to emphasize.

5.   Discuss the following questions with the students:
      a) *Refer to day 9 in the Student Book. Choose the trait that is the hardest for you to show - virtue, truthfulness, or kindness. Explain.*
      b) *Look at the Bible verse on day 9 in the Student Book for the trait you chose. How does the behavior of your book characters compare to this verse? Explain.*
      c) *What ways can you demonstrate the verse you chose in your own life?*

6.   Hand out one index card to each student. Have the students list actions they will take to help them live according to the verse they chose.

7.   On the other side of the card, have the students divide the card into 3-4 sections, by drawing vertical lines. Instruct the students to break the chosen verse into sections and draw a quick picture or symbol to stand for each section of the verse. When the students look at the pictures, it should remind them of each part of the verse.

8.   The Bible verse may be written on the bottom or on the back of the card if you choose to have the students do so.

9.   Have the students post their cards in a place where they will see them often.

Independent   **Level 6/7/8**

Focus: Godly Character Traits - Personal Assessment

Preparation:
1.   The students each need an index card or note card for today.

Lesson:
1.   The students complete the activities in the *Student Book* and read the assigned pages for day 14 on their own.

2.   The directions instruct the students to come and show you the completed assignment for day 14, including the completed index card or note card for posting.

Teacher Directed   **All Levels Together**

Preparation:

1.   Choose which **one** of the following project options you would like your students to complete as a culminating project for this genre. Each option is explained in detail on the pages that follow. For ease in planning, you should choose the same option for each of the students.

a) **Option 1:** You may choose a character based project, which focuses on the Godly character trait for this genre. The directions for these projects are more general. The project does not involve any of the books from the unit. It does include a final reflection form.

b) **Option 2:** You may choose a book based project, which is an individual project that is tailored to the student's individual level. Students will choose one of the books they read for this genre to use for the project. In order to choose this option, you must purchase *Book Projects to Send Home* by Lori Sanders and Linda Kimble for your particular students' levels. There is one book for each of the three levels. The project directions are very detailed and include a final reflection for each project.

c) **Option 3:** Your final option is to choose a group project, which requires two or more students working together. This project is based on a common book the students have all read or had read aloud to them. The **one** book the project is based upon should fit into the genre studied in this unit.

2.   Have the directions for the project copied for each student. Make sure to read over the directions for the project option you chose in order to know what supplies you will need to have available for the projects.

3.   The plans allow 5 work days for the projects to be completed. This time allotment includes the planning and any presenting of the projects. The plans assume that the students will use only their normal amount of reading time to complete the projects.

Lesson:

1.   Say, *Today we will be starting our culminating project for folk tales. You will have 5 days, counting today, to work on your project. Your projects are due at the end of that time on _____. (give due date)*

2.   Introduce the project you have chosen for this unit. Go through the directions and make sure students have a copy of the directions, so they can work as independently as possible. Show them where the needed supplies are located.

3.   Then, have students read the assigned pages for day 15 to finish the folk tale books. Students may begin the project after the reading is complete.

Folk Tale - Day 15 - **Option 1**

Focus: Godly Character Trait Project   **Fruits of the Spirit**

Project Notes:

1.   Teach children to act upon the virtues studied in this unit.

2.   You will explore several Bible passages to better understand the meaning of virtues or "fruits of the spirit". The Bible discussion needs to be completed by day 16. Read the passage Matthew 3:10-11. Discuss the following questions with your students:
      a) *What do you think John the Baptist is talking about in verse 10?* (A fruit tree bears fruit and as Christians we should "bear fruit" through our good deeds.)
      b) *In verse 11 what is the difference between the way John baptized and the way Jesus baptizes?* (Water is an outward sign and the Holy Spirit is an inward change.)

3.   Read the passage Galations 5:22-26. Discuss the following question with your students:
      a) *What does the Holy Spirit produce in us?* (List the fruits of the Spirit that are mentioned in the passage.)

4.   Read the passage John 15:1-8. Discuss the following questions with your students:
      a) *Who is the vine?* (Christ)
      b) *Who is the gardener?* (God)
      c) *Who are the branches?* (The followers of Christ)
      d) *What does this passage tell us?* (The only way to live a good life is to stay close to Christ, just like branches attached to the vine. Others need to see our faith in the way we treat them, or in the "fruit" we bear.)

5.   Read the passage 2 Peter 1:5-8. Discuss the following question with your students:
      a) *What does this passage tell us to do?* (To act upon our faith in order to grow as a Christian. One way to act upon our faith is through showing kindness and love to others.)

6.   As a group, discuss actions you could take to show kindness or love to others during the next week. Students may choose an action to do for someone individually or one action to do as a group. Some examples include baking something to deliver to someone, visiting someone who is sick or lonely, mowing the lawn for someone who isn't able to do so, sending a card to someone in need, or calling a person who needs encouragement.

7.   On day 19, reproduce the reflection form included in this guide for each student to complete.

Unit 6

Focus: Book Based Project   **Individual Projects by Level**

Project Notes:

1.   This is an individual project tailored to the students' individual levels.

2.   In order to choose this option, you must purchase *Book Projects to Send Home* by Lori Sanders and Linda Kimble (McGraw-Hill, 2004) for your particular students' levels. There is one project book for each of the 3 levels. The books include detailed reproducible directions, work schedules, and reflection forms.

3.   The students each need to choose **one** book from those that **were read in this genre**. That book is the basis for the project.

4.   The project titles, corresponding page numbers, and levels in the *Book Projects to Send Home* books are listed below.

Use Grade 2 of *Book Projects to Send Home*   **Level 2/3**

Project Title: Main Character Mobile   Page Numbers: 23-26

Preparation:

1.   Read the project description box and the materials to provide section on p. 23. The rest of the items on p. 23 are optional ideas to use if you enjoy teaching through themes.

2.   Copy pp. 24-26 for your students. Save p. 26 for the students to complete on day 19 as a reflection on their project. This is listed in the plans for day 19.

Use Grade 4 of *Book Projects to Send Home*   **Level 4/5**

Note: The project directions are written for use with a biography. The students will use their folk tale character instead.

Project Title: Meet a Famous Figure   Page Numbers: 15-18

Preparation:

1.   Read the project description box and the materials to provide section on p. 15. The rest of the items on p. 15 are optional ideas to use if you enjoy teaching through themes.

2.   Copy pp. 16-18 and 47 for your students. Have students change the wording from biography to folk tale. Students need to change the interview questions on p.16, so they can be answered by the folk tale character.

Folk Tale - Day 15 - **Option 2**

3.	Save p. 47 for the students to complete on day 19 as a reflection on their project. This is listed in the plans for day 19.

4.	Instruct students to think of the schedule on p. 17 as steps to complete, rather than a time frame for each part of the project. The students will be working solely on completing the projects for 5 reading days, instead of doing them gradually for 4 weeks as the project book suggests.

5.	The students have already completed the project requirements listed under week 1 in the schedule on p. 17. They will not need to choose another folk tale to read.

6.	The presentation guidelines listed on p. 17 will be changed to a folk tale character interview instead.

Use Grade 5 of *Book Projects to Send Home*   **Level 6/7/8**
Note: Although these projects are listed for grade 5, they are very challenging to complete which makes them appropriate for level 6/7/8.

Project Title: Role-Play   Page Numbers: 31-34

Preparation:
1.	Read the project description box and the materials to provide section on p. 31. The rest of the items on p. 31 are optional ideas to use if you enjoy teaching through themes.

2.	Copy pp. 32-34 and 47 for your students. You may want to remove the "Dear Fifth Grader" greeting on p. 32. Save p. 47 for the students to complete on day 19 as a reflection on their projects. This is listed in the plans for day 19.

3.	Instruct students to think of the schedule on p. 33 as steps to complete, rather than a time frame for each part of the project. The students will be working solely on completing the projects for 5 reading days, instead of doing them gradually for 4 weeks as the project book suggests.

4.	The students have already completed the project requirements listed under week 1 on the schedule on p. 33. They will not need to choose another book to read.

Focus: <u>**Group Project**</u>   <u>**Play**</u>

Notes:

1.   In order to choose this option, you must have two or more students (unless you are willing to do part of the project with your student).

2.   This project is based on **one** common book the students have all read or had read aloud to them. The book the project is based upon <u>should fit into the genre studied in this unit.</u>

3.   The group chooses **one exciting scene** to perform as a one act play. Encourage students to choose a shorter scene, so they have time to create costumes and scenery and practice their parts.

4.   Reproduce the planning form included in this guide for students to use as they are planning the one act play.

5.   Each group member needs to have a role in the play. The role can be an acting role, a narrating role, or a directing role. Group members meet to determine who is responsible for each role.

6.   Actors and narrators may choose to read their parts directly from the book, to read their parts from copies of the book pages, or to memorize their parts.

7.   All group members must participate in creating costumes and scenery. You need to supervise this part of the preparation, so students are able to finish by day 19.

8.   Group members must be prepared to share their one act play on day 19. You may want to videotape the performance, so students can see their one act play.

9.   On day 19, students present the one act play. Reproduce the reflection form included in this guide for each student to complete.

One Act Play Planning Sheet

Name: _____

Book Title: _____

1. Choose one short, exciting scene from your book to use for the one act play.

2. List the page numbers for the scene: pp. _____

3. Write the names of the characters in the scene and tell who will perform each role. List the person who will be the director.

   _____

   _____

   _____

4. Who will be the narrator? What will the narrator say to introduce the play? What will the narrator say throughout the play?

   _____

   _____

   _____

5. What costumes will you wear? _____

   _____

   _____

6. What props will you use, and what scenery will you need?

   _____

   _____

   _____

Independent / Teacher Directed   **All Levels**

Focus: Project Work

Preparation:
1. For details, read the directions for the project option you chose.

Lesson:
1. Check students' progress to make sure each student understands what to do and is on schedule to finish by day 19.

2. Meet with students as a group, if this is needed.

Independent / Teacher Directed   **All Levels**

Focus: Project Completion

Preparation:
1. For details, read the directions for the project option you chose.

2. Have the reflection forms copied for each student to match the project option you chose.

Lesson:
1. Briefly check students' progress. Students should finish their projects today.

2. Have students share their projects with each other or with you.

3. Hand out the reflection form that matches the project option you chose. Have the students complete the reflection and show you.

4. You are ready to choose the next genre your students will study. Look ahead to prepare the kickoff for the upcoming genre.

Fruits of the Spirit Reflection

1. What action did you take this week to show kindness and love to others? _____
_____.

2. What did you learn from your actions?_____
_____
_____.

3. What would you do differently if you could do this project again?_____
_____.

4. What did you learn about the Fruits of the Spirit? _____
_____
_____
_____.

_____   _____
Signature of student   Date

One Act Play Reflection

1. During the one act play, I felt that I did a good job of _____

_____.

2. I think that I could have done a better job of_____

_____.

3. If I could do the one act play project again, I would _____

_____

_____.

4. From the one act play, I learned _____

_____

_____.

5. My favorite part of this project was_____

_____

_____.

_____   _____
    Signature of student   Date

Nonfiction

GENRE: NONFICTION

Definition:
Informational books and factual stories based upon real people and events.

Common Characteristics:
1. Is well-researched by the author in order to provide information that is correct.
2. Supports facts with data, pictures, charts, diagrams, and photographs.
3. Presents detailed information in a direct, factual way.
4. Includes different points of view of a topic.
5. Has a table of contents and may include an index.

Story Element Emphasis: Main Idea or Theme

Definition of Main Idea:
The details in the text working together to support one idea. The main idea can be determined for a paragraph, section, chapter, or an entire text.

Definition of Theme:
The main purpose, lesson, or big idea in the text.

Godly Character Trait Emphasis: Obedience

Definition:
A willingness to do what is asked or required without complaint.

Subqualities:
1. attentiveness
2. cooperativeness
3. meekness

Teacher Directed   **All Levels Together**

Focus: Genre Kickoff

Preparation:

1.   The goal of the kickoff is to introduce students of all ages to the upcoming genre in a fun and entertaining manner.

2.   Decide how much time you want to spend on the kickoff. You can spend one normal reading class period, several hours, or even a whole day. After the kickoff, you begin with day 1 in the teacher's plans.

3.   Read through the list of ideas below and choose those that interest you for this genre's kickoff. You are welcome to add your own ideas that fit within this genre. Refer to the cover page for a definition and common characteristics for each genre. Introduce the name and definition of the genre to begin the kickoff.

Possible Kickoff Ideas:

1.   Give students several examples of facts and opinions. Next, have students use nonfiction magazines or short nonfiction books to find their own examples of facts and opinions. Students share their own examples, and the rest of the group discusses whether each example is a fact or an opinion.

2.   Guide students through one or more science experiments. Have students write their observations and list conclusions. Discuss the differences between facts and opinions.

3.   Help students make a labeled model of how something works or the different parts of something. For example, they could make a topographical map using a salt, water, and flour mixture; a model of your teeth using red clay for the gums and soy beans for the different types of teeth; models of various animal tracks in plaster; the layers of human skin using colored play dough; or the inside of an animal's body using balloons and colored string for the organs. The model needs to be based on factual information.

4.   Go on a nature walk and watch for one specific item in nature, such as types of trees, leaves, bugs, grasses, clouds, or birds. Collect specimens, sketch the different types of the item, or photograph them. Then, use nonfiction books to categorize or diagnose your findings.

5.   Focus on the different types of one thing you can view and compare factually, such as structures of bridges, types of architecture, or periods of art. Prepare your students ahead of time, by providing them with nonfiction books that have pictures demonstrating the different types of items you'll be viewing.

6. Do one activity that shows students how to do something that is unfamiliar, such as folding origami paper, watching clouds, or cooking a difficult dish. Then, provide students with hobby books that show the steps required to do something new. Have each student choose one new skill to practice and demonstrate for the group.

7. Visit a museum and discuss the differences between what is fact and what is opinion in the written details that accompany each exhibit.

8. Focus on one country in the world during one of its historical time periods. Choose several factual areas to replicate, such as the clothing, food, music, art, games, architecture, celebrations, or customs of that country. Design activities to involve the students in recreating that country's historical time era.

9. Share *Brain Quest* questions and answers in partners or as a group. If you have a different game with factual information, play that instead.

10. Poll students about their opinions of what the answer is to a certain question. Then, provide a fact that answers the question. For example, you might ask students to give their opinion on "What animal is the largest living mammal in the world?" Then, you would provide students with the fact "The blue whale is the largest living mammal in the world." Repeat the polling and answering process with each question you ask.

Questions to discuss at the end of the kickoff:
1. What is nonfiction? (Refer to the definition on the cover page for this genre.)

2. What did you learn about nonfiction from today's activities?

3. What are some common characteristics of nonfiction books?

4. What is the difference between a fact and an opinion?

5. Why is nonfiction important as a genre?

Teacher Directed   **All Levels Together**

Focus: Prereading Activity - K- W Chart
Preparation:
1.   Prior to meeting with the students for day 1, follow the directions for *Getting Started* listed in the back of this guide.

2.   Have the first book and one *Assigned Reading Calendar* ready for each student.

Lesson:
1.   Say, *Today we will be doing a prereading activity to help you think about the next book you will be reading.*

2.   Give students the first book they will be reading for this genre. Discuss the following questions with the students:
        a) *Look through the table of contents. What is the book about?*
        b) *What makes your book nonfiction?*
        c) *Does the book have pictures, charts, maps, or photographs? Find one and share it with the group.*
        d) *As you page through the book, what are some topic words that seem important?*
        e) *What makes the words you shared look important?*

3.   Have students open their *Student Book* to the K-W Chart on day 1. Tell students they will be listing what they know about the topic of their nonfiction book. They will also write any questions they have about this topic.

4.   Students write what is known about the topic on the left side of the chart. This is information students know without looking in the book. On the right side of the chart, students write the questions they have about this topic. Students get ideas for questions by looking through the book.

5.   The directions instruct the students to come and show you the completed assignment.

6.   Have students open their *Student Books* to the *Assigned Reading Calendar* for this genre. Help each student fill in the page numbers to be read for days 1-5.

7.   Have students read the assigned pages for day 1 on their own.

Teacher Directed   **Level 2/3**

Focus: Story Discussion and Optional Phonics or Vocabulary Work

Preparation:

1.   You may choose to have students at this level review phonics or complete a vocabulary assignment. Use your own program for the phonics review. Refer to the Appendix for a reproducible vocabulary assignment. The lesson on this day is much shorter to compensate for the additional time you may spend on phonics or on vocabulary work.

Lesson:

1.   Optional phonics or vocabulary work

2.   Listen to your students read the assigned pages out loud to you. Use the Reading Strategies list and the Qualities of Good Reading list provided in the Appendix to help you know what to emphasize.

3.   Discuss the following questions with your students:
        a) *What did you find out that you didn't know before you began reading this book?*
        b) *Is the information presented as a series of facts, or is it presented as a story?*
        c) *How is a nonfiction book different from other types of books?*

Independent / Teacher Directed   **Level 4/5**

Focus: Story Element Instruction - Main Idea

Lesson:

1.   Tell the students to read the assigned pages on their own, leaving 3-4 pages to read aloud to you.

2.   Listen to your students read several pages. Use the Qualities of Good Reading list provided in the Appendix to help you know what to emphasize.

3.   Introduce the following definition for *main idea: The details in the text working together to support one idea. The main idea can be determined for a paragraph, section, chapter, or an entire text.*

4.   Select a paragraph from the 3-4 pages the students read aloud to you. Reread the paragraph out loud.

5.   Ask students to tell you what they think the paragraph is saying.

6.   Have students find the main idea of the paragraph and read that sentence aloud. Show students that the other sentences give details which support the main idea.

7.   Guide students to see that the remaining sentences provide details which support the main idea.

8.   Select a different paragraph from the pages the students read aloud to you. Repeat steps 4-7 for the paragraph you selected.

9.   Discuss with students the one main idea for the 3-4 page section they read aloud to you. Have students summarize what happened in a single sentence. Students will use this main idea to complete day 2 in the *Student Book.*

10. Have students open their *Student Books* to the Main Idea Tree on day 2. Tell students that just as roots support a tree, details support the main idea.

11. Work with the students to write the main idea, from number 9, on the the tree. List at least one supporting detail from the text for each root in the ground. You may want to write answers on a marker board as you discuss them, so the students can copy them. Then, the students can concentrate on the discussion rather than on spelling and capitalization.

Independent   **Level 6/7/8**

Focus: Vocabulary Builder - Inspect It

Preparation:
1.   Have a dictionary and a thesaurus available.

Lesson:
1.   The students complete the activities in the *Student Book* and read the assigned pages for day 2 on their own.

2.   The directions instruct students to come and show you the completed Inspect It vocabulary assignment.

Teacher Directed   **Level 2/3**

Focus: Story Element Instruction - Main Idea

Lesson:

1.   Listen to your students read the assigned pages out loud to you. Use the Reading Strategies list and the Qualities of Good Reading list provided in the Appendix to help you know what to emphasize.

2.   Ask one student to tell about something important that has happened in his life. Have the student share as much information about the important event as possible. Group members may ask the student questions to learn more details.

3.   Use the directions that follow to model how to use paraphrasing to state the main idea of the student's event. Tell students that they have heard all of the details of the event. Now, they need to choose one idea that shows only the most important information. This is called the main idea. List suggestions for the main idea on a marker board or a large piece of paper.

4.   Use the suggestions the students listed to write one sentence that summarizes the main idea.

5.   Introduce the following definition for *main idea: The details in the text working together to support one idea. The main idea can be determined for a paragraph, section, chapter, or an entire text.*

6.   Select a paragraph from the pages the students read aloud to you. Reread the paragraph out loud.

7.   Ask students what they think the paragraph is telling them.

8.   Have students find one sentence in the paragraph that gives the main idea.

9.   Show students that the other sentences give details which support the main idea.

10.   Select a different paragraph from the pages the students read aloud to you. Repeat steps 6-9 for the paragraph you selected.

Independent   <u>**Level 4/5**</u>

Focus: Story Element Extension - Nonfiction Notes

Lesson:
1.   Tell the students to read the assigned pages for day 3 on their own.

2.   Tell them to complete the Nonfiction Notes on day 3 in their *Student Book* when they finish reading.

3.   The directions instruct students to come and show you the completed assignment.

Teacher Directed / Independent   <u>**Level 6/7/8**</u>

Focus: Story Element Discussion - Main Idea

Lesson:
1.   The students read the assigned pages for day 3 on their own.

2.   The students meet with you to discuss the following questions:
       a) *Is the information presented clearly? How can you tell?*
       b) *Does the book provide up-to-date, or current, information?* (Check the publishing date.)
       c) *Why is it important to use several resources when you are learning about a topic?* (Different resources may have different information due to what information was available when the book was published.)
       d) *Does the book make you want to learn more about the topic? Why, or why not?*

3.   Introduce the following definition for *main idea: The details in the text working together to support one idea. The main idea can be determined for a paragraph, section, chapter, or an entire text.*

4.   Go over the Main Idea Ladder in the *Student Book* under day 3.

5.   Have the students work to complete day 3 on their own.

6.   The directions instruct students to come and show you the completed assignment.

Teacher Directed

Level 2/3

Focus: Godly Character Traits - Examples

Preparation:
1. Think of examples you can share from your own life for each of the following traits: *obedience* and *attentiveness*. (Definitions are listed in the lesson below.)

Lesson:
1. Introduce the following definition and scripture passage for *obedience:*
   a) *Obedience is a willingness to do what is asked or required without complaint.*
   b) *Key Scripture verse: Teach me O Lord to follow your decrees; then I will keep them to the end. Give me understanding, and I will keep your law and obey it with all my heart. Psalms 119:33,34*

2. Share an example of *obedience* from your own life.

3. Help the students think of an example of *obedience* from their own lives.

4. Introduce the following definition and scripture passage for *attentiveness:*
   a) *Attentiveness is giving your full attention to something so that you may receive knowledge and gain understanding.*
   b) *Key Scripture verse: My son, pay attention to what I say; listen closely to my words. Do not let them out of your sight, keep them within your heart. Proverbs 4:20,21*

5. Repeat steps 2 and 3 for the trait *attentiveness.*

6. Instruct your students to search for examples of *obedience* and *attentiveness* as they read part or all of the assigned pages out loud to you. Use the Reading Strategies list and the Qualities of Good Reading list provided in the Appendix to help you know what to emphasize.

7. Discuss the following questions with your students:
   a) *What are some examples of obedience or attentiveness in your nonfiction book?*
   b) *Are examples of the opposite traits of disobedience or inattentiveness shown in the book? Explain.*
   c) *How are obedience and attentiveness an important part of the topic you are studying?*

Independent / Teacher Directed   **Level 4/5**

Focus: Godly Character Traits - Examples

Lesson:
1. Tell the students to read and complete the Godly Character Sheet on day 4 in the *Student Book* on their own.

2. The students also silently read the assigned pages for day 4, leaving 3-4 pages to read aloud to you.

3. The students should come and show you when both are completed.

4. Review the Godly Character Sheet on day 4 in the *Student Book*, so the students and you will know what traits you are searching for in the nonfiction book. *(obedience, attentiveness, cooperativeness)*

5. Listen to your students read 3-4 pages aloud. Use the Qualities of Good Reading list provided in the Appendix to help you know what to emphasize.

6. Discuss the following questions with the students:
    a) *What is an example of obedience in your nonfiction book?*
    b) *What is an example of attentiveness in your nonfiction book?*
    c) *How is cooperativeness shown in your nonfiction book?*
    d) *Are examples of the opposite traits of disobedience, inattentiveness, or self-centeredness shown in the book? Explain.*
    e) *What examples of God's sovereignty do you find in your nonfiction book?*

Independent   **Level 6/7/8**

Focus: Godly Character Traits - Examples

Lesson:
1. The students complete the activities in the *Student Book* and read the assigned pages for day 4 on their own.

2. The directions instruct students to come and show you the completed Godly Character page.

Teacher Directed / Independent   **All Levels Together**

Focus: Comprehension Check - Factual Fun

Lesson:

1.   Say, *We will be sharing interesting facts from our nonfiction books today.*

2.   Give students 15 minutes to complete the Factual Fun planning form on day 5 in the *Student Book.*

3.   Have each student share the parts they chose with the group.

4.   Allow group members to ask questions after the person has shared the facts from the book.

5.   When all students have finished sharing, have students read the assigned pages in their nonfiction book for day 5 on their own.

Teacher Directed   **All Levels Together**

Focus: Prereading Activity - Questions and Answers

Preparation:
1.   If students are beginning new books today, make sure to have the number of pages to be read each day calculated and have those books ready to hand out. (See the *Getting Started* section, item #7, in the back of this guide for details.)

2.   If students are not beginning new books today, they use the books they are currently reading for today's activities.

Lesson:
1.   Say, *Today we will be doing a prereading activity to help you think about the next book you will be reading or the next part of the book you will be reading.*

2.   Say, *Look at the Table of Contents. Scan the headings and subheadings or chapter titles to help you "see" what is in the book.*

3.   Discuss the following questions with the students:
      a) *What things have you learned about the book from the Table of Contents?*
      b) *Is the information in the book presented as a series of facts, or is it presented as a story? Explain.*

4.   Tell students they will write questions about the topics of their nonfiction books. These should be questions that require students to search for the answers.

5.   Discuss the following questions with the students:
      a) *How do we punctuate a question?* (with a question mark at the end of the sentence)
      b) *How do you know if a sentence is a question?* (It ends with a question mark, and it asks something.)
      c) *What kinds of words do we find at the beginning of a question?* (asking words - such as *how, where, when, what, who, why*)
      d) *What would be a question you could ask about the topic of your book?* (Have students share ideas. Guide the students to see that questions should be about something important and should require students to search for the answer.)
      e) For example, a question asking, *How many arms does an octopus have?* is not a question that requires much thought to answer. An example of a better question might be, *What does the octopus use its arms to do?*

6. Have students open their *Student Books* to Questions and Answers on day 6 and write their questions. Students should get ideas for questions by looking through the nonfiction book. Students will answer as many of the questions as possible on day 10.

7. Help students update their *Assigned Reading Calendar* for days 6-10.

8. The directions instruct the students to come and show you the completed assignment.

9. Have students read the assigned pages for day 6 on their own.

Teacher Directed   **Level 2/3**

Focus: Story Discussion and Optional Phonics <u>or</u> Vocabulary Work

Preparation:
1.   You may choose to have students at this level review phonics <u>or</u> complete a vocabulary assignment. Use your own program for the phonics review. Refer to the Appendix for a reproducible vocabulary assignment. The lesson on this day is much shorter to compensate for the additional time you may spend on phonics or on vocabulary work.

Lesson:
1.   Optional phonics or vocabulary work

2.   Listen to your students read the assigned pages out loud to you. Use the Reading Strategies list and the Qualities of Good Reading list provided in the Appendix to help you know what to emphasize.

3.   Discuss the following questions with your students:
   a) *What is something new you've learned from this book?*
   b) *How does the author show you information in the book?*
   c) *How can you find information quickly?* (Show the students how to use the Table of Contents and the Index to find information.)

Independent / Teacher Directed   **Level 4/5**

Focus: Story Element Instruction - Main Idea Discussion

Lesson:
1.   Tell the students to read the assigned pages on their own, leaving 3-4 pages to read aloud to you.

2.   Listen to your students read several pages. Use the Qualities of Good Reading list provided in the Appendix to help you know what to emphasize.

3.   Review the following definition for *main idea: The details in the text working together to support one idea. The main idea can be determined for a paragraph, section, chapter, or an entire text.*

4.   Introduce the following definition for *theme: The main purpose, lesson, or big idea in the text.*

5.   Work with the students to complete Main Idea Discussion on day 7 in the
        Student Book. The main idea should be a single sentence summarizing
        the important ideas. You may want to write the answers on a marker board as
        you discuss them, so the students can copy them. Then, the students can
        concentrate on the discussion rather than on spelling and capitalization.

Independent   **Level 6/7/8**

Focus: Vocabulary Builder - Inspect It

Preparation:
1.   Have a dictionary and a thesaurus available.

Lesson:
1.   The students complete the activities in the *Student Book* and read the assigned
        pages for day 7 on their own.

2.   The directions instruct students to come and show you the completed
        Inspect It vocabulary assignment.

<u>Teacher Directed</u>   **<u>Level 2/3</u>**

Focus: Story Element Instruction - Main Idea

Preparation:
1.   You need a large piece of paper or a marker board for the lesson.

Lesson:
1.   Listen to your students read part or all of the assigned pages out loud to you. Use the Reading Strategies list and the Qualities of Good Reading list provided in the Appendix to help you know what to emphasize.

2.   Review the following definition for *main idea: The details in the text working together to support one idea. The main idea can be determined for a paragraph, section, chapter, or an entire text.*

3.   Ask students to summarize the important ideas for the pages they read today. Write the ideas the students share on a marker board or a large piece of paper.

4.   Using the ideas from number 3, discuss with students the <u>one</u> main idea for the section they read aloud to you. Have students summarize what happened in a single sentence. Students will use this main idea to complete day 8 in the *Student Book.*

5.   Show students that the other ideas give details which support the main idea.

6.   Have students open their *Student Books* to the Main Idea Tower on day 8. Tell students that just as the blocks support each other when you build a block tower, the details support the main idea.

7.   Work with the students to write the main idea, from number 4, in the top block of the tower. List at least one supporting detail from the text for each block in the tower. You may want to write answers on a marker board as you discuss them, so the students can copy them. Then, the students can concentrate on the discussion rather than on spelling and capitalization.

<u>Independent</u>   **<u>Level 4/5</u>**

Focus: Story Element Extension - Fascinating Facts

Lesson:
1.   Tell the students to read the assigned pages for day 8 on their own.

2.   Tell them to complete Fascinating Facts on day 8 in their *Student Books* when they finish reading.

3.   The directions instruct students to come and show you the completed assignment.

Teacher Directed / Independent   **Level 6/7/8**

Focus: Story Element Instruction - Theme Card

Preparation:
1.   You need one index card for each student.

Lesson:
1.   The students read the assigned pages for day 8 on their own.

2.   The students meet with you to discuss the following questions:
       a) *How is the nonfiction genre different from the fiction genre?* (Nonfiction includes factual information, tables, graphs, charts, real-life photographs, data, table of contents, index, glossary etc.)
       b) *What is the author's purpose for writing the book?*
       c) *How do you decide if an example in the book is a main idea or a supporting detail?*

3.   Review the following definition for *main idea: The details in the text working together to support one idea. The main idea can be determined for a paragraph, section, chapter, or an entire text.*

4.   Introduce the following definition for *theme: The main purpose, lesson, or big idea in the text.*

5.   Introduce the Theme Card on day 8 in the *Student Book*. Make sure the students understand what to do. Then, have the students work on their own.

6.   The directions instruct students to come and show you the completed assignment.

Teacher Directed   **Level 2/3**

Focus: Godly Character Traits - Biblical Comparisons

Preparation:
1.   Find a short children's book of the Bible story about Abraham leaving Ur with his family as God instructed him to do. Otherwise, you will need to read the story directly from the Bible in Genesis 12:1-5.

Lesson:
1.   Review the following definitions and scripture passages:
        a) *Obedience is a willingness to do what is asked or required without complaint.*
        b) *Key Scripture verse: Teach me O Lord to follow your decrees; then I will keep them to the end. Give me understanding, and I will keep your law and obey it with all my heart. Psalms 119:33,34*
        c) *Attentiveness is giving your full attention to something so that you may receive knowledge and gain understanding.*
        d) *Key Scripture verse: My son, pay attention to what I say; listen closely to my words. Do not let them out of your sight, keep them within your heart. Proverbs 4:20,21*

2.   Read the children's book, or the Bible passage Genesis 12:1-5, about Abraham leaving Ur with his family as God instructed him to do. Instruct your students to listen for examples of *obedience* and *attentiveness* in the story being read.

3.   Discuss the following question with your students:
        a) *How did Abraham's actions show obedience and attentiveness?*

4.   Record the students' responses in the *Student Book* on day 9 under the Biblical Character column. (Possible answers include the following: *Obedience* when Abraham left Ur to go to Haran and then to Canaan as God instructed him to do; *Attentiveness* when Abraham made sure to listen carefully to God's instructions to leave his country, his people, and his father's household.)

5.   Listen to your students read the assigned pages for day 9 out loud to you. Remind the students to be searching for *obedience* and *attentiveness.*

6.   Using the questions listed below, compare Abraham's actions with the examples in the nonfiction book. Record the responses on day 9 in the *Student Book* under the Book Examples column.
        a) *What is an example of obedience in your nonfiction book?*
        b) *What is an example of attentiveness in your nonfiction book?*
        c) *What does the Biblical character, Abraham, teach us about obedience and attentiveness?*

Independent / Teacher Directed   **Level 4/5**

Focus: Godly Character Traits - Biblical Comparisons

Preparation:
1.   Find a short children's book of the Bible story about Moses and the burning bush. Otherwise, the students read the story directly from the Bible in Exodus chapter 3 and chapter 4:1-19.

Lesson:
1.   Tell the students to review the Godly Character Traits listed on day 9 in the *Student Book* on their own. Then, have the students silently read the story of Moses and the burning bush, either from the book you provided or from the Bible in Exodus chapter 3 and chapter 4:1-19.

2.   Have students do their best to complete the Biblical Character column on the Godly Character Story Sheet for Moses on day 9 in the *Student Book.*

3.   Students silently read the assigned pages in the nonfiction book for day 9, saving 3 or 4 pages to read aloud to you.

4.   The students meet with you to finish the assignment for day 9. Listen to your students read several pages. Use the Qualities of Good Reading list provided in the Appendix to help you know what to emphasize.

5.   Discuss the following questions with the students as you review what they have already done in the *Student Book* for day 9.   Complete the remaining columns in the *Student Book* for day 9.
       a) How did Moses' behavior show *obedience, attentiveness*, and *cooperativeness?* (Possible answers include the following: *Obedience* when Moses went to Egypt and left Midian with his wife and sons as God had instructed him to do; *Attentiveness* as Moses listened to God's directions and asked God questions about the things he did not understand; *Cooperativeness* as Moses gladly accepted his brother, Aaron, to speak to the people for him due to his feelings of inadequacy as a speaker.)
       b) *What is an example of obedience in your nonfiction book?*
       c) *What is an example of attentiveness in your nonfiction book?*
       d) *What is an example of cooperativeness in your nonfiction book?*
       e) *What does the Biblical character, Moses, teach us about obedience, attentiveness, and cooperativeness?*

Independent   <u>**Level 6/7/8**</u>

Preparation:
1.   The students need a Bible for today's lesson.

Focus: Godly Character Traits - Biblical Comparisons

Lesson:
1.   The students complete the activities in the *Student Book* and read the assigned pages for day 9 on their own.

2.   The directions instruct the students to come and show you the completed Godly Character Story page. (Possible examples for the traits Jesus showed in Matthew 26:36-56 include the following: *Obedience* in verses 53-54 as Jesus explained that He could call on His Father to send the angels to fight for Him, but then the scripture would not be fulfilled; *Attentiveness* in verse 41 as Jesus warned Peter to watch and pray, to avoid temptation; *Cooperativeness* in verse 52 as Jesus went with the soldiers without doing battle; *Meekness* in verses 39 and 42, as Jesus always prayed for God's will to be done.)

Teacher Directed / Independent   **Level 2/3**

Focus: Comprehension Check - Questions and Answers

Lesson:
1.   Review the questions the students wrote on day 6 in the *Student Book*. Students will answer these questions on their own after reading the assigned pages today.

2.   Listen to your students read part of the assigned pages out loud to you. Use the Reading Strategies list and the Qualities of Good Reading list provided in the Appendix to help you know what to emphasize.

3.   The students finish the assigned reading and complete Questions and Answers from day 6 on their own. The directions instruct the students to come and show you the completed assignment.

Independent   **Level 4/5**

Focus: Comprehension Check - Questions and Answers

Lesson:
1.   Tell the students to review the questions written on day 6 in the *Student Book*. The students will be answering these questions on their own after reading the assigned pages for day 10.

2.   You may choose to have the students leave 3-4 pages to read aloud to you. The directions instruct the students to come and show you the completed assignment from day 6.

Independent   **Level 6/7/8**

Focus: Comprehension Check - Questions and Answers

Lesson:
1.   The students complete the activities in the *Student Book* and read the assigned pages for day 10 on their own.

2.   The directions instruct the students to come and show you the completed Questions and Answers assignment from day 6.

Teacher Directed   **All Levels Together**

Focus: Prereading Activity - Curious Questions

Preparation:

1.   If students are beginning new books today, make sure to have the number of pages to be read each day calculated and have those books ready to hand out. (See the *Getting Started* section, item #7, in the back of this guide for details.)

2.   If students are not beginning new books today, they use the books they are currently reading for today's activities.

Lesson:

1.   Say, *Today we will be doing a prereading activity to help you think about the next book you will be reading or the next part of the book you will be reading.*

2.   Guide students to look at the book jacket, title page, forward, introduction or any other information given about the author as you discuss the following questions:
        a) *Is the author qualified to write about the topic in the book? Explain.*
        b) *What research did the author need to do before writing the book?*
        c) *Why is it important that nonfiction books be well researched?*

3.   Guide students to search through the table of contents, index, glossary, charts, tables, graphs, pictures, and photographs as you discuss the following questions:
        a) *How is the information in the book organized?* (Have students give examples from the table of contents, titles, and headings.)
        b) *Is information easy to find in the book?* (Have students give examples from the table of contents, index, and glossary.)
        c) *What is the purpose of the charts, tables, graphs, pictures, and photographs?* (Have students give examples by using the illustrations in the book.)

4.   Tell students to search through the assigned pages for today and choose one interesting illustration.

5.   Have students open the *Student Book* to Curious Questions on day 11. Students write questions about the illustration they chose. The directions instruct the students to come and show you the completed assignment.

6.   Help students update their *Assigned Reading Calendar* for days 11-15.

7.   Have students read the assigned pages for day 11 on their own.

Teacher Directed   **Level 2/3**

Focus: Story Discussion and Optional Phonics <u>or</u> Vocabulary Work

Preparation:
1.   You may choose to have students at this level review phonics <u>or</u> complete a
        vocabulary assignment. Use your own program for the phonics review. Refer to
        the Appendix for a reproducible vocabulary assignment. The lesson on this day
        is much shorter to compensate for the additional time you may spend on
        phonics or on vocabulary work.

Lesson:
1.   Optional phonics or vocabulary work

2.   Listen to your students read the assigned pages out loud to you. Use the
        Reading Strategies list and the Qualities of Good Reading list provided in the
        Appendix to help you know what to emphasize.

3.   Discuss the following questions with your students:
        a) *Is the book easy to understand? Why, or why not?*
        b) *What is the most interesting part?*
        c) *Does this book remind you of any other book? Explain.*

Independent / Teacher Directed   **Level 4/5**

Focus: Story Element Instruction - Theme Map

Lesson:
1.   Tell the students to read the assigned pages on their own, leaving 3-4 pages to
        read aloud to you.

2.   Listen to your students read several pages. Use the Qualities of Good Reading
        list provided in the Appendix to help you know what to emphasize.

3.   Review the following definition for *main idea: The details in the text working
        together to support one idea. The main idea can be determined for a
        paragraph, section, chapter, or an entire text.*

4.   Review the following definition for *theme: The main purpose, lesson, or big
        idea in the text.*

5.   Work with the students to complete the Theme Map on day 12 in the *Student Book.* Write the theme in the middle. Write phrases from the book that support the theme on the lines. Answer the two questions at the bottom. You may want to write the answers on a marker board as you discuss them, so the students can copy them. Then, the students can concentrate on the discussion.

Independent   **Level 6/7/8**

Focus: Vocabulary Builder - Inspect It

Preparation:
1.   Have a dictionary and a thesaurus available.   .

Lesson:
1.   The students complete the activities in the *Student Book* and read the assigned pages for day 12 on their own.

2.   The directions instruct students to come and show you the completed Inspect It vocabulary assignment.

<u>Teacher Directed</u>   **<u>Level 2/3</u>**

Focus: Story Element Instruction - Theme

Preparation:
1.   You need a large piece of paper or a marker board for the lesson.

Lesson:
1.   Listen to your students read the assigned pages out loud to you. Use the Reading Strategies list and the Qualities of Good Reading list provided in the Appendix to help you know what to emphasize.

2.   Review the following definition for *main idea: The details in the text working together to support one idea. The main idea can be determined for a paragraph, section, chapter, or an entire text.*

3.   Introduce the following definition for *theme: The main message, lesson, or big idea in the text.*

4.   Discuss the following questions with your students:
      a) What *are some possible themes for this book?* (List students' responses on a marker board or a large piece of paper. Try to limit each theme idea to one sentence.)
      b) *Which one of the themes we listed matches the main focus of the text the best?* (Guide students to choose the theme that all of the details in the text work together to support.)
      c) *Based on the theme we chose, what do you think is the author's purpose for writing this book?*

<u>Independent</u>   **<u>Level 4/5</u>**

Focus: Story Element Extension - Main Idea Sequencer

Lesson:
1.   Tell the students to read the assigned pages for day 13 on their own.

2.   Tell them to complete the Main Idea Sequencer on day 13 in their *Student Books* when they finish reading.

3.   The directions instruct students to come and show you the completed assignment.

Unit 7

Teacher Directed / Independent   **Level 6/7/8**

Focus: Story Element Discussion - Theme: Fact or Opinion

Lesson:
1.   The students read the assigned pages for day 13 on their own.

2.   The students meet with you to discuss the following questions:
   a) *Is the information in the book presented as a series of facts, or is it presented as a story?*
   b) *What is the difference between a fact and an opinion?* (A fact is something known to have happened or to be true. An opinion is a personal view or conclusion.)
   c) *Since the definition of nonfiction is information books and true stories based on facts, how are opinions used in nonfiction books?* (The book shows research on the part of the author and illustrator in order to accurately portray information. Various viewpoints of a subject are often presented.)
   d) *Some literature is written to persuade the reader to consider a theme from a certain perspective. The author has certain beliefs he wants the reader to accept. Does the author in your nonfiction book have a perspective he is promoting?*
   e) *Do you agree with the author's perspective?* (Explain the importance of checking several sources for information, instead of accepting everything you read as being factual.)

3.   Introduce the Fact and Opinion Chart in the *Student Book* for day 13. Review the difference between a fact and an opinion. Help the students get started.

4.   Have the students work to complete the rest of the Fact and Opinion Chart on their own.

5.   The directions instruct students to come and show you the completed assignment.

Teacher Directed   **Level 2/3**

Focus: Godly Character Traits - Personal Assessment

Preparation:
1.   You will need an index card or note card for each of your students today.

Lesson:
1.   Review the following definitions and scripture passages:
   a) _Obedience_ is a willingness to do what is asked or required without complaint.
   b) _Key Scripture verse_: Teach me O Lord to follow your decrees; then I will keep them to the end. Give me understanding, and I will keep your law and obey it with all my heart. Psalms 119:33,34
   c) _Attentiveness_ is giving your full attention to something so that you may receive knowledge and gain understanding.
   d) _Key Scripture verse:_ My son, pay attention to what I say; listen closely to my words. Do not let them out of your sight, keep them within your heart. Proverbs 4:20,21

2.   Listen to your students read the assigned pages for day 14 out loud to you.

3.   Discuss the following questions with the students:
   a) _How could the nonfiction book do a better job of showing the traits of obedience and attentiveness in connection with God's word? Explain._
   b) _Choose the trait that is harder for you to show, obedience or attentiveness. Explain._

4.   Hand out one index card to each student. Have the students write the trait they chose and 3 ways to work on showing the trait more often in their own lives.

5.   On the other side of the card, have the students draw themselves portraying this trait. The students may also write the matching Bible verse if you choose for them to do so.

6.   Have the students post their cards in a place where they will see them often.

Independent / Teacher Directed   **Level 4/5**

Focus: Godly Character Traits - Personal Assessment

Preparation:
1.   You will need an index card or note card for each of your students today.
Unit 7

Lesson:

1.   Tell the students to review the Godly Character Traits listed on day 9 in the *Student Book* on their own.

2.   Have the students silently read the assigned pages in the nonfiction book for day 14, saving 3-4 pages to read aloud to you.

3.   Meet with the students to finish the assignment for day 14.

4.   Listen to your students read 3-4 pages. Use the Qualities of Good Reading list provided in the Appendix to help you know what to emphasize.

5.   Discuss the following questions with the students:
      a) *Refer to day 9 in the Student Book. Choose the trait that is the hardest for you to show - obedience, attentiveness, or cooperativeness. Explain.*
      b) *Look at the Bible verse and the definition on day 9 in the Student Book for the trait you chose. How is that trait shown in your nonfiction book? Explain.*
      c) *What ways can you demonstrate the trait and verse you chose in your own life?*

6.   Hand out one index card to each student. Have students list actions they will take to help them live according to the verse they chose.

7.   On the other side of the card, have the students divide the card into 3-4 sections, by drawing vertical lines. Instruct the students to break the chosen verse into sections and draw a quick picture or symbol to stand for each section of the verse. When the students look at the pictures, it should remind them of each part of the verse.

8.   The Bible verse may be written on the bottom or on the back of the card if you choose to have the students do so.

9.   Have the students post their cards in a place where they will see them often.

Independent   **Level 6/7/8**

Focus: Godly Character Traits - Personal Assessment

Preparation:
1.   The students each need an index card or note card for today.

Lesson:

1.   The students complete the activities in the *Student Book* and read the assigned pages for day 14 on their own.

2.   The directions instruct the students to come and show you the completed assignment for day 14, including the completed index card or note card for posting.

Teacher Directed   **All Levels Together**

Preparation:
1.   Choose which **one** of the following project options you would like your students to complete as a culminating project for this genre. Each option is explained in detail on the pages that follow. For ease in planning, you should choose the same option for each of the students.
        a) **Option 1:** You may choose a character based project, which focuses on the Godly character trait for this genre. The directions for these projects are more general. The project does not involve any of the books from the unit. It does include a final reflection form.
        b) **Option 2:** You may choose a book based project, which is an individual project that is tailored to the student's individual level. Students will choose one of the books they read for this genre to use for the project. In order to choose this option, you must purchase *Book Projects to Send Home* by Lori Sanders and Linda Kimble for your particular students' levels. There is one book for each of the three levels. The project directions are very detailed and include a final reflection for each project.
        c) **Option 3:** Your final option is to choose a group project, which requires two or more students working together. This project is based on a common book the students have all read or had read aloud to them. The **one** book the project is based upon should fit into the genre studied in this unit.

2.   Have the directions for the project copied for each student. Make sure to read over the directions for the project option you chose in order to know what supplies you will need to have available for the projects.

3.   The plans allow 5 work days for the projects to be completed. This time allotment includes the planning and any presenting of the projects. The plans assume that the students will use only their normal amount of reading time to complete the projects.

Lesson:
1.   Say, *Today we will be starting our culminating project for nonfiction. You will have 5 days, counting today, to work on your project. Your projects are due at the end of that time on _____. (give due date)*

2.   Introduce the project you have chosen for this unit. Go through the directions and make sure students have a copy of the directions, so they can work as independently as possible. Show them where the needed supplies are located.

3.   Then, have students read the assigned pages for day 15 to finish the nonfiction books. Students may begin the project after the reading is complete.

Nonfiction - Day 15 - **Option 1**

Focus: <u>Godly Character Trait Project</u>   <u>Obedience Objects</u>

Project Notes:

1.   Students will carry one object each day to remind them of the obedience traits.

2.   On day 15, refer to day 4 or day 9 in the texts. Review the definition and key scripture verse for *obedience.*

3.   Read the Bible passage Exodus 24:12. Emphasize that God gave Moses tablets of stone with his commandments written on them. Tell students they will carry a stone with them all day as a reminder to be obedient. Give each student a small stone or a rock. Students need to have the rock with them at all times. If students need a reminder to be obedient say, *Remember the stone.*

4.   On day 16, have students put their stone from the previous day in a box or a container. This should be a container that students will be allowed to decorate and keep at the end. Refer to day 4 or day 9 in the texts. Review the definition and key scripture verse for *attentiveness.* Discuss how the word *sight* in the verse relates to the trait *attentiveness.*

5.   Tell students they will carry an object with big eyes all day as a reminder to be attentive. Suggestions for the object include a ping pong ball, a walnut, or a golf ball with a face drawn on it that includes big eyes. Students need to have the object with them at all times. If students need a reminder to be attentive say, *Remember the eyes.*

6.   On day 17, have students put their object from the previous day in their box or container. If you do <u>not</u> have students in level 4/5 or level 6/7/8, repeat steps 2 and 3 listed above. If you <u>do</u> have students in level 4/5 or level 6/7/8, refer to day 4 or day 9 in the texts. Review the definition and key scripture verse for *cooperativeness.* Discuss how the word *unity* in the verse and the words *joining together* in the definition relate to the trait *cooperativeness.*

7.   If you have students in level 4/5 or level 6/7/8, tell students they will carry 2 paper clips joined or linked together all day as a reminder to be cooperative. Students need to have the linked paper clips with them at all times. If students need reminding to be cooperative say, *Remember the paper clips.*

8.   On day 18, have students put their object from the previous day in their box or container. If you do <u>not</u> have students in level 6/7/8, repeat steps 4 and 5 listed above.

Unit 7

9.   If you <u>do</u> have students in level 6/7/8, refer to day 4 or day 9 in the texts. Review the definition and key scripture verse for *meekness.* Discuss how the word *gentleness* in the verse and the word *resistance* in the definition relate to the trait *meekness.*

10.   If you have students in level 6/7/8, tell students they will carry a cotton ball all day as a reminder to be meek. Students need to have the cotton ball with them at all times. If students need reminding to be cooperative say, *Remember the cotton.*

11.   On day 19, have students put their object from the previous day in their box or container. Discuss the following questions with your students:
        a) How did the objects help remind you of the traits you were studying?
        b) What did you learn about obedience this week?
        c) What reminders does God give us of his word?
        d) How can we "carry" God's reminders with us each day?

12.   Have students write the definitions and key verses that they studied on cards to keep inside their container. Then, the students may decorate the outside of their container.

13.   Reproduce the reflection form included in this guide for each student to complete on day 19.

Focus: Book Based Project   Individual Projects by Level

Project Notes:

1.   This is an individual project tailored to the students' individual levels.

2.   In order to choose this option, you must purchase *Book Projects to Send Home* by Lori Sanders and Linda Kimble (McGraw-Hill, 2004) for your particular students' levels. There is one project book for each of the 3 levels. The books include detailed reproducible directions, work schedules, and reflection forms.

3.   The students each need to choose **one** book from those that **were read in this genre**. That book is the basis for the project.

4.   The project titles, corresponding page numbers, and levels in the *Book Projects to Send Home* books are listed below.

Use Grade 2 of *Book Projects to Send Home*   **Level 2/3**

Project Title: Nature's Wonders Accordion Book   Page Numbers: 27-30

Preparation:

1.   Read the project description box and the materials to provide section on p. 27. If your students did not read about nature, the accordion book needs to be adapted to be about the topic your students did study. The rest of the items on p. 27 are optional ideas to use if you enjoy teaching through themes.

2.   Copy pp. 28-30 for your students. Remember to adjust the pages as needed for the topic your students studied. Save p. 30 for the students to complete on day 19 as a reflection on their project. This is listed in the plans for day 19.

3.   If your students read about animals, you might consider the *Stuffed Animal Research* project on pp. 39-42 as an alternative.

Use Grade 4 of *Book Projects to Send Home*   **Level 4/5**

Project Title: Flip-Fact Book   Page Numbers: 11-14

Preparation:

1.   Read the project description box and the materials to provide section on p. 11. The rest of the items on p. 11 are optional ideas to use if you enjoy teaching through themes.

2.   Copy pp. 12-14 and 47 for your students. Save p. 47 for the students to complete on day 19 as a reflection on their project. This is listed in the plans for day 19.

3.   Instruct students to think of the schedule on p. 13 as steps to complete, rather than a time frame for each part of the project. The students will be working solely on completing the projects for 5 reading days, instead of doing them gradually for 4 weeks as the project book suggests.

4.   The students have already completed the project requirements listed under week 1 in the schedule on p. 13. They will not need to choose another book to read.

5.   Students <u>do not need</u> to follow the card catalog format to write a description of their Flip-Fact Book unless you choose for them to do so. You may choose whether or not to follow the presentation guidelines listed on p. 13.

Use Grade 5 of _Book Projects to Send Home_   **Level 6/7/8**
Note: Although these projects are listed for grade 5, they are very challenging to complete which makes them appropriate for level 6/7/8.

Project Title: Flip-It Fact Book   Page Numbers: 19-22

Preparation:
1.   Read the project description box and the materials to provide section on p. 19. Students do not need to write the proposal part. The rest of the items on p. 19 are <u>optional</u> ideas to use if you enjoy teaching through themes.

2.   Copy pp. 20-22 and 47 for your students. You may want to remove the "Dear Fifth Grader" greeting on p. 20. Remember that students <u>do not</u> need to write the proposal about what they hope to learn from the reading. Questions are written <u>after</u> the book is read, rather than before. Save p. 47 for the students to complete on day 19 as a reflection on their projects. This is listed in the plans for day 19.

3.   Instruct students to think of the schedule on p. 21 as steps to complete, rather than a time frame for each part of the project. The students will be working solely on completing the projects for 5 reading days, instead of doing them gradually for 4 weeks as the project book suggests.

4.   The students have already completed the project requirements listed under week 1 on the schedule on p. 21. They will not need to choose another book to read or need to write the paragraph.

Focus: <u>Group Project</u>   <u>Museum Exhibits</u>

Project Notes:

1.   In order to choose this option, you must have two or more students (unless you are willing to do part of the project with your student).

2.   This project is based on **one** common book the students have all read or had read aloud to them. The book the project is based upon <u>should fit into the genre studied in this unit.</u>

3.   The group chooses interesting facts from the nonfiction book that they would like to represent as exhibits in a museum.

4.   Facts are listed on large paper or on a marker board as students share them.

5.   Each group member must be responsible for three facts off the list. Each fact becomes an exhibit in the museum.

6.   Each exhibit must have a card explaining one fact and a specimen or object to represent the fact.

7.   Objects or specimens must be three-dimensional. These can be created or found, as long as they go with the fact on the card. For example, a fact about an eye might use a ping pong ball with the parts of the eye drawn on it.

8.   Have students complete the reproducible planning form included in this guide, after they have chosen their three facts.

9.   Although, each group member must be responsible for <u>at least</u> three facts with three exhibits, students may make more exhibits if they have time.

10.   On day 19, students set up their exhibits and tour the museum. Reproduce the reflection form included in this guide for each student to complete.

Museum Exhibits
(Planning Sheet)

Name:_____

These are the three facts I have chosen to make into museum exhibits:

1. _____

   _____

2. _____

   _____

3. _____

   _____

This is how I plan to show the facts listed above:

1. _____

   _____

2. _____

   _____

3. _____

   _____

I need the following materials to make my museum exhibits:_____

_____

_____

_____

Show the teacher this page when you are finished.

Nonfiction - Days 16-18

Independent / Teacher Directed   **All Levels**

Focus: Project Work

Preparation:
1.   For details, read the directions for the project option you chose.

Lesson:
1.   Check students' progress to make sure each student understands what to do
        and is on schedule to finish by day 19.

2.   Meet with students as a group, if this is needed.

Nonfiction - Day 19

Independent / Teacher Directed   **All Levels**

Focus: Project Completion

Preparation:
1.   For details, read the directions for the project option you chose.

2.   Have the reflection forms copied for each student to match the project option
        you chose.

Lesson:
1.   Briefly check students' progress. Students should finish their projects today.

2.   Have students share their projects with each other or with you.

3.   Hand out the reflection form that matches the project option you chose. Have
        the students complete the reflection and show you.

4.   You are ready to choose the next genre your students will study. Look ahead to
        prepare the kickoff for the upcoming genre.

Obedience Objects Reflection

1. What did you learn from carrying your obedience objects with you? _____

_____

_____.

2. Which obedience trait did you improve the most? Explain. _____

_____

_____.

3. Which obedience trait do you need to practice more? Explain. _____

_____

_____.

4. Which part of the project was your favorite? Why was it your favorite?

_____

_____

_____.

_____   _____
Signature of student   Date

Museum Exhibits Reflection

1. On the museum exhibits project, I felt that I did a good job of_____

_____.

2. I think that I could have done a better job of_____

_____.

3. If I could do the museum exhibits project again, I would_____

_____

_____.

4. From the museum project, I learned _____

_____

_____

_____.

5. My favorite part of the museum exhibits project was _____

_____

_____.

_____   _____
Signature of student   Date

Humor

GENRE: HUMOR

Definition:
> Stories, jokes, and poems that have the quality of inciting laughter and are highly entertaining.

Common Characteristics:
1. Contains clever wordplay, paradoxes, or zany wit.
2. Can be realistic or fantastic.
3. Often includes amusing adventures with an escalating pattern of comical events.
4. Focuses on human nature as a character struggles with a problem that ends up differently than planned with hilarious results.
5. Includes silly humor in fantasy stories that have a ridiculous twist.

Story Element Emphasis: Cause and Effect

Definition of Cause:
> A decision, behavior, or incident that happens and produces an effect.

Definition of Effect:
> A consequence that occurs as a result of a cause.

Godly Character Trait Emphasis: Joy

Definition:
> Rejoicing, despite your troubles, because God's daily presence within you is not based on your circumstances.

Subqualities:
1. thankfulness
2. enthusiasm
3. creativity

Teacher Directed   **All Levels Together**

Focus: Genre Kickoff

Preparation:

1.   The goal of the kickoff is to introduce students of all ages to the upcoming genre in a fun and entertaining manner.

2.   Decide how much time you want to spend on the kickoff. You can spend one normal reading class period, several hours, or even a whole day. After the kickoff, you begin with day 1 in the teacher's plans.

3.   Read through the list of ideas below and choose those that interest you for this genre's kickoff. You are welcome to add your own ideas that fit within this genre. Refer to the cover page for a definition and common characteristics for each genre. Introduce the name and definition of the genre to begin the kickoff.

Possible Kickoff Ideas:

1.   Place a variety of joke books that feature appropriate humor around one room. Tell students to silently read the joke book that is nearest to them. Use a flashlight to spotlight students at random. The student in the spotlight reads one joke to the group from whatever joke book he is currently reading. Students move to a new joke book at your signal. Continue spotlighting students as they move from one joke book to the next.

2.   Encourage students to wear their clothes backwards, dress in silly hats, slippers, sunglasses, oversized clothes, or mismatched shoes and socks. Read aloud various jokes that have appropriate humor to the group. Have students select one of their favorite jokes to write on paper to post in their room. After all, laughter is contagious!

3.   Make juice with a touch of humor to serve to the group. Use food coloring to change the color of a juice with a distinctive taste. Perhaps you could turn orange juice into red juice or lemonade into blue lemonade. The students taste buds will get a "funny" surprise when they take their first sip.

4.   Set out some of your family photographs. Do not set out photographs of sacred or special events that should not be seen in a humorous way. Encourage students to think of funny sayings or captions for the photographs. Have students share their ideas with the group. Make sure the humor is appropriate.

5.   Dress like the main character in the next humorous book you plan to read aloud to the group. Use props to tell the beginning of the story from the main character's perspective. Then, give a short book talk that includes details about the humorous book. Begin reading the book aloud.   Unit 8

6. Play a silly game as a group that inspires laughter, such as Charades, Spoons, Hot Potato, or Twister.

7. Read aloud the picture book *Animals Should Definitely Not Wear Clothing* by Judi Barrett or *Uses for Mooses and Other Popular Pets* by Mike Thaler. Have students follow the pattern in the book by choosing one animal to draw either wearing human clothing or using its body to perform a household task, depending on which of the two books you read aloud.

8. Play and sing songs that are funny or silly as a group.

9. Have students write a silly alliteration using another family member's name. An alliteration is repeating the same letter sound at the beginning of each word in a group. Alliterations are often called tongue twisters, like *Peter Piper picked a peck of pickled peppers . . .* Have students share their alliterations with the group. Give the group a chance to repeat the alliteration quickly 3 or more times.

10. Host a silly stunts show for your students. Prepare events for the students to participate in, such as an egg toss, two-legged race, bobbing for apples, water gun fight, sack race, blowing bubbles, or a water balloon toss.

11. Sit in a circle as a group. Share a funny memory you have about something that happened to you. Have students volunteer their own funny memories about something that happened to them.

12. Watch an appropriate funny video. Possibilities might include a video of an old time comedy show, an appropriate standup comic, or a humorous feature film. Screen the video prior to showing it to your students to make sure the content is appropriate and that the humor does not contradict your family values.

Questions to discuss at the end of the kickoff:
1. What are some characteristics of the humor genre? (Refer to the definition on the cover page for this genre.)

2. What is the difference between silly and realistic humor?

3. Why is it necessary that humor be used in an appropriate way?

4. What did you learn about humor from today's activities?

5. Why is humor important as a genre?

Unit 8

Teacher Directed   **All Levels Together**

Focus: Prereading Activity - Secret Passages

Preparation:

1.   Prior to meeting with the students for day 1, follow the directions for *Getting Started* listed in the back of this guide.

2.   Have the first book and one *Assigned Reading Calendar* ready for each student.

3.   You will need a folder or barrier of some sort between you and the students, so you can hide the covers of the books with the passages for today's lesson. If you have only 1 student, you will need to have several books from this genre beside the book he or she will be reading.

Lesson:

1.   Say, *Today we will be doing a prereading activity to help you think about the next book you will be reading.*

2.   Set out the books the students will be reading, but <u>do not tell</u> them who will be reading which book. Allow the students to <u>briefly</u> look at the titles, covers, and illustrations for a few minutes.

3.   Say, *I will be reading several sentences from one of these books to you. Your job will be to guess which book has that passage.*

4.   Hide all the books behind your "barrier" and read a few sentences from one of the books. Then, set out the books in front of the students and have them guess which book had that passage. Have students give reasons for their choices.

5.   After each student has guessed, show students which book contains the passage.

6.   Continue steps 3, 4, and 5 until you have read several parts from each book.

7.   Give students the books you have chosen for them.

8.   Allow them time to carefully read the title, look at the front cover, read the synopsis, and look at the illustrations.

9.   Discuss the following questions with your students:
     a) *What makes your book humorous?*
     b) *What questions do you have about your book?*
     c) *What made you think of those questions?*

10. Have students open their *Student Books* to the *Assigned Reading Calendar* for this genre. Help each student fill in the page numbers to be read for days 1-5.

11. Have students read the assigned pages for day 1 on their own.

Teacher Directed   **Level 2/3**

Focus: Story Discussion and Optional Phonics <u>or</u> Vocabulary Work

Preparation:
1.   You may choose to have students at this level review phonics <u>or</u> complete a vocabulary assignment. Use your own program for the phonics review. Refer to the Appendix for a reproducible vocabulary assignment. The lesson on this day is much shorter to compensate for the additional time you may spend on phonics or on vocabulary work.

Lesson:
1.   Optional phonics or vocabulary work

2.   Listen to your students read the assigned pages out loud to you. Use the Reading Strategies list and the Qualities of Good Reading list provided in the Appendix to help you know what to emphasize.

3.   Discuss the story with your students:
       a) *Retell one funny part from the story.*
       b) *What things do you have in common with the main character?*
       c) *Explain where the story takes place and describe the mood of the story.*

Independent / Teacher Directed   **Level 4/5**

Focus: Story Element Instruction - Cause and Effect

Preparation:
1.   You need a large piece of paper or a marker board to record answers.

Lesson:
1.   Tell the students to read the assigned pages on their own, leaving 3-4 pages to read aloud to you.

2.   Listen to your students read several pages. Use the Qualities of Good Reading list provided in the Appendix to help you know what to emphasize.

3.   Introduce the following terms and definitions:
       a) *A cause is a decision, behavior, or incident that happens and produces an effect.*
       b) *An effect is a consequence that occurs as a result of a cause.*

4. Give the following examples of cause and effect:
    a) *Cause: It is raining. Effect: I put up my umbrella.*
    b) *Cause: I am hungry. Effect: I eat a meal.*

5. Play a game of cause and effect with the students. Name each cause listed below and have the students name a possible effect.
    a) *Cause: My alarm clock rings.* (Possible effect: I get up and turn it off.)
    b) *Cause: The doorbell rings.* (Possible effect: I answer the door.)
    c) *Cause: The car has a flat tire.* (Possible effect: I change the tire.)

6. Name each effect listed below and have the students name a possible cause.
    a) *Effect: The sink is full of dirty dishes.* (Possible cause: We just ate a meal.)
    b) *Effect: I have to mow the lawn.* (Possible cause: The grass has grown.)
    c) *Effect: Everyone sang, "Happy Birthday" to me.* (Possible cause: It is my birthday.)

7. Discuss the questions listed below with the students. List the responses on a large piece of paper or a marker board.
    a) *What problems do the characters have in the story?* (List the problems under a column labeled *effects.*)
    b) *What caused those problems to happen?* (List the answers under a column labeled *causes* and draw an arrow to link it to the effect.)

Independent   **Level 6/7/8**

Focus: Vocabulary Builder - Clue Finder

Lesson:
1. The students complete the activities in the *Student Book* and read the assigned pages for day 2 on their own.

2. The directions instruct students to come and show you the completed Clue Finder vocabulary assignment.

Teacher Directed   **Level 2/3**

Focus: Story Element Instruction - Cause and Effect

Preparation:

1.   You need a large piece of paper or a marker board for drawing causes and effects.

Lesson:

1.   Listen to your students read the assigned pages out loud to you. Use the Reading Strategies list and the Qualities of Good Reading list provided in the Appendix to help you know what to emphasize.

2.   Introduce the following terms and definitions:
       a) *A cause is a decision, behavior, or incident that happens and produces an effect.*
       b) *An effect is a consequence that occurs as a result of a cause.*

3.   Give the following examples of cause and effect. Have students act out the effect.
       a) *Cause: I am thirsty. Effect: I get a drink.*
       b) *Cause: I am tired. Effect: I rest or sleep.*

4.   Play a game of cause and effect with the students. Make two columns on the marker board. Label one *cause* and the other one *effect*. Draw each cause listed below on the marker board and have the students draw a possible effect. Connect each cause to its effect with an arrow.
       a) *Cause: The telephone rings.* (Possible effect: I answer the telephone.)
       b) *Cause: I fall down and scrape my knee.* (Possible effect: I put a band-aid over the scrape.)

5.   Draw each effect listed below on the marker board and have the students draw a possible cause. Connect each effect to its cause with an arrow.
       a) *Effect: The dog's feet were muddy.* (Possible cause: The dog was in the mud outside.)
       b) *Effect: I need a haircut.* (Possible cause: My hair has grown.)

6.   Have students open their *Student Books* to day 3, Cause and Effect Pictures. Help students choose two examples of cause and effect from the story they are reading. Students can write the causes and effects first. They can do the drawing on their own.

7.   The directions instruct the students to come and show you the completed assignment.

Independent   **Level 4/5**

Focus: Story Element Extension - Cause and Effect Reflection

Lesson:
1.   Tell the students to read the assigned pages for day 3 on their own.

2.   Tell them to complete the Cause and Effect Reflection on day 3 in their *Student Book* when they finish reading.

3.   The directions instruct students to come and show you the completed assignment.

Teacher Directed / Independent   **Level 6/7/8**

Focus: Story Element Discussion - Cause and Effect Chart

Lesson:
1.   The students read the assigned pages for day 3 on their own.

2.   The students meet with you to discuss the following questions:
        a) *Is the humor in the story silly or realistic? Describe situations from the book that support your answer.*
        b) *Which characters would be good influences? How can you support your answer?*
        c) *Which characters would be bad influences? How can you support your answer?*

3.   Introduce the following terms and definitions:
        a) *A cause is a decision, behavior, or incident that happens and produces an effect.*
        b) *An effect is a consequence that occurs as a result of a cause.*

4.   Give the following examples of cause and effect.
        a) *Cause: The clouds are dark and heavy. Effect: It begins to rain.*
        b) *Cause: My watch stopped working. Effect: I got a new battery for my watch.*

5.   Have the students give you several examples of causes and effects. Introduce the Cause and Effect Chart in the *Student Book* under day 3. Complete one or more examples with the students as needed.

6.   Have the students work on their own to finish the Cause and Effect Chart. The directions instruct students to come and show you the completed assignment.

Teacher Directed   **Level 2/3**

Focus: Godly Character Traits - Examples

Preparation:
1.   Think of examples you can share from your own life for each of the following
        traits: *joy* and *thankfulness*. (Definitions are listed in the lesson below.)

Lesson:
1.   Introduce the following definition and scripture passage for *joy:*
        a) <u>*Joy*</u> *is rejoicing, despite your troubles, because God's daily presence within*
           you is not based on your circumstances.
        b) <u>*Key Scripture verse*</u>*: Glory in his holy name; let the hearts of those who seek*
           the Lord rejoice. Look to the Lord and his strength; seek his face always.
           1 Chronicles 16:10-11

2.   Share an example of *joy* from your own life.

3.   Help the students think of an example of *joy* from their own lives.

4.   Introduce the following definition and scripture passage for *thankfulness:*
        a) <u>*Thankfulness*</u> *is showing gratitude by expressing appreciation to others.*
        b) <u>*Key Scripture verse*</u>*: Therefore, since we are receiving a kingdom that*
           cannot be shaken, let us be thankful, and so worship God acceptably with
           reverence and awe. Hebrews 12:28

5.   Repeat steps 2 and 3 for the trait *thankfulness.*

6.   Instruct your students to search for examples of *joy* and *thankfulness* as they
        read part or all of the assigned pages out loud to you. Use the Reading
        Strategies list and the Qualities of Good Reading list provided in the Appendix
        to help you know what to emphasize.

7.   Discuss the following questions with your students:
        a) *How do the characters show joy? Or thankfulness?*
        b) *Did the characters show the opposite traits of despair or self-pity? Explain.*
        c) *What could the characters do differently to be more joyful or thankful?*

Independent / Teacher Directed   **Level 4/5**

Focus: Godly Character Traits - Examples

Lesson:
1.   Tell the students to read and complete the Godly Character Sheet on day 4 in the *Student Book* on their own.

2.   The students also silently read the assigned pages for day 4, leaving 3-4 pages to read aloud to you.

3.   The students should come and show you when both are completed.

4.   Review the Godly Character Sheet on day 4 in the *Student Book*, so the students and you will know what traits you are searching for in the humorous book. *(joy, thankfulness,* and *enthusiasm)*

5.   Listen to your students read 3-4 pages aloud. Use the Qualities of Good Reading list provided in the Appendix to help you know what to emphasize.

6.   Discuss the following questions with the students:
       a) *How did the characters show joy?*
       b) *How did the characters show thankfulness?*
       c) *How did the characters show enthusiasm?*
       d) *Did the characters show the opposite traits of despair? Or self-pity? Or apathy? Explain.*
       e) *What might Jesus have done differently if He had been the character in the book?*

Independent   **Level 6/7/8**

Focus: Godly Character Traits - Examples

Lesson:
1.   The students complete the activities in the *Student Book* and read the assigned pages for day 4 on their own.

2.   The directions instruct students to come and show you the completed Godly Character page.

Teacher Directed / Independent   **Level 2/3**

Focus: Comprehension Check - Story Notes

Lesson:

1.   Go over the directions for Story Notes on day 5 in the *Student Book*. Students complete this assignment on their own after reading the assigned pages.

2.   Listen to your students read part or all of the assigned pages out loud to you. Use the Reading Strategies list and the Qualities of Good Reading list provided in the Appendix to help you know what to emphasize.

3.   The students finish the assigned reading and complete Story Notes on their own. The directions instruct the students to come and show you the completed assignment.

Independent   **Level 4/5**

Focus: Comprehension Check - Character Close-up

Lesson:

1.   Tell the students to complete the Character Close-up on day 5 in the *Student Book* on their own.

2.   The students read the assigned pages for day 5 on their own. You may choose to have the students leave 3-4 pages to read aloud to you.

3.   The directions instruct students to come and show you the completed assignment.

Independent   **Level 6/7/8**

Focus: Comprehension Check - Book Highlights

Lesson:

1.   The students complete the activities in the *Student Book* and read the assigned pages for day 5 on their own.

2.   The directions instruct students to come and show you the completed Book Highlights assignment.

Teacher Directed   **All Levels Together**

Focus: Prereading Activity - Concentration

Preparation:
1.   If students are beginning new books today, make sure to have the number of pages to be read each day calculated and have those books ready to hand out. (See the *Getting Started* section, item #7, in the back of this guide for details.)

2.   If students are <u>not</u> beginning new books today, they use the books they are currently reading for today's activities.

3.   Choose one <u>important</u> picture from each of the students' humorous books. The pictures need to show characters, setting, and an important event, if possible. You may need to use the cover, if there are no other pictures in the book.

Lesson:
1.   Say, *Today we will be doing a prereading activity to help you think about the next book you will be reading or the next part of the book you will be reading.*

2.   Show each student the picture you selected from their humorous book.

3.   Tell students they have two minutes to look at the picture and remember as much of what they see as possible.

4.   After two minutes, have students put the picture out of sight.

5.   Have students open their *Student Books* to day 6, Concentration. Give students a time limit of 5 minutes to write down as much information from the picture as they can remember.

6.   After 5 minutes, allow students to see the picture again to check and add to their answers.

7.   Give the following directions for students to follow in their *Student Books*:
     a) *Circle any details that have to do with the characters in the story.*
     b) *Put an "x" by any details that describe the setting in the story.*
     c) *Make a check next to any details that are humorous.*
     d) *Choose the detail that is most important and put a star by it. Share the detail that you marked. Why do you think that detail is most important?*
     e) *What is the problem or conflict in your book?*

8. Give students a little time to look at the cover, read over the synopsis, and quickly page through the book.

9. Help students update the *Assigned Reading Calendar* for days 6-10.

10. Have students read the assigned pages for day 6 on their own.

Teacher Directed   **Level 2/3**

Focus: Story Discussion and Optional Phonics <u>or</u> Vocabulary Work

Preparation:
1.   You may choose to have students at this level review phonics <u>or</u> complete a vocabulary assignment. Use your own program for the phonics review. Refer to the Appendix for a reproducible vocabulary assignment. The lesson on this day is much shorter to compensate for the additional time you may spend on phonics or on vocabulary work.

Lesson:
1.   Optional phonics or vocabulary work

2.   Listen to your students read the assigned pages out loud to you. Use the Reading Strategies list and the Qualities of Good Reading list provided in the Appendix to help you know what to emphasize.

3.   Discuss the following questions with your students:
        a) *What problems do the characters have in the story?*
        b) *How would you solve the problems?*
        c) *What do you think will happen next? Explain.*

Independent / Teacher Directed   **Level 4/5**

Focus: Story Element Instruction - Cause and Effect Chart

Lesson:
1.   Tell the students to read the assigned pages on their own, leaving 3-4 pages to read aloud to you.

2.   Tell students to open their *Student Books* to day 7, Cause and Effect Chart. Have students list six important events from their humorous books on their own. Students <u>do not</u> do the cause and effect part in their *Student Books.* They complete that part of the assignment later with you.

3.   Listen to your students read several pages. Use the Qualities of Good Reading list provided in the Appendix to help you know what to emphasize.

4. Review the following definitions:
    a) *A cause is a decision, behavior, or incident that happens and produces an effect.*
    b) *An effect is a consequence that occurs as a result of a cause.*

5. Have students give you an example of a cause and effect from their books.

6. Explain to the students that often a decision, action, or event happens that causes an effect. Then, that effect becomes a cause for another effect and so on. The causes and effects become one chain of events all linked together. Read the following example to the students:
    a) *Cause: You need to get up early. Effect: You set the alarm.*
    b) *The effect then becomes a cause. Cause: You set the alarm. Effect: Your alarm rings.*
    c) *The effect then becomes a cause. Cause: Your alarm rings. Effect: You get up.*

7. Have students open their *Student Books* to day 7. Work with the students to complete the Cause and Effect Chart, which demonstrates a chain of events.

8. Point out that decisions, behaviors, or incidents never stand alone. Each one is always followed by an effect.

Independent   **Level   6/7/8**

Focus: Vocabulary Builder - Clue Finder

Lesson:
1. The students complete the activities in the *Student Book* and read the assigned pages for day 7 on their own.

2. The directions instruct students to come and show you the completed Clue Finder vocabulary assignment.

Teacher Directed / Independent   **Level 2/3**

Focus: Story Element Instruction - Cause and Effect Chain of Events

Preparation:
1.   You may choose to use a copy of one of the following books by Laura Numeroff to read as an illustration of a chain of events: *If You Give a Mouse a Cookie, If You Give a Moose a Muffin,* or *If you Give a Pig a Pancake.*

2.   You need at least 5 index cards for each student.

Lesson:
1.   Listen to your students read the assigned pages out loud to you. Use the Reading Strategies list and the Qualities of Good Reading list provided in the Appendix to help you know what to emphasize.

2.   Review the definitions of *cause* and *effect* listed below. Then, have students act out their own examples of cause and effect.
       a) *A cause is a decision, behavior, or incident that happens and produces an effect.*
       b) *An effect is a consequence that occurs as a result of a cause.*

3.   Explain to students that often a decision, behavior, or incident happens that causes an effect. Then, that effect becomes a cause for another effect and so on. The causes and effects become one chain of events all linked together.

4.   Read one of the books by Laura Numeroff to your students, *If You Give a Mouse a Cookie, If You Give a Moose a Muffin,* or *If You Give a Pig a Pancake.* Give an example from the book you read of a chain of events. If you do not have a copy of one of the books to read, give the example listed below:
       a) *Cause: You get dirty playing outside. Effect: You take a bath.*
       b) *The effect then becomes a cause. Cause: You take a bath. Effect: You are all wet.*
       c) *The effect then becomes a cause. Cause: You are all wet. Effect: You dry off with a towel.*

5.   Create a chain of events from the students' humorous books they are reading. Decide the first event in the story and write it on an index card numbered *1.* Discuss the following questions with the students:
       a) *What was the effect of the first event?* (Have students write the effect on another index card numbered *2.*)

b) *The effect you wrote on card 2 becomes the cause for the next event. What happened next because of event number 2?* (Write the effect on an index card numbered *3.*)

c) *The effect you wrote on card 3 becomes the cause for the next event. What happened next because of event number 3?* (Have students write the effect on an index card numbered *4.*)

6. Students continue sequencing as many events as you choose. Tape the cards onto yarn or string in sequence to make a chain of events.

7. Point out that decisions, behaviors, or incidents never stand alone. Each one is always followed by an effect.

Independent   Level 4/5

Focus: Story Element Extension - Positive Influence or Effects

Lesson:
1. Tell the students to read the assigned pages for day 8 on their own.

2. Tell them to complete Positive Influence on day 8 in their *Student Books* when they finish reading.

3. The directions instruct students to come and show you the completed assignment.

Teacher Directed / Independent   Level 6/7/8

Focus: Story Element Instruction - Cause and Effect Journal

Lesson:
1. The students read the assigned pages for day 8 on their own.

2. The students meet with you to discuss the following questions:
    a) *Would you like to be friends with the main character? Why or why not?*
    b) *Which part of the story best describes the setting?*
    c) *What possible solutions are there for solving the problem in the story?*

3. Introduce the Cause and Effect Journal on day 8 in the *Student Book*. Make sure the students understand what to do. Then, have the students work on their own. The directions instruct students to come and show you the completed assignment.

Teacher Directed   **Level 2/3**

Focus: Godly Character Traits - Biblical Comparisons

Preparation:
1.   Find a short children's book of the Bible story about Jesus' birth. Otherwise, you will need to read the story directly from the Bible in Luke 2:1-20.

Lesson:
1.   Review the following definitions and scripture passages:
   a) *Joy is rejoicing, despite your troubles, because God's daily presence within you is not based on your circumstances.*
   b) *Key Scripture verse: Glory in his holy name; let the hearts of those who seek the Lord rejoice. Look to the Lord and his strength; seek his face always. 1 Chronicles 16:10-11*
   c) *Thankfulness is showing gratitude by expressing appreciation to others.*
   d) *Key Scripture verse: Therefore, since we are receiving a kingdom that cannot be shaken, let us be thankful, and so worship God acceptably with reverence and awe. Hebrews 12:28*

2.   Read the children's book, or the Bible passage Luke 2:1-20, about Jesus' birth. Instruct your students to listen for examples of *joy* and *thankfulness* in the story being read.

3.   Discuss the following question with your students:
   a) *How did the shepherd's actions show joy and thankfulness?*

4.   Record the students' responses in the *Student Book* on day 9 under the Biblical Character column. (Possible answers include the following: *Joy* as the shepherds hurried to Bethlehem to see the baby Messiah, just as the angel of the Lord told them; *Joy* as the shepherds spread the news about the Messiah's birth; *Thankfulness* as the shepherds returned praising God for all the things they had seen and heard.)

5.   Listen to your students read the assigned pages for day 9 out loud to you. Remind the students to be searching for examples of *joy* and *thankfulness.*

6.   Using the questions listed below, compare the shepherds with the main character in the humorous book. Record the responses on day 9 in the *Student Book* under the Book Character column.
   a) *How does the character in your book show joy and thankfulness?*
   b) *What would the Biblical characters, the shepherds, do differently from the character in your book?*

Independent / Teacher Directed   **Level 4/5**

Focus: Godly Character Traits - Biblical Comparisons

Preparation:
1.   The students need a Bible to read 2 Chronicles chapter 29:1-11 and chapter 30 about King Hezekiah purifying the temple in Jerusalem.

Lesson:
1.   Tell the students to review the Godly Character Traits listed on day 9 in the *Student Book* alone. Then, have the students silently read the story of King Hezekiah from the Bible in 2 Chronicles chapter 29:1-11 and chapter 30.

2.   Students do their best to complete the Biblical Character column on the Godly Character Story Sheet for King Hezekiah on day 9 in the *Student Book.*

3.   Students silently read the assigned pages in the humorous book for day 9, saving 3 or 4 pages to read aloud to you.

4.   The students meet with you to finish the assignment for day 9. Listen to your students read several pages. Use the Qualities of Good Reading list provided in the Appendix to help you know what to emphasize.

5.   Discuss the following questions with the students as you review what they have already done in the *Student Book* for day 9. Complete the remaining columns in the *Student Book* for day 9.
   a) *How did Hezekiah's behavior show joy, thankfulness, and enthusiasm?*
      (Possible answers include the following: *Joy* as Hezekiah praised the Lord and celebrated the Feast of Unleavened Bread along with those who were in Jerusalem, in chapter 30 verses 21 and 26; *Thankfulness* as Hezekiah encouraged the Levites to give fellowship offerings to express gratitude to God; *Thankfulness* as Hezekiah provided bulls, sheep, and goats for the assembly as the festival continued another seven days; *Enthusiasm* when Hezekiah sent a proclamation throughout Israel calling the people to celebrate the Passover and return to the Lord; *Enthusiasm* as Hezekiah had the people remove the pagan idols and alters.)
   b) *How did the person in your book behave like the Biblical character, Hezekiah?* (List the answers in the *Student Book.*)
   c) *How did the person in your book behave differently from Hezekiah?* (List the answers in the *Student Book.*)
   d) *Which trait was shown least often by the book character?* (Explain in the *Student Book.*)

<u>Independent</u>   **<u>Level 6/7/8</u>**

Focus: Godly Character Traits - Biblical Comparisons

Preparation:
1.   The students need a Bible for today's lesson.

Lesson:
1.   The students complete the activities in the *Student Book* and read the assigned pages for day 9 on their own.

2.   The directions instruct the students to come and show you the completed Godly Character Story page. (Examples of the traits Paul talked about in the passage might include the following: *Joy* as he talks about hope in Romans 12:12; *Joy* when he talks about rejoicing with others in Romans 12:15; *Thankfulness* as Paul points out that our gifts come from God and we should use them for His glory; *Enthusiasm* as Paul tells us to never be lacking in zeal and to keep the spiritual fervor in Romans 12:11; *Creativity* as Paul urges us not to be conformed by the pattern of the world, but to be transformed in Romans 12:2.)

Teacher Directed   **All Levels Together**

Focus: Comprehension Check - Lots of Laughter

Lesson:
1.   Say, *When you read a humorous book, the author makes sure to have funny parts in the story that leave you laughing. Today you will be choosing parts of your book to share that you think are very humorous.*

2.   Have the students complete the Lots of Laughter planning form for day 10 in the *Student Book.*

3.   Have each student share the parts they chose with the group. After the person has shared a funny part, all group members may say, *Ha! Ha!* together.

4.   Allow group members to ask questions after the person has shared about the book.

5.   When all students have finished sharing, have students read the assigned pages in their humorous book for day 10.

Teacher Directed   **All Levels Together**

Focus: Prereading Activity - Book Examination

Preparation:

1.   If students are beginning new books today, make sure to have the number of pages to be read each day calculated and have those books ready to hand out. (See the *Getting Started* section, item #7, in the back of this guide for details.)

2.   If students are <u>not</u> beginning new books today, they use the books they are currently reading for today's activities.

Lesson:

1.   Say, *Today we will be doing a prereading activity to help you think about the next book you will be reading or the next part of the book you will be reading.*

2.   Discuss the following questions with your students:
        a) *Find the dedication in your humorous book. What can you learn about the book from reading the dedication?*
        b) *Read the title of the book. What hints does reading the title give you about the book?*
        c) *Look carefully at the illustration on the cover. What information did you discover about the story?*
        d) *Find the synopsis of the book. What characters, settings, and problems are mentioned?*
        e) *Do you see any reviews, recommendations, or awards for the book? What can you learn from reading those?*
        f) *What makes this book humorous?*
        g) *What predictions can you make about the book after reviewing the items we just discussed?*

3.   Help students update the *Assigned Reading Calendar* for days 11-15.

4.   Have students read the assigned pages for day 11 on their own.

Teacher Directed   **Level 2/3**

Focus: Story Discussion and Optional Phonics <u>or</u> Vocabulary Work

Preparation:
1.   You may choose to have students at this level review phonics <u>or</u> complete a vocabulary assignment. Use your own program for the phonics review. Refer to the Appendix for a reproducible vocabulary assignment. The lesson on this day is much shorter to compensate for the additional time you may spend on phonics or on vocabulary work.

Lesson:
1.   Optional phonics or vocabulary work

2.   Listen to your students read the assigned pages out loud to you. Use the Reading Strategies list and the Qualities of Good Reading list provided in the Appendix to help you know what to emphasize.

3.   Discuss the following questions with your students:
        a) *Compare your life to the main character's life. What things are the same?*
        b) *Contrast your life with the main character's life. Which things are different?*
        c) *Do you approve of the main character's behavior? Why, or why not?*

Independent / Teacher Directed   **Level 4/5**

Focus: Story Element Instruction - Multiple Causes and Effects

Lesson:
1.   Tell the students to read the assigned pages alone, leaving 3-4 pages to read aloud to you.

2.   Listen to your students read several pages. Use the Qualities of Good Reading list provided in the Appendix to help you know what to emphasize.

3.   Discuss the following questions with your students:
        a) *Is the setting realistic? Explain.*
        b) *Could any of the problems in the story have been avoided? Explain.*
        c) *What do you like about the main character?*

4.   Review the definitions on the next page and have the students each give you examples of cause and effect.

a) *A cause is a decision, behavior, or incident that happens and produces an effect.*

b) *An effect is a consequence that occurs as a result of a cause.*

5.   Explain to students that sometimes one cause can have several different effects, or one effect can have several different things that cause it to happen. Read the following examples to the students:

a) *Cause: It was a hot day. Effect 1: We didn't go outside. Effect 2: We kept the air conditioning on in the house.*

b) *Cause 1: I needed carrot seeds for my science project. Cause 2: We were out of milk. Effect: We went shopping at the grocery store.*

6.   Work with the students to complete Multiple Causes and Effects on day 12 in the *Student Book*. You may want to write the answers on a marker board as you discuss them, so the students can copy them. Then, the students can concentrate on the discussion rather than on spelling and capitalization.

Independent   **Level 6/7/8**

Focus: Vocabulary Builder - Clue Finder
Lesson:

1.   The students complete the activities in the *Student Book* and read the assigned pages for day 12 on their own.

2.   The directions instruct students to come and show you the completed Clue Finder vocabulary assignment.

Teacher Directed   **Level 2/3**

Focus: Story Element Instruction - Cause and Effect

Preparation:
1.   You need at least 5 index cards for each pair of students. If you have only one student, you will be the student's partner.

Lesson:
1.   Listen to your students read the assigned pages out loud to you. Use the Reading Strategies list and the Qualities of Good Reading list provided in the Appendix to help you know what to emphasize.

2.   Review the following definitions:
       a) *A cause is a decision, behavior, or incident that happens and produces an effect.*
       b) *An effect is a consequence that occurs as a result of a cause.*

3.   Divide an index card in half. Write *cause* on one half and *effect* on the other half. You may choose to do the writing for your students, since that is not the focus of the lesson.

4.   Have each student think of an example of a cause and effect from the humorous story they are reading. Write the cause on the correct half of the index card and the effect on the other half of the index card.

5.   Cut the card in half, between the cause and the effect.

6.   Repeat steps 2-5 to make 4 more cause and effect index cards. You need 5 causes with 5 matching effects for each pair of students.

7.   Instruct students to play *Concentration* in partners using the 5 cause cards with the 5 matching effect cards. Students put all the cards face down in rows and turn two over at a time. If they turn over a matching cause and effect, they may keep the two cards and have another turn. If they turn over two cards that do not match, their turn is over. The cards are placed face down again for the partner to take a turn. The student with the most pairs at the end of the game is the winner.

Independent   **Level 4/5**

Focus: Story Element Extension - A Sense of Humor

Lesson:
1.   Tell the students to read the assigned pages for day 13 on their own.

2.   Tell them to complete A Sense of Humor on day 13 in their *Student Book* when they finish reading.

3.   The directions instruct students to come and show you the completed assignment.

Teacher Directed / Independent   **Level 6/7/8**

Focus: Story Element Discussion - Cause and Effect Events

Lesson:
1.   The students read the assigned pages for day 13 on their own.

2.   The students meet with you to discuss the following questions:
        a) *What would you do differently from the main character?*
        b) *What problem in your own life or your family's life reminds you of the problem in the story?*

3.   Review the following definitions and have each student give you an example of a cause and effect:
        a) *A cause is a decision, behavior, or incident that happens and produces an effect.*
        b) *An effect is a consequence that occurs as a result of a cause.*

4.   Explain to students that sometimes one cause can have several different effects, or one effect can have several different things that cause it to happen.

5.   Discuss the following questions with the students:
        a) *What is an example from your life of one cause that has several effects?*
        (If students have a difficult time with this, give them the following example: Cause: You did not finish your schoolwork. Effect 1: You have a consequence. Effect 2: You must finish your schoolwork.)

b) *What is an example from your life of one effect having several causes?*
(If students have a difficult time with this, give them the following example: Effect: Your project was done on time. Cause 1: You waited until the last minute to do your project and had to work hard to finish. Cause 2: You planned ahead and had plenty of time to finish.)

6.   Introduce Key Events in the *Student Book* under day 13. Have the students work on their own to complete it.

7.   The directions instruct students to come and show you the completed assignment.

Teacher Directed   **Level 2/3**

Focus: Godly Character Traits - Personal Assessment

Preparation:
1.   You will need an index card or note card for each of your students today.

Lesson:
1.   Review the following definitions and scripture passages:
      a) *Joy is rejoicing, despite your troubles, because God's daily presence within you is not based on your circumstances.*
      b) *Key Scripture verse: Glory in his holy name; let the hearts of those who seek the Lord rejoice. Look to the Lord and his strength; seek his face always.*
      1 Chronicles 16:10-11
      c) *Thankfulness is showing gratitude by expressing appreciation to others.*
      d) *Key Scripture verse: Therefore, since we are receiving a kingdom that cannot be shaken, let us be thankful, and so worship God acceptably with reverence and awe. Hebrews 12:28*

2.   Listen to your students read the assigned pages for day 14 out loud to you.

3.   Discuss the following questions with the students:
      a) *Which trait was shown less often by the book character, joy or thankfulness? Explain.*
      b) *Choose the trait that is harder for you to show, joy or thankfulness. Explain.*

4.   Hand out one index card to each student. Have the students write the trait they chose and 3 ways to work on showing the trait more often in their own lives.

5.   On the other side of the card, have the students draw themselves portraying this trait. The students may also write the matching Bible verse if you choose for them to do so.

6.   Have the students post their cards in a place where they will see them often.

Independent / Teacher Directed   **Level 4/5**

Focus: Godly Character Traits - Personal Assessment

Preparation:

1.	You will need an index card or note card for each of your students today.

Lesson:

1.	Tell the students to review the Godly Character Traits listed on day 9 in the *Student Book* on their own.

2.	Have the students silently read the assigned pages in the humorous book for day 14, saving 3-4 pages to read aloud to you.

3.	Meet with the students to finish the assignment for day 14.

4.	Listen to your students read 3-4 pages. Use the Qualities of Good Reading list provided in the Appendix to help you know what to emphasize.

5.	Discuss the following questions with the students:
	a) *Refer to day 9 in the Student Book. Choose the trait that is the hardest for you to show - joy, thankfulness, or enthusiasm. Explain.*
	b) *Look at the Bible verse on day 9 in the Student Book for the trait you chose. How does the behavior of your book characters compare to this verse? Explain.*
	c) *What ways can you demonstrate the verse you chose in your own life?*

6.	Hand out one index card to each student. Have students list actions they will take to help them live according to the verse they chose.

7.	On the other side of the card, have the students divide the card into 3-4 sections, by drawing vertical lines. Instruct the students to break the chosen verse into sections and draw a quick picture or symbol to stand for each section of the verse. When the students look at the pictures, it should remind them of each part of the verse.

8.	The Bible verse may be written on the bottom or on the back of the card if you choose to have the students do so.

9.	Have the students post their cards in a place where they will see them often.

Independent   **Level 6/7/8**

Focus: Godly Character Traits - Personal Assessment

Preparation:

1.   The students each need an index card or note card for today.

Lesson:

1.   The students complete the activities in the *Student Book* and read the assigned pages for day 14 on their own.

2.   The directions instruct the students to come and show you the completed assignment for day 14, including the completed index card or note card for posting.

Teacher Directed   **All Levels Together**

Preparation:
1.   Choose which **one** of the following project options you would like your students to complete as a culminating project for this genre. Each option is explained in detail on the pages that follow. For ease in planning, you should choose the same option for each of the students.

    a) **Option 1:** You may choose a character based project, which focuses on the Godly character trait for this genre. The directions for these projects are more general. The project does not involve any of the books from the unit. It does include a final reflection form.

    b) **Option 2:** You may choose a book based project, which is an individual project that is tailored to the student's individual level. Students will choose one of the books they read for this genre to use for the project. In order to choose this option, you must purchase *Book Projects to Send Home* by Lori Sanders and Linda Kimble for your particular students' levels. There is one book for each of the three levels. The project directions are very detailed and include a final reflection for each project.

    c) **Option 3:** Your final option is to choose a group project, which requires two or more students working together. This project is based on a common book the students have all read or had read aloud to them. The **one** book the project is based upon should fit into the genre studied in this unit.

2.   Have the directions for the project copied for each student. Make sure to read over the directions for the project option you chose in order to know what supplies you will need to have available for the projects.

3.   The plans allow 5 work days for the projects to be completed. This time allotment includes the planning and any presenting of the projects. The plans assume that the students will use only their normal amount of reading time to complete the projects.

Lesson:
1.   Say, *Today we will be starting our culminating project for humor. You will have 5 days, counting today, to work on your project. Your projects are due at the end of that time on _____. (give due date)*

2.   Introduce the project you have chosen for this unit. Go through the directions and make sure students have a copy of the directions, so they can work as independently as possible. Show them where the needed supplies are located.

3.   Then, have students read the assigned pages for day 15 to finish the humorous books. Students may begin the project after the reading is complete.

Focus: <u>**Godly Character Trait Project**</u>   <u>**Verses to Stand Upon**</u>

Project Notes:

1.   Teach students why we can have an attitude of joy even in times of trouble.

2.   Have students meet as a group. Review the definition and key verse for joy.
       a) *<u>Joy</u> is rejoicing, despite your troubles, because God's daily presence within*
            you is not based on your circumstances.
       b) *<u>Key Scripture verse</u>: Glory in his holy name; let the hearts of those who seek*
            the Lord rejoice. Look to the Lord and his strength; seek his face always.
            1 Chronicles 16:10-11

3.   Discuss the following questions with the students:
       a) *Who do you know that always seems to be cheerful or full of joy?*
       b) *Do you think that the people you listed never have any troubles or*
            hardships?
       c) *Then, how can these people always be cheerful?*
       d) *What do the definition and key scripture verse for joy teach us about being*
            joyful in times of trouble?

4.   Reproduce the Verses to Stand Upon Letter included in this guide. To
       demonstrate the trait *thankfulness,* have each student send a copy of the letter
       to one cheerful person. The letter thanks the person for being a joyful example.
       It also asks the person to write one favorite Bible verse and return the letter to
       the student.

6.   In order to remember to be joyful, even in times of trouble, students will make a
       personal collection of favorite Bible verses. The verses <u>do not</u> need to be
       specific to the topic of *joy.* The verse from the letter will be added to this
       collection. Students will work on their collections on days 16-18.

7.   Some possible ways for students to create their collection include:
       a) asking others for their favorite verses
       b) using a children's Bible or book of verses for ideas
       c) referring to a Biblical index or other reference book to search for verses
       d) reviewing verses that have been memorized
       e) rereading a devotional or Bible study book for suggestions

8.   Reproduce the Verses to Stand Upon planning form included in this guide.
       Have students complete the form as they plan their collections. Make sure that
       students set reasonable expectations for their collections.

9.   On day 19, students will view each other's collections. Reproduce the reflection
       form included in this guide for each student to complete.

Verses to Stand Upon Letter

Dear _____,

I have been studying the character trait joy in school. I have noticed that you always seem to be cheerful or full of joy.

I wanted to send you this letter to thank you for being a joyful example. I know that your life must have trouble and hardship too. Yet, you seem to be joyful whenever I see you.

One scripture verse I have been studying that refers to joy is as follows:

> *Glory in his holy name; let the hearts of those who seek*
> *the Lord rejoice. Look to the Lord and his strength;*
> *seek his face always. 1 Chronicles 16:10-11*

I am working on being joyful like you, even in times of trouble. As a project for the study of joy, I am making a collection of favorite Bible verses to remind me that the heavenly Father is always with me.

I would appreciate knowing your favorite Bible verse so that I can include it in my collection. Please write your favorite Bible verse in the space at the bottom of this letter. Return the verse to me at the following address:

_____

_____

_____

Thanks for your help! I look forward to seeing your smiling face again soon.

Sincerely,

_____

Please write your favorite Bible verse on the lines below.

_____

_____

_____

_____

Verses to Stand Upon Planning Form

Name:_____

Note: You have 4 work periods to complete your collection of favorite Bible verses.

How many verses will you have in your collection by day 19 (list a number)? _____

What sources do you plan to use to find verses for your collection?_____

_____

_____

Where will you put your collection of verses (circle one)?   booklet
                                                                    file box
                                                                    lidded can
                                                                    binder
                                                                    other

What will you need to write your verses on so that they fit in your "container"?

_____

How do you plan to make your collection special? _____

_____

_____

What help will you need from others to complete your collection?_____

_____

_____

Show the teacher this page when you are finished.

Focus: Book Based Project   **Individual Projects by Level**

Project Notes:
1.   In order to choose this option, you must purchase *Book Projects to Send Home* by Lori Sanders and Linda Kimble (McGraw-Hill, 2004) for your particular students' levels. There is one project book for each of the 3 levels. The books include detailed reproducible directions, work schedules, and reflection forms.

2.   The students each need to choose **one** book from those that **were read in this genre**. That book is the basis for the project.

3.   The project titles, corresponding page numbers, and levels in the *Book Projects to Send Home* books are listed below.

Use Grade 2 of *Book Projects to Send Home*   **Level 2/3**

Project Title: Character Tube Puppet   Page Numbers: 7-10

Preparation:
1.   Read the project description box, the materials to provide section, and the tips to introduce on p. 7. The rest of the items on p. 7 are <u>optional</u> ideas to use if you enjoy teaching through themes.

2.   Copy pp. 8-10 for your students. Save p. 10 for the students to complete on day 19 as a reflection on their project. This is listed in the plans for day 19.

Use Grade 4 of *Book Projects to Send Home*   **Level 4/5**

Project Title: Character Puppet   Page Numbers: 7-10

Preparation:
1.   Read the project description box and the materials to provide section on p. 7. The rest of the items on p. 7 are <u>optional</u> ideas to use if you enjoy teaching through themes.

2.   Copy pp. 8-10 and 47 for your students. Save p. 47 for the students to complete on day 19 as a reflection on their project. This is listed in the plans for day 19.

3.   Instruct students to think of the schedule on p. 9 as steps to complete, rather than a time frame for each part of the project. The students will be working solely on completing the projects for 5 reading days, instead of doing them gradually for 4 weeks as the project book suggests.

4.   The students have already completed the project requirements listed under week 1 in the schedule on p. 9. They will not need to choose another book to read.

5.   The presentation guidelines listed on p. 9 will be modified for use at home.

Use Grade 5 of _Book Projects to Send Home_   **Level 6/7/8**

Note: Although these projects are listed for grade 5, they are very challenging to complete which makes them appropriate for level 6/7/8.

Project Title: Mystery Marionette   Page Numbers: 35-38

Preparation:
1.   Read the project description box and the materials to provide section on p. 35. The rest of the items on p. 35 are optional ideas to use if you enjoy teaching through themes.

2.   Copy pp. 36-38 and 47 for your students. You may want to remove the "Dear Fifth Grader" greeting on p. 36. Save p. 47 for the students to complete on day 19 as a reflection on their projects. This is listed in the plans for day 19.

3.   Instruct students to think of the schedule on p. 37 as steps to complete, rather than a time frame for each part of the project. The students will be working solely on completing the projects for 5 reading days, instead of doing them gradually for 4 weeks as the project book suggests.

4.   The students have already completed the project requirements listed under week 1 on the schedule on p. 37. They will not need to choose another book to read.

Focus: Group Project   **Puppet Performance**

Project Notes:

1.   In order to choose this option, you must have two or more students (unless you are willing to do part of the project with your student).

2.   This project is based on **one** common book the students have all read or had read aloud to them. The book the project is based upon should fit into the genre studied in this unit.

3.   Students plan and perform a puppet show, using one scene from the book.

4.   The students have the following options for puppets:
        a) make traditional puppets
        b) use gloves and tape a picture of the character to the middle 3 fingers, leaving the thumb and pinky free to move as the character's arms
        c) choose stuffed animals, other plush toys, or dolls and add costumes or props to each toy so that they represent the characters.

5.   The puppet theater may be as simple as a table or trunk to sit behind, or as complex as a large box with a window cut out. Scenery can consist of a drawn background or only simple props placed on the stage.

6.   Reproduce the form included in this guide for students to complete as they plan the show. The group chooses **one humorous scene** to perform as a puppet show. Encourage students to choose a shorter scene, so they have time to create puppets and scenery and practice their parts.

7.   Each group member needs to have a role in the puppet show. The role can be an acting role, a narrating role, or a directing role. Group members meet to determine who is responsible for each role.

8.   Actors and narrators may choose to read their parts directly from the book or from copies of the book pages, or memorize their parts.

9.   All group members must participate in creating puppets and scenery or props. You need to supervise this part of the preparation, so students finish by day 19.

10.   Group members share their puppet show on day 19. You may want to video tape the performance, so students can see their puppet show.

11.   On day 19, students present the puppet show. Reproduce the reflection form included in this guide for each student to complete.

Puppet Performance Planning Sheet

Name: _____

Book Title: _____

1. Choose one short, humorous scene from your book to use for the puppet show.

2. List the page numbers for the scene: pp. _____

3. Write the names of the characters in the scene and who will be responsible for the puppet for each role. List the person who will be the director.

   _____

   _____

   _____

4. Who will be the narrator? What will the narrator say to introduce the performance? What will the narrator say throughout the performance?

   _____

   _____

   _____

   _____

5. How will you make the puppets?_____

   _____

   _____

6. What props will you use, and what scenery will you make?

   _____

   _____

7. What will you use as a puppet theater? _____

Unit 8

Independent / Teacher Directed   **All Levels**

Focus: Project Work

Preparation:
1.   For details, read the directions for the project option you chose.

Lesson:
1.   Check students' progress to make sure each student understands what to do and is on schedule to finish by day 19.

2.   Meet with students as a group, if this is needed.

Independent / Teacher Directed   **All Levels**

Focus: Project Completion

Preparation:
1.   For details, read the directions for the project option you chose.

2.   Have the reflection forms copied for each student to match the project option you chose.

Lesson:
1.   Briefly check the students' progress. Students should finish their projects today.

2.   Have students share their projects with each other or with you.

3.   Hand out the reflection form that matches the project option you chose. Have the students complete the reflection and show you.

4.   You are ready to choose the next genre your students will study. Look ahead to prepare the kickoff for the upcoming genre.

Verses to Stand Upon Reflection

1. From making a collection of favorite Bible verses, I learned_____

_____

_____.

2. The verse in the collection that is my personal favorite is_____

_____

_____.

3. By sending a letter to one person that is *joyful*, I learned _____

_____

_____.

4. My favorite part of this project was_____

_____.

_____   _____
Signature of student   Date

Puppet Performance Reflection

1. During the puppet performance, I felt that I did a good job of_____

_____.

2. I think that I could have done a better job of_____

_____.

3. If I could do the puppet performance again, I would_____

_____

_____.

4. From the puppet performance, I learned _____

_____

_____.

5. My favorite part of this project was _____

_____

_____.

_____   _____
Signature of student   Date

Realistic Fiction

GENRE: REALISTIC FICTION

Definition:
>   An invented story that seems real and is set in modern times.

Common Characteristics:
1. Has characters who are fictional, but act in a realistic manner.
2. Includes colorful descriptions of characters, settings, and experiences.
3. Utilizes dialogue to convey information about the characters and the plot.
4. Involves the main characters in the conflict.
5. Has a rational plot, concluding with a realistic answer to the problem.

Story Element Emphasis: Perspective and Point of View

Definition of Perspective:
>   How you perceive or view a subject or thing; your point of view.

Literary Definition of Point of View:
>   The author's "voice" or method chosen to tell the events of a story.

Godly Character Trait Emphasis: Integrity

Definition:
>   Being honest and doing what is right, even when no one else is watching, so that you may be blameless in the eyes of the Lord.

Subqualities:
1. dependability
2. self-acceptance
3. leadership

Teacher Directed   **All Levels Together**

Focus: Genre Kickoff

Preparation:

1. The goal of the kickoff is to introduce students of all ages to the upcoming genre in a fun and entertaining manner.

2. Decide how much time you want to spend on the kickoff. You can spend one normal reading class period, several hours, or even a whole day. After the kickoff, you begin with day 1 in the teacher's plans.

3. Read through the list of ideas below and choose those that interest you for this genre's kickoff. You are welcome to add your own ideas that fit within this genre. Refer to the cover page for a definition and common characteristics for each genre. Introduce the name and definition of the genre to begin the kickoff.

Possible Kickoff Ideas:

1. Have students draw a realistic scene on a large window or glass door by using dry erase markers. It is important to check that the markers can be erased easily and are low odor.

2. Post a paper or marker board with the following three categories listed on it: *Nonfiction, Realistic Fiction, Fantasy.* Select sentences to read to the group that fall into any of the three categories. Read the sentences one at a time and have the group decide which category fits the sentence. Discuss that the primary question to consider is, *How real is it?*

3. Provide a variety of short folk tales that the students recognize. Have students choose one of the folk tales you provided to rewrite as a realistic story. Students may choose to work alone or in partners. If the group is small, you may want to rewrite the tale as a group.

4. Realistic fiction books are noted for their colorful description of characters, settings, and experiences. Choose one section with vivid description from a realistic fiction book to read aloud to your students. Have students draw what you are describing. Seat students so they are unable to see each other's papers. Read the description many times, so students can incorporate as many of the details from the book as possible. At the end of the drawing time, students may share their drawings and compare them for similarities.

5.   Prior to meeting with the students, select and write down one <u>very important</u> word, phrase, and sentence from <u>each</u> realistic book you have chosen for the students to read. Set out one copy of each realistic fiction book you used. The students' job is to guess which realistic book best fits the word, phrase, and sentence you read to them. Pause after sharing the first word, for students to make their predictions. Then, share the phrase from the same book as the word, and pause again for students to revise their predictions. Finally, share the sentence from the same book as the word and the phrase. Allow students to make their final predictions. Tell students the correct answer. Repeat the process for the second book, and so on.

6.   Think of a variety of realistic situations for students to role play. Decide whether or not to use props.

7.   Realistic fiction books are noted for their colorful descriptions. Take a walk to a place you have chosen ahead of time. Prepare for students to sit in one place and write or draw a vivid description of the place. Have students position themselves, so they are unable to see anyone else's paper. Share the descriptions after a set amount of time.

8.   Read aloud a short, realistic fiction book. Instruct students to listen to the details about the main characters and the settings carefully. Students will need to think of real people that remind them of each of the characters. They also need to think of real places that remind them of each setting. Last, have students share what things they have in common with the main character, or how they are similar.

9.   Give each pair of students a paper with the name of one character, a description of a realistic setting, a realistic problem, and one mood. The partners need to quickly plan how to work the four elements on their paper into a dialogue, or conversation. The partners then share their dialogue with the rest of the group. The group needs to assess whether the dialogue sounded realistic, and whether or not it made sense.

10.   List a variety of realistic problems. Share the problems one at a time with the group. Have each student write down a realistic solution to the problem. Share the solutions prior to going on to the next problem. Any students who provide a realistic solution to the problem receive one point. At the end of the problem-solving session, award the student with the most points a realistic reward, such as the title of *Family Problem-Solver*.

Questions to discuss at the end of the kickoff:

1. What are some characteristics of the realistic fiction genre? (Refer to the definition on the cover page for this genre.)

2. How can you tell the difference between realistic fiction and historical fiction?

3. What is the difference between nonfiction and realistic fiction?

4. What did you learn about realistic fiction from today's activities?

5. Why do we read realistic fiction?

Realistic Fiction - Day 1

Teacher Directed   **All Levels Together**

Focus: Prereading Activity - Helpful Hints

Preparation:
1.   Prior to meeting with the students for day 1, follow the directions for *Getting Started* listed in the back of this guide.

2.   Have the first book and one *Assigned Reading Calendar* ready for each student.

Lesson:
1.   Say, *Today we will be doing a prereading activity to help you think about the next book you will be reading.*

2.   Give students the first book they will be reading for this genre.

3.   Have students open their *Student Books* to day 1, Helpful Hints. They will be following along in their *Student Books* and writing answers to the questions below as you discuss them.
      a) *Who is the author? Have you read anything else by this author? If so, what?*
      b) *What clues to the story are given in the title?*
      c) *What interesting details do you notice on the cover?*

4.   Say, *Quickly page through the book. Choose three pages to read to yourself. The pages should be from different places in the book. List the important information you discovered after reading each page.*

5.   Have students share some of the important information they discovered.

6.   Say, *Read the synopsis of the book.*

7.   Discuss the following questions with the students:
      a) *What did you learn from reading the synopsis of the book?*
      b) *What questions do you have about the story?*
      c) *What makes your book realistic?*

8.   Have students open their *Student Books* to the *Assigned Reading Calendar* for this genre. Help each student fill in the page numbers to be read for days 1-5.

9.   Have students read the assigned pages for day 1 on their own.

Unit 9

Teacher Directed   **Level 2/3**

Focus: Story Discussion and Optional Phonics <u>or</u> Vocabulary Work

Preparation:
1.   You may choose to have students at this level review phonics <u>or</u> complete a vocabulary assignment. Use your own program for the phonics review. Refer to the Appendix for a reproducible vocabulary assignment. The lesson on this day is much shorter to compensate for the additional time you may spend on phonics or on vocabulary work.

Lesson:
1.   Optional phonics or vocabulary work

2.   Listen to your students read the assigned pages out loud to you. Use the Reading Strategies list and the Qualities of Good Reading list provided in the Appendix to help you know what to emphasize.

3.   Discuss the following questions with your students:
        a) *What do you have in common with the characters?*
        b) *What is the problem that needs to be solved in the story?*
        c) *Is the setting realistic? Why, or why not?*

Independent / Teacher Directed   **Level 4/5**

Focus: Story Element Instruction - Author's Perspective

Preparation:
1.   You need a large piece of paper or a marker board.

Lesson:
1.   Tell the students to read the assigned pages on their own, leaving 3-4 pages to read aloud to you.

2.   Assign students the Author's Perspective in the *Student Book* for day 3. Students need to complete the page in the *Student Book* prior to meeting with you.

3.   Meet with the students to listen to them read several pages. Use the Qualities of Good Reading list provided in the Appendix to help you know what to emphasize.

4. Introduce the following definition and examples for *perspective:*
   a) *Perspective is how you perceive or view a subject or thing; your point of view.*
   b) *Example: What is your perspective on what time you should go to bed?* (Have students' share their views.)
   c) *My perspective on what time you should go to bed is . . .* (Share your view.)

5. Have students think of their own example of perspective to share.

6. Say, *Today we will be discussing the perspective of the author who wrote the story you are reading.*

7. Read the book synopsis. Use the <u>completed Author's Perspective page</u> in the *Student Book,* along with the book synopsis as you discuss the following questions with the students:
   a) *What do you know about the personality or interests of the author?*
   b) *What links do you find between the things you noted about the author and the story?* (Examples: The list of book titles tells us the author likes to write realistic stories, such as the one we are reading. The dedication shows us the author has a son, which could be the reason the main character is a boy. The "About the Author" section says the author lives in a small town, and the setting in the book is similar.)
   c) *How could an author's perspective affect a story?*

<u>Independent</u>   **<u>Level 6/7/8</u>**

Focus: Vocabulary Builder - Similar Sentences

Preparation:
1. Have a dictionary and a thesaurus available.

Lesson:
1. The students complete the activities in the *Student Book* and read the assigned pages for day 2 on their own.

2. The directions instruct students to come and show you the completed Similar Sentences vocabulary assignment.

Teacher Directed   **Level 2/3**

Focus: Story Element Instruction - Perspective

Preparation:
1.   You need a large piece of paper or a marker board and markers.

Lesson:
1.   Listen to your students read part or all of the assigned pages out loud to you. Use the Reading Strategies list and the Qualities of Good Reading list provided in the Appendix to help you know what to emphasize.

2.   Introduce the following definition and examples for *perspective:*
       a) *Perspective is how you perceive or view something; your point of view.*
       b) *Example 1: What is your perspective on how often you can have candy?* (Have students' share their views.)
       c) *My perspective on how often you can have candy is . . .* (Share your view.)
       d) *Example 2: What is your perspective on which sport is the most fun?* (Have students' share their views.)
       e) *My perspective on which sport is the most fun is . . .* (Share your view.)

3.   Say, *Today we will find out how a person's perspective affects what they write.*

4.   Discuss the following questions with the students as you write their responses on a large piece of paper or a marker board:
       a) *List the names and ages of your family members.*
       b) *Describe the town where you live.*
       c) *Name some of your favorite things.*
       d) *Tell about some things you dislike.*

5.   Say, *If you wrote a realistic fiction book, what things that we listed would you include in your book?* (Explain to students that their perspective affects what they write. The way you view things becomes part of the story.)

6.   Discuss the following questions with the students:
       a) *How would the book you are reading change if it was written from your perspective, instead of the author's perspective?*
       b) *What could we do to find out more about the author's perspective?* (You could read any information supplied in the book about the author. For example, you could read the dedication, introduction, foreword, other titles written by the author, or the *About the Author* section.)
       c) *Use clues from the story you are reading to guess what sorts of things the author likes or dislikes.*

Realistic Fiction - Day 3

Independent   **Level 4/5**

Focus: Story Element Extension - If I Wrote a Realistic Fiction Book

Lesson:
1.   Tell the students to read the assigned pages for day 3 on their own.

2.   Tell them to complete If I Wrote a Realistic Fiction Book on day 3 in their *Student Book* when they finish reading.

3.   The directions instruct students to come and show you the completed assignment.

Teacher Directed / Independent   **Level 6/7/8**

Focus: Story Element Discussion - Author's Perspective

Preparation:
1.   You need two short editorials or letters to the editor from a newspaper or a magazine.

Lesson:
1.   The students silently read the assigned pages for day 3 on their own.

2.   Have the students read the two short editorials or letters to the editor, prior to meeting with you.

3.   Introduce the following definition for *perspective:*
        a) *Perspective is how you perceive or view something; your point of view.*

4.   Have students give you examples of perspective.

5.   Say, *Today we will be discussing how perspective affects what a person writes.*
        The students meet with you to discuss the following questions:
        a) *Why did each person write the editorial or the letter to the editor?*
        b) *What sorts of things does each writer like or dislike?*
        c) *What is each writer's perspective?*
        d) *How do the writer's perspectives differ?*

6.   Introduce the Author's Perspective in the *Student Book* under day 3.

7.   Have the students work to complete day 3 on their own. The directions instruct students to come and show you the completed assignment.

Unit 9

Teacher Directed   **Level 2/3**

Focus: Godly Character Traits - Examples

Preparation:
1.   Think of examples you can share from your own life for each of the following traits: *integrity* and *dependability.* (Definitions are listed in the lesson below.)

Lesson:
1.   Introduce the following definition and scripture passage for *integrity:*
      a) <u>*Integrity*</u> *is being honest and doing what is right, even when no one else is watching, so that you may be blameless in the eyes of the Lord.*
      b) <u>*Key Scripture verse:*</u> *For the grace of God that brings salvation has appeared to all men. It teaches us to say "No" to ungodliness and worldly passions, and to live self-controlled, upright and godly lives in this present age. Titus 2:11,12*

2.   Share an example of *integrity* from your own life.

3.   Help the students think of an example of *integrity* from their own lives.

4.   Introduce the following definition and scripture passage for *dependability:*
      a) <u>*Dependability*</u> *is being reliable and keeping your word, so that others can trust you to do what you say.*
      b) <u>*Key Scripture verse:*</u> *When a man makes a vow to the Lord or takes an oath to obligate himself by a pledge, he must not break his word but must do everything he said. Numbers 30:2*

5.   Repeat steps 2 and 3 for the trait *dependability.*

6.   Instruct your students to search for examples of *integrity* and *dependability as* they read part or all of the assigned pages out loud to you. Use the Reading Strategies list and the Qualities of Good Reading list provided in the Appendix to help you know what to emphasize.

7.   Discuss the following questions with your students:
      a) *How do the main characters show integrity? Or dependability?*
      b) *Did the characters show the opposite traits of dishonesty or unreliability? Explain.*
      c) *What could the characters do differently to show more integrity or dependability?*

Independent / Teacher Directed   **Level 4/5**

Focus: Godly Character Traits - Examples

Lesson:

1.   Tell the students to read and complete the Godly Character Sheet on day 4 in the *Student Book* on their own.

2.   The students also silently read the assigned pages for day 4, leaving 3-4 pages to read aloud to you.

3.   The directions instruct the students to come and show you the completed assignment.

4.   Review the Godly Character Sheet on day 4 in the *Student Book*, so the students and you will know what traits you are searching for in the book. *(integrity, dependability,* and *self-acceptance)*

5.   Listen to your students read 3-4 pages aloud. Use the Qualities of Good Reading list provided in the Appendix to help you know what to emphasize.

6.   Discuss the following questions with the students:
      a) *How did the main characters show integrity?*
      b) *How did the main characters show dependability?*
      c) *How did the main characters show self-acceptance?*
      d) *Did the main characters show the opposite traits of dishonesty? Or unreliability? Or self-pity? Explain.*
      e) *What might Jesus have done differently if He had been the character in the book?*

Independent   **Level 6/7/8**

Focus: Godly Character Traits - Examples

Lesson:
1.   The students complete the activities in the *Student Book* and read the assigned pages for day 4 on their own.

2.   The directions instruct students to come and show you the completed Godly Character page.

Teacher Directed / Independent

All Levels Together

Focus: Comprehension Check - The Main Event

Preparation:
1.   You need 3 to 5 index cards for each student.

Lesson:
1.   Say, *Today you will choose three or more important events from your book.*
       (Level 2/3 chooses 3 events, Level 4/5 chooses 4 events, Level 6/7/8 chooses 5
       events.)
       a) *You need one index card for each event you choose.*
       b) *Write a detailed explanation of <u>one</u> event on each index card.*
       c) *Choose the one card you feel explains the most important event. Illustrate
          that event on the blank side of the card to show its importance.*
       d) *You may color your illustration if you have time.*
       e) *You have about 30 minutes to complete your cards.*
       f) *After 30 minutes, we will meet together to do an activity using your cards.*

2.   Have the students complete the index cards and meet as a group after 30
       minutes have passed.

3.   Instruct students to trade cards with another group member.

4.   Students read the cards they received and try to sequence the cards in the
       order they think the events occur in the story.

5.   When students have finished sequencing, have them check with the author of
       the cards to see if the sequence is correct.

6.   Discuss the following questions with the students:
       a) *What clues helped you decide how to sequence the cards you received?*
       b) *What information was missing on the cards you received that you wanted to
          know?*
       c) *Was the most important event in the beginning of the sequence? Why not?*
       d) *How can you tell the cards you received are from a realistic story?*

7.   Have students read the assigned pages in their realistic fiction book for day 5
       on their own.

Teacher Directed / Independent   **All Levels Together**

Focus: Prereading Activity - Character Description

Preparation:

1.   If students are beginning new books today, make sure to have the number of pages to be read each day calculated and have those books ready to hand out. (See the *Getting Started* section, item #7, in the back of this guide for details.)

2.   If students are not beginning new books today, they use the books they are currently reading for today's activities.

Lesson:

1.   Say, *Today we will be doing a prereading activity to help you think about the next book you will be reading or the next part of the book you will be reading.*

2.   Have students open their *Student Books* to day 6, Character Description.

3.   Go over the directions for the assignment with the students. Instruct students to quickly page through their realistic fiction books, read the synopsis, and look at any illustrations. Student should use this information to help them make their predictions for the main character.

4.   Emphasize that students do not write anything on the *Changes* lines for today's assignment.

5.   Help students update their *Assigned Reading Calendar* for days 6-10.

6.   The directions instruct the students to come and show you the completed assignment.

7.   Have students read the assigned pages for day 6 on their own.

<u>Teacher Directed</u>   **<u>Level 2/3</u>**

Focus: Story Discussion and Optional Phonics <u>or</u> Vocabulary Work

Preparation:
1.   You may choose to have students at this level review phonics <u>or</u> complete a
     vocabulary assignment. Use your own program for the phonics review. Refer to
     the Appendix for a reproducible vocabulary assignment. The lesson on this day
     is much shorter to compensate for the additional time you may spend on
     phonics or on vocabulary work.

Lesson:
1.   Optional phonics or vocabulary work

2.   Listen to your students read the assigned pages out loud to you. Use the
     Reading Strategies list and the Qualities of Good Reading list provided in the
     Appendix to help you know what to emphasize.

3.   Discuss the following questions with your students:
     a) *What do you like about the characters?*
     b) *What would you do to solve the problem in the story?*
     c) *What place reminds you of the setting in the story? Why does this place
        remind you of the setting?*

<u>Independent / Teacher Directed</u>   **<u>Level 4/5</u>**

Focus: Story Element Instruction - Perspective

Preparation:
1.   Select 2 or more stories the students <u>have already read</u> to use as examples of
     perspective. You must be able to clearly determine whose side of the story is
     being told for each example.

Lesson:
1.   Tell the students to read the assigned pages on their own, leaving 3-4 pages to
     read aloud to you.

2.   Listen to your students read several pages. Use the Qualities of Good Reading
     list provided in the Appendix to help you know what to emphasize.

3.   Review the following definition for *perspective*:
     a) *Perspective is how you perceive or view a subject or thing; your point of view.*

4. Say, *Today we will be discussing the meaning of perspective as 'whose side of the story is being told'.*

5. Give students the following example of perspective:
   a) *If you bumped into your little brother and knocked him down, your side of the story might be that it was an accident.*
   b) *However, your little brother's side of the story might be that you did it on purpose.*

6. Show students the books you chose to use as examples. Decide whose side of the story is being told in each book. (For example: In *Cinderella*, the story shows Cinderella's perspective. If it was written from the stepsisters' perspective, Cinderella would be shown as ungrateful and undeserving of happiness.)

7. Discuss the following questions with the students:
   a) *Whose perspective or whose side of the story is being told in the realistic fiction book you are reading? Explain.*
   b) *How would the story change if it was told from a different character's perspective?*

8. Choose one important event from the story to role play.

9. Role play the event as it is written. Then, role play the same event from a different character's perspective.

Independent   **Level 6/7/8**

Focus: Vocabulary Builder - Similar Sentences

Preparation:
1. Have a dictionary and a thesaurus available.

Lesson:
1. The students complete the activities in the *Student Book* and read the assigned pages for day 7 on their own.

2. The directions instruct students to come and show you the completed Similar Sentences vocabulary assignment.

Teacher Directed / Independent

Focus: Story Element Instruction - Perspective

Preparation:
1.   You may choose either number 2 or number 3 listed below to prepare for today's lesson.

2.   Choose a picture book that is a retelling of a story from a new point of view, such as *The True Story of the Three Little Pigs* by John Scieszka. Or, choose a book that shows differing points of view, such as *The Pain and the Great One* by Judy Blume.

3.   Select 2 or more familiar stories the students have already read to use as examples of perspective. You must be able to clearly determine whose side of the story is being told for each example.

Lesson:
1.   Listen to your students read the assigned pages out loud to you. Use the Reading Strategies list and the Qualities of Good Reading list provided in the Appendix to help you know what to emphasize.

2.   Review the following definition for *perspective:*
       a) *Perspective is how you perceive or view a subject or thing; your point of view.*

3.   Say, *Today we will be discussing the meaning of perspective as 'whose side of the story is being told'.*

4.   Give students the following example of perspective:
       a) *If there are muddy tracks across the kitchen floor, your side of the story might be that your sister did it.*
       b) *However, your sister's side of the story might be that you forgot to take your shoes off and tracked the mud in the kitchen yourself.*

5.   If you chose a picture book that shows different points of view to read to your students, read the selection aloud. Discuss the contrasting point of views demonstrated by the story. Then, go on to number 7 on the next page.

6.   If you selected 2 or more stories the students have already read, show students the books as examples. Help the students decide whose side of the story is being told in each book. (For example: In *The Three Little Pigs* the pigs' side of the story is told. If the wolf's side of the story was being told, the pigs may have been shown as unfriendly neighbors who refused to let the wolf join them. A storm could have been responsible for blowing the pigs' houses down.)

7. Discuss the following question with the students:
   a) *Whose perspective or whose side of the story is being told in the realistic fiction book you are reading? Explain.*

8. Go over the directions for Pen Pals in the *Student Book* for day 8.

9. Have students complete the letter on their own.

10. The directions instruct the students to come and show you the completed assignment.

Independent   **Level 4/5**

Focus: Story Element Extension - Switch It

Lesson:

1. Tell the students to read the assigned pages for day 8 on their own.

2. Tell them to complete Switch It on day 8 in their *Student Book* when they finish reading.

3. The directions instruct students to come and show you the completed assignment.

Teacher Directed / Independent   **Level 6/7/8**

Focus: Story Element Discussion - Perspective

Lesson:

1. The students read the assigned pages for day 8 on their own.

2. Prior to meeting with you, have students choose 2 books that they have read in the past. Set them aside for use with number 5 in this lesson.

3. The students meet with you to discuss the following questions:
   a) *How does the author make the characters seem real to you?*
   b) *Does the setting seem realistic? Why, or why not?*

4. Review the following definition for *perspective*:
   a) *Perspective is how you perceive or view a subject or thing; your point of view.*

5. Say, *Today we will be discussing the meaning of perspective as 'whose side of the story is being told'.*

6. Give students the following example for perspective:
   a) *If you are going through the items in your pencil box when you are supposed to be working, your side of the story may be that you need a pencil sharpener.*
   b) *However, your teacher's side of the story might be that you are wasting time when you are supposed to be working.*

7. Use the 2 books the students chose. Decide whose side of the story is being told in each book. (For example: In *The Little Red Hen,* the story shows the Little Red Hen's perspective. If it was written from one of the other animal's perspective, the Little Red Hen may have been shown as bossy and unwilling to share.)

8. Discuss the following questions with the students:
   a) *Whose perspective or whose side of the story is being told in the realistic fiction book you are reading? Explain.*
   b) *How would the story change if it was told from a different character's perspective?*

9. Introduce Take My Advice on day 8 in the *Student Book*. Make sure the students understand what to do. Then, have the students work on their own.

10. The directions instruct students to come and show you the completed assignment.

Teacher Directed   **Level 2/3**

Focus: Godly Character Traits - Biblical Comparisons

Preparation:
1. Find a short children's book of the Bible story about the boy, Samuel, being called by the Lord. Otherwise, you will need to read the story directly from the Bible in 1 Samuel chapter 3.

Lesson:
1. Review the following definitions and scripture passages:
    a) *Integrity is being honest and doing what is right, even when no one else is watching, so that you may be blameless in the eyes of the Lord.*
    b) *Key Scripture verse: For the grace of God that brings salvation has appeared to all men. It teaches us to say "No" to ungodliness and worldly passions, and to live self-controlled, upright and godly lives in this present age. Titus 2: 11,12*
    c) *Dependability is being reliable and keeping your word, so that others can trust you to do what you say.*
    d) *Key Scripture verse: When a man makes a vow to the Lord or takes an oath to obligate himself by a pledge, he must not break his word but must do everything he said. Numbers 30:2*

2. Read the children's book or the Bible passage 1 Samuel chapter 3 about the boy, Samuel, being called by the Lord. Instruct your students to listen for examples of *integrity* and *dependability* in the story being read.

3. Discuss the following question with your students:
    a) *How did Samuel's actions show integrity and dependability?*

4. Record the students' responses in the *Student Book* on day 9 under the Biblical Character column. (Possible answers include the following: *Dependability* as Samuel came to Eli three times in the night, because he thought Eli was calling him; *Integrity* as Samuel told Eli what God had said, even though he was afraid to tell Eli; *Integrity* as the Lord called Samuel to be a prophet as he grew up.)

5. Listen to your students read the assigned pages for day 9 out loud to you. Remind the students to be searching for examples of *integrity* and *dependability*.

6. Using the questions listed on the next page, compare Samuel with the main character in the realistic fiction book. Record the responses on day 9 in the *Student Book* under the Book Character column.

a) *How does the character in your book show integrity and dependability?*
b) *What would the Biblical character, Samuel, do differently from the character in your book?*

Independent / Teacher Directed   **Level 4/5**

Focus: Godly Character Traits - Biblical Comparisons

Preparation:
1.   Each student needs a Bible for today's lesson.

Lesson:
1.   Tell the students to review the Godly Character Traits listed on day 9 in the *Student Book* on their own. Then, have the students silently read the story of Job from the Bible in Job chapters 1 and 2.

2.   Have students do their best to complete the Biblical Character column on the Godly Character Story Sheet for Job on day 9 in the *Student Book*.

3.   Students silently read the assigned pages in the realistic fiction book for day 9, saving 3 or 4 pages to read aloud to you.

4.   The students meet with you to finish the assignment for day 9. Listen to your students read several pages. Use the Qualities of Good Reading list provided in the Appendix to help you know what to emphasize.

5.   Discuss the following questions with the students as you review what they have already done in the *Student Book* for day 9. Complete the remaining columns in the *Student Book* for day 9.
a) *How did Job's behavior show integrity, dependability, and self-acceptance?* (Possible answers include the following: *Integrity* in chapter 2 verses 3 and 9, as the Lord and Job's wife each refer to Job's integrity; *Dependability* in chapter 2 verse 10, when Job talks about accepting and trusting God through the good and the bad times; *Self-acceptance* in chapter 1 verses 20-22, as Job accepted the way he was and what had happened to him by continuing to praise the Lord.)
b) *How did the person in your book behave like the Biblical character, Job?* (List the answers in the *Student Book*.)
c) *How did the person in your book behave differently from Job?* (List the answers in the *Student Book*.)
d) *Which trait was shown least often by the book character?* (Explain in the *Student Book*.)

Independent   **Level 6/7/8**

Focus: Godly Character Traits - Biblical Comparisons

Preparation:
1.   The students need a Bible for today's lesson.

Lesson:
1.   The students complete the activities in the *Student Book* and read the assigned pages for day 9 on their own.

2.   The directions instruct the students to come and show you the completed Godly Character Story page. (Examples of the traits shown by Deborah might include the following: *Integrity* in Judges 4 verse 5, as the Israelites came to Deborah to have their disputes settled; *Dependability* in Judges 4 verse 10, as Deborah went with Barak as she had promised; *Self-Acceptance* in Judges 4 verse 14, as Deborah allowed Barak to have the glory and carry out God's command; *Leadership* in Judges 4 verses 6-9, as Deborah summoned Barak with God's command and agreed to accompany Barak in order to get him to go.)

Teacher Directed / Independent   **All Levels Together**

Focus: Comprehension Check - Character Description

Lesson:

1.   Say, *Today you will be reviewing the predictions you made about your book character on day 6.*

2.   Have students open their *Student Books* to day 6, Character Description.

3.   Tell students that they have two directions to follow for today's assignment. First, students need to read their previous predictions and circle any parts of the predictions that were correct. Second, students need to write any additional details or any corrections on the *Changes* line for each question.

4.   Since the *Changes* line includes both additional details and corrections, students should have something written on each *Changes* line before showing you the completed assignment.

5.   Have students read the assigned pages for day 10 on their own.

6.   The directions instruct the students to come and show you the completed assignment.

Teacher Directed   **All Levels Together**

Focus: Prereading Activity - Prereading Map

Preparation:

1.   If students are beginning new books today, make sure to have the number of pages to be read each day calculated and have those books ready to hand out. (See the *Getting Started* section, item #7, in the back of this guide for details.)

2.   If students are <u>not</u> beginning new books today, they use the books they are currently reading for today's activities.

Lesson:

1.   Say, *Today we will be doing a prereading activity to help you think about the next book you will be reading or the next part of the book you will be reading.*

2.   Give students a little time to look at the cover, read the synopsis, and quickly page through the book.

3.   Have students open their *Student Books* to the Prereading Map on day 11. As you discuss the following questions, students should write their answers to the first questions in the squares. They should write the answers to the second questions on the lines by the squares.
      a) *What is a realistic fiction book? What makes your book realistic?*
      b) *Who are the main characters in your book? What do you notice about them from looking through your book?*
      c) *What places are important in this story? Do you know anything about these places?*
      d) *What seems to be the problem or conflict in this story? What do you know about this kind of problem?*
      e) *What might be some possible solutions to the problem or conflict in the book? How would you solve the problem in the story?*

4.   Help students update their *Assigned Reading Calendar* for days 11-15.

5.   Have students read the assigned pages for day 11 on their own.

Teacher Directed   **Level 2/3**

Focus: Story Discussion and Optional Phonics <u>or</u> Vocabulary Work

Preparation:

1. You may choose to have students at this level review phonics <u>or</u> complete a vocabulary assignment. Use your own program for the phonics review. Refer to the Appendix for a reproducible vocabulary assignment. The lesson on this day is much shorter to compensate for the additional time you may spend on phonics or on vocabulary work.

Lesson:

1. Optional phonics or vocabulary work

2. Listen to your students read the assigned pages out loud to you. Use the Reading Strategies list and the Qualities of Good Reading list provided in the Appendix to help you know what to emphasize.

3. Discuss the following questions with your students:
   a) *Choose one character. Why is this character important to the story?*
   b) *What other story reminds you of this story? Explain.*
   c) *What do you think is going to happen? What clues helped you make this prediction?*

Independent / Teacher Directed   **Level 4/5**

Focus: Story Element Instruction - Point of View

Lesson:

1. Tell the students to read the assigned pages on their own, leaving 3-4 pages to read aloud to you.

2. Listen to your students read several pages. Use the Qualities of Good Reading list provided in the Appendix to help you know what to emphasize.

3. Introduce the following definition for *literary point of view:*
   a) *Point of view is the author's "voice" or method chosen to tell the events of a story.*
   b) *The three types of point of view discussed today will be first person, second person, and third person.*

4.   Have students open their *Student Books* to day 12, Point of View Practice. Work with the students to follow the directions and practice writing in first person, second person, and third person.

5.   Discuss the following questions with your students:
      a) *Is your realistic fiction book in first person (like the note to another character), second person (like the ad to you), or third person (like the reporter)?*

Independent   **Level 6/7/8**

Focus: Vocabulary Builder - Similar Sentences

Preparation:
1.   Have a dictionary and a thesaurus available.

Lesson:
1.   The students complete the activities in the *Student Book* and read the assigned pages for day 12 on their own.

2.   The directions instruct students to come and show you the completed Similar Sentences vocabulary assignment.

Teacher Directed   **Level 2/3**

Focus: Story Element Instruction - Point of View

Preparation:
1.   Select one story that the students remember well. It should be a story with a strong main character. Use dress-up clothes and props to create costumes that look like the main character in the book you selected. Have the book ready to show the students.

2.   You also need the following props to create reporter costumes: microphones, note pads, and pens.

Lesson:
1.   Listen to your students read the assigned pages out loud to you. Use the Reading Strategies list and the Qualities of Good Reading list provided in the Appendix to help you know what to emphasize.

2.   Introduce the following definition for *point of view* :
       a) *Point of view is the author's "voice" or method chosen to tell the events of a story.*

3.   Say, *Today's lesson will help you understand two types of point of view, first person and third person.*

4.   Introduce the following definition for the *first person point of view:*
       a) *The author becomes the character whose telling the story.*

5.   Show students the book that you selected with the strong main character. Tell students they will "become" the main character in that book, just like the first person point of view. Give students the dress-up clothes and props to create costumes that look like the main character in the book you selected.

6.   Tell students they must walk out in costume and introduce themselves as the main character. *Hello, I am* _____. Then, you may ask the students a few questions having to do with their character. The students must begin their answers with, *I* _____.

7.   Introduce the following definition for the *third person point of view:*
       a) *The author is an observer who reports what is happening.*

8.   Give students the microphones, note pads, and pens. Tell students that they are reporters. Their job is to think of several questions to ask the main character in their realistic fiction book. They are reporting about the character as an observer, just like the third person point of view.

9.   Discuss the following questions with your students:
       a) *From which point of view is your realistic fiction book written? Is it from the first person, where the writer becomes the character, or from the third person, where the writer is reporting about the character?*
       b) *What is the main difference between first person and third person?*

Independent   Level 4/5

Focus: Story Element Extension - Who Am I?

Lesson:
1.   Tell the students to read the assigned pages for day 13 on their own.

2.   Tell them to complete Who Am I on day 13 in their *Student Book* when they finish reading.

3.   The directions instruct students to come and show you the completed assignment.

Teacher Directed / Independent   Level 6/7/8

Focus: Story Element Discussion - Point of View

Lesson:
1.   The students read the assigned pages for day 13 on their own.

2.   The students meet with you to discuss the following questions:
       a) *How do the characters change in the story?*
       b) *What changes would you make to the setting location? Explain.*
       c) *Could the problem in the story have been avoided? If so, how?*

3.   Have students open their *Student Books* to day 13. Follow the directions in the *Student Book* to discuss and evaluate with the students, which point of view is shown in the realistic fiction book the students are reading.

Teacher Directed   **Level 2/3**

Focus: Godly Character Traits - Personal Assessment

Preparation:
1.   You will need an index card or note card for each of your students today.

Lesson:
1.   Review the following definitions and scripture passages:
        a) _Integrity_ *is being honest and doing what is right, even when no one else is watching, so that you may be blameless in the eyes of the Lord.*
        b) _Key Scripture verse_: *For the grace of God that brings salvation has appeared to all men. It teaches us to say "No" to ungodliness and worldly passions, and to live self-controlled, upright and godly lives in this present age. Titus 2:11,12*
        c) _Dependability_ *is being reliable and keeping your word, so that others can trust you to do what you say.*
        d) _Key Scripture verse:_ *When a man makes a vow to the Lord or takes an oath to obligate himself by a pledge, he must not break his word but must do everything he said. Numbers 30:2*

2.   Listen to your students read the assigned pages for day 14 out loud to you.

3.   Discuss the following questions with the students:
        a) *Which trait was shown less often by the book character, integrity or dependability? Explain.*
        b) *Choose the trait that is harder for you to show, integrity or dependability. Explain.*

4.   Hand out one index card to each student. Have the students write the trait they chose and 3 ways to work on showing the trait more often in their own lives.

5.   On the other side of the card, have the students draw themselves portraying this trait. The students may also write the matching Bible verse if you choose for them to do so.

6.   Have the students post their cards in a place where they will see them often.

Independent / Teacher Directed   **Level 4/5**

Focus: Godly Character Traits - Personal Assessment

Preparation:
1.   You will need an index card or note card for each of your students today.

Lesson:
1.   Tell the students to review the Godly Character Traits listed on day 9 in the *Student Book* on their own.

2.   Have the students silently read the assigned pages in the realistic fiction book for day 14, saving 3-4 pages to read aloud to you.

3.   Meet with the students to finish the assignment for day 14.

4.   Listen to your students read 3-4 pages. Use the Qualities of Good Reading list provided in the Appendix to help you know what to emphasize.

5.   Discuss the following questions with the students:
      a) *Refer to day 9 in the Student Book. Choose the trait that is the hardest for you to show - integrity, dependability, or self-acceptance. Explain.*
      b) *Look at the Bible verse on day 9 in the Student Book for the trait you chose. How does the behavior of the book characters compare to this verse? Explain.*
      c) *What ways can you demonstrate the verse you chose in your own life?*

6.   Hand out one index card to each student. Have students list actions they will take to help them live according to the verse they chose.

7.   On the other side of the card, have the students divide the card into 3-4 sections, by drawing vertical lines. Instruct the students to break the chosen verse into sections and draw a quick picture or symbol to stand for each section of the verse. When the students look at the pictures, it should remind them of each part of the verse.

8.   The Bible verse may be written on the bottom or on the back of the card if you choose to have the students do so.

9.   Have the students post their cards in a place where they will see them often.

Independent   **Level 6/7/8**

Focus: Godly Character Traits - Personal Assessment

Preparation:
1.   The students each need an index card or note card for today.

Lesson:
1.   The students complete the activities in the *Student Book* and read the assigned pages for day 14 on their own.

2.   The directions instruct the students to come and show you the completed assignment for day 14, including the completed index card or note card for posting.

Preparation:
1.   Choose which **one** of the following project options you would like your students to complete as a culminating project for this genre. Each option is explained in detail on the pages that follow. For ease in planning, you should choose the same option for each of the students.
      a) **Option 1:** You may choose a character based project, which focuses on the Godly character trait for this genre. The directions for these projects are more general. The project does not involve any of the books from the unit. It does include a final reflection form.
      b) **Option 2:** You may choose a book based project, which is an individual project. Students will choose one of the books they read for this genre to use for the project. The project directions are detailed and include a final reflection form.
      c) **Option 3:** Your final option is to choose a group project, which requires two or more students working together. This project is based on a common book the students have all read or had read aloud to them. The **one** book the project is based upon should fit into the genre studied in this unit.

2.   Have the directions for the project copied for each student. Make sure to read over the directions for the project option you chose in order to know what supplies you will need to have available for the projects.

3.   The plans allow 5 work days for the projects to be completed. This time allotment includes the planning and any presenting of the projects. The plans assume that the students will use only their normal amount of reading time to complete the projects.

Lesson:
1.   Say, *Today we will be starting our culminating project for realistic fiction. You will have 5 days, counting today, to work on your project. Your projects are due at the end of that time on _____. (give due date)*

2.   Introduce the project you have chosen for this unit. Go through the directions and make sure students have a copy of the directions, so they can work as independently as possible. Show them where the needed supplies can be found.

3.   Then, have students read the assigned pages for day 15 to finish the realistic fiction books. Students may begin the project after the reading is complete.

Focus: **Godly Character Trait Project**   **Integrity Investigation**

Project Notes:

1.   Teach students to recognize integrity through the use of short stories or articles.

2.   Reproduce the Integrity Investigation Planning Form included in this guide. Review the definitions and key verses for the traits your students studied.

3.   Choose several <u>short</u> stories or articles to read aloud to your students. It is helpful to have some selections be nonfiction and some be fiction. Tell students to listen for examples of the traits they studied.

4.   After each short story or article, discuss the following questions with your students:
   a) What examples of *integrity* did you notice? What examples of *dishonesty* did you notice?
   b) What examples of *dependability* did you notice? What examples of *unreliability* did you notice?
   c) If you have students in level 4/5 or level 6/7/8 ask, what examples of *self-acceptance* did you notice? What examples of *timidity* did you notice?
   d) If you have students in level 6/7/8 ask, what examples of *leadership* did you notice? What examples of *self-pity* did you notice?

5.   Tell students that their assignment for days 16-18 is to find <u>one</u> short story or article which shows examples of the traits they studied. Have students circle the traits on their Integrity Investigation form that they are responsible for finding.
   a) Students in level 2/3 will search for <u>one</u> story or article with examples of *integrity* and *dependability.*
   b) Students in level 4/5 will search for <u>one</u> story or article with examples of *integrity, dependability,* and *self-acceptance.*
   c) Students in level 6/7/8 will search for <u>one</u> story or article with examples of *integrity, dependability, self-acceptance,* and *leadership.*

6.   The students need to complete the Integrity Investigation Planning Form for the book they select.

7.   Then, students must practice reading the short story or article aloud so they may share it with the group on day 19.

8.   On day 19, have a special integrity sharing time. Be seated in a cozy place and serve enjoyable snacks and refreshments. The students will share their books and planning forms with the group. Reproduce the reflection form included in this guide for each student to complete on day 19.

Integrity Investigation Planning Form

Name: _____

Definitions:

INTEGRITY is being honest and doing what is right, even when no one else is watching, so that you may be blameless in the eyes of the Lord.

DEPENDABILITY is being reliable and and keeping your word, so that others can trust you to do what you say.

SELF-ACCEPTANCE is believing that you are special because you are made in God's image, so that others might see Him reflected in you.

LEADERSHIP is guiding and directing others by setting a good example as you work together for a common purpose.

Key Verses:

INTEGRITY - For the grace of God that brings salvation has appeared to all men. It teaches us to say "No" to ungodliness and worldly passions, and to live self-controlled, upright and godly lives in this present age. Titus 2:11,12

DEPENDABILITY - When a man makes a vow to the Lord or takes an oath to obligate himself by a pledge, he must not break his word but must do everything he said. Numbers 30:2

SELF-ACCEPTANCE - I praise you because I am fearfully and wonderfully made; your works are wonderful, I know that full well. Psalms 139:14

LEADERSHIP - Follow my example, as I follow the example of Christ. 1 Corinthians 11:1

Directions:

1.   Circle the traits listed above that you studied in this unit. Your teacher will tell you which traits to circle, if you are unsure.

2.   Find <u>one</u> short story or article which shows examples of each trait you circled.

3.   Complete the Integrity Investigation Planning Form on the next page for the story or article you select.

4.   Practice reading the <u>short</u> story or article aloud, so you are prepared to share it with the group on day 19.

5.   Be prepared to share your answers from your Integrity Investigation Planning Form with the group as well.

Note: This planning form is continued on the next page.

Integrity Investigation Planning Form
(continued)

Name:_____

Story or Article Title: _____

Remember: You only need to complete the parts of the planning form that match the traits you circled on the previous page.

Here are some of the examples of *integrity* that I noticed in my selection:

_____

_____

_____

Here are some of the examples of *dependability* that I noticed in my selection:

_____

_____

_____

Here are some of the examples of *self-acceptance* that I noticed in my selection:

_____

_____

_____

Here are some of the examples of *leadership* that I noticed in my selection:

_____

_____

_____

Show the teacher this page when you are finished.

Focus: **Book Based Project**   **Time Line**

Project Notes:

1.   The students each need to choose **one** book from those that **were read in this genre**. That book is the basis for the project.

2.   Each student makes a time line of the book's important events.
       a) Each chapter of the book is one section of the time line.
       b) If the book doesn't have chapters, students can be assigned a certain
          number of sections to complete.

3.   Reproduce the Time Line Planning Form included in this guide for each student.

4.   Cut white paper in long strips to resemble a time line.
       a) Students draw vertical lines to divide the paper into the number of sections
          needed for their book.
       b) Students may need several strips of paper to have enough room for all the
          sections.
       c) The strips will be joined together to create one time line for each student.

5.   Each section of the time line needs to include the following things:
       a) Label each section of the time line with the chapter number.
       b) For books that do not have chapters, label the sections of the time line
          Event 1, Event 2, Event 3, and so on.
       c) Summarize the most important events from the chapter in writing.
       d) Draw a picture to portray the events from that chapter.
       e) Color the pictures if there is enough time.

6.   On day 19, students present the completed time line by having each student
       read and explain the sections of their time line. Reproduce the reflection form
       included in this guide for each student to complete.

Time Line Planning Sheet

Name:_____

Title of the Book: _____

1. How many sections will there be in your time line?_____

2. You will use white paper cut in long strips to resemble a time line.

3. Draw vertical lines to divide the paper into the number of sections you need.

4. Label each section of the time line with the chapter number. For books that do not have chapters, label the sections of the time line *Event 1, Event 2, Event 3, . . .*

5. Summarize the most important events from the chapter or section of the book in writing. List the important events for each section of the time line on the lines below. You may continue on another sheet of paper if your time line has more than 8 sections.

    Section 1: _____

    Section 2: _____

    Section 3: _____

    Section 4: _____

    Section 5: _____

    Section 6: _____

    Section 7: _____

    Section 8: _____

6. Draw a picture for each section of the time line to show the important events.

7. Color the pictures if you have time.

8. If you have 4 working days, not counting today, how many sections of the time line do you need to complete each day? _____ sections each day

Show the teacher this page when you are finished.

Focus: Group Project   **Variety Show**
Project Notes:

1.   In order to choose this option, you must have two or more students (unless you are willing to do part of the project with your student).

2.   This project is based on **one** common book the students have all read or had read aloud to them. The book the project is based upon should fit into the genre studied in this unit.

3.   Students plan a variety of acts to perform that provide information about the book and entertain the audience. Students meet as a group to decide the types of acts each student will plan and perform. Each act should be 1-5 minutes in length.

4.   Each student must participate in at least two acts. Acts may be planned and performed individually or with other students. The role of director and of master of ceremonies count as one act each.

5.   Reproduce the Variety Show planning form included in this guide. Have students complete the form. Possible ideas for acts include the following:
a) Write a song to sing about the book.
b) Write a poem to recite about the book.
c) Dress up as a character. Give a speech from that character's point of view.
d) Act out a short scene with dialogue from the book.
e) Pantomime an important part of the story.
 f) Draw large pictures of the main characters to display. Write important things each character says or does. Read one at a time to the audience and have them guess which character matches each statement.
g) Do a puppet show, using stuffed toys or dolls, of an important part of the story.
h) Write about some situations that happen in the book and ask the audience for their opinion about what to do. Then, share how each situation happened in the book.
i) Choral read an important part of the story. Assign individual students parts to read expressively and have the group read some parts all together.
j) Create a large background scene of the settings in the book to display.
k) Give a speech that explains what you have in common with a character.

6.   On days 15-17, students plan and practice their acts. Students meet as a group to practice the variety show on day 18. The director directs the practices and helps acts gather props and needed items. The master of ceremonies introduces each act and gives the opening and closing remarks.

7.   On day 19, students perform the variety show for an audience. Reproduce the reflection form included in this guide for each student to complete.

Unit 9

Variety Show Planning Sheet

Name: _____

Title of the Book: _____

Notes: You must participate in at least two acts. Acts may be planned and performed alone or with other students. Each act should be 1-5 minutes in length. The role of director and of master of ceremonies count as one act each.

Plan for Act 1:

1. I plan to do _____ for one of my acts.

2. I will work: (Circle one of the following options:)   alone   with others

3. My plan for the act includes the following details: _____

_____

_____

_____

4. I need the following supplies for my act:_____

_____

Plan for Act 2:

1. I plan to do _____ for my other act.

2. I will work: (Circle one of the following options:)   alone   with others

3. My plan for the act includes the following details: _____

_____

_____

_____

4. I need the following supplies for my act:_____

_____

Show the teacher this page when you are finished.

Realistic Fiction - Days 16-18

Independent / Teacher Directed   **All Levels**

Focus: Project Work

Preparation:
1.   For details, read the directions for the project option you chose.

Lesson:
1.   Check students' progress to make sure each student understands what to do and is on schedule to finish by day 19.

2.   Meet with students as a group, if this is needed.

Realistic Fiction - Day 19

Independent / Teacher Directed   **All Levels**

Focus: Project Completion

Preparation:
1.   For details, read the directions for the project option you chose.

2.   Have the reflection forms copied for each student to match the project option you chose.

Lesson:
1.   Briefly check students' progress. Students should finish their projects today.

2.   Have students share their projects with each other or with you.

3.   Hand out the reflection form that matches the project option you chose. Have the students complete the reflection and show you.

4.   You are ready to choose the next genre your students will study. Look ahead to prepare the kickoff for the upcoming genre.

Integrity Investigation Reflection

1. During the integrity investigation, I felt that I did a good job of _____

_____.

2. I think that I could have done a better job of_____

_____.

3. If I could do the integrity investigation again, I would _____

_____

_____.

4. From the integrity investigation I learned_____

_____

_____.

5. My favorite part of the investigation was _____

   because _____.

_____   _____
Signature of student   Date

Time Line Reflection

1. On my time line, I felt that I did a good job of _____

_____.

2. I think that I could have done a better job of _____

_____.

3. If I could do my time line project again, I would _____

_____

_____.

4. From making a time line of my book, I learned_____

_____

_____

_____.

5. I thought the most important part of my time line was_____

_____

_____.

_____   _____
    Signature of student   Date

Variety Show Reflection

1. For the variety show, I felt that I did a good job of _____

_____.

2. I think that I could have done a better job of_____

_____.

3. If I could do the variety show project again, I would _____

_____

_____.

4. From doing the variety show, I learned _____

_____

_____

_____.

5. My favorite part of the variety show project was_____

_____.

_____   _____

Signature of student   Date

Getting Started

GETTING STARTED

1. Read the cover page at the beginning of each genre to aid in selecting the genre you will do first. For a general overview of the units, you can read the *Program Structure* and *Unit Overview* provided in the front of this guide.

2. Read the *Student Placement* section. This will help you determine which instructional level each student needs to be placed in to begin the program. Reproduce the *Genre Log* found in the Appendix. Write each student's name in the log and circle the level where you placed each student in the program.

3. Read the *Student Book* section. You will need one *Student Book* for each student that matches the instructional level. You may also choose to order one copy of the reproducible *Book Projects to Send Home* by Lori Sanders and Linda Kimball for each level that you have students placed in the program. *Book Projects to Send Home* are a one time purchase due to the fact that the project directions included in each book are reproducible.

4. Read the *Literature Pacing and Selection* section. Select appropriate literature for each student. Choose a pace for each student to read the literature. Update the *Genre Log* by writing the book selections for each student on the *Title* lines. Complete the *Pacing* column by circling the number of reading days you allotted for each book.

5. You may want to choose a book to read aloud to the group that corresponds with the genre you selected. This is an <u>optional</u> idea that is encouraged, but not required for this program. A common read-aloud book is needed in order to choose the <u>group</u> project option on day 15 in the plans. If you do not wish to read a book from the genre aloud to the group, you may choose one of the other project options listed on day 15.

6. Read the descriptions of the three project options on day 15 in the daily plans for the genre you chose. Decide which project option you would like to do and circle that option on the *Genre Log* for each student. Save the *Genre Log* in a folder as a record of the selections each student has been assigned in each genre. This log becomes important as students move through the levels, so you can vary selections and projects the next time you teach the genre.

7. Open each *Student Book* to the *Assigned Reading Calendar* found after the cover page of the genre you selected. A reproducible copy of the *Assigned Reading Calendar* can also be found in the Appendix of this Teacher's Guide. Follow the directions below to prepare the *Assigned Reading Calendar(s):*

- Write each student's name on his own calendar.
- Check the box next to the pace you selected for each student.
- Write the book title(s) of the book(s) you selected for each student.
- Divide the number of pages in each student's book, by the number of reading days you allotted for that book. This will give you the number of pages each student needs to read daily in order to complete the book at the pace you chose for them. Write the number of pages to be read daily on the corresponding student's *Assigned Reading Calendar.*
- Students will write in the page numbers for each day of the calendar with your help on day 1.
- The daily plans remind you to have students update the *Assigned Reading Calendar* as needed on days 1, 6, and 11 in each unit.

8. Read the *Time Allotment* section. This will guide you in setting aside enough work time for students in each level.

9. Read the kickoff ideas that are found after the cover page of the genre you selected.

10. Plan and have the genre kickoff.

11. Follow the plans for day 1 in the genre you selected. Continue following the daily plans until you have completed the genre unit. To see an overview of the plans in a unit, categorized by day and level, refer to the *General Daily Format* section in the front of this guide.

12. Begin with step 1 of *Getting Started* and follow these steps again.

STUDENT PLACEMENT

The plans assume that students participating in this program have mastered phonics and are in the oral reading stage or above it. For the purposes of this program, the oral reading stage is defined as readers who need practice reading aloud until they are able to read proficiently.

Students at the oral reading stage, regardless of age, should be placed in level 2/3. Students who are able to read silently, with some monitoring, may be placed in level 2/3 or level 4/5. Students able to read independently for pleasure, may be placed in level 4/5 or level 6/7/8.

Any students that are new to this program should be placed in level 2/3 or level 4/5. Level 6/7/8 builds on the concepts introduced in levels 2/3 and 4/5 and is more independent.

The program intends for students to remain in the same level of instruction for two years, before moving up to the next level. For example, students in level 2/3 can work through all nine units in one year, reading books at the second grade level. The next year, they repeat level 2/3, reading books at the third grade level. Due to the structure of the activities, reading different books from one year to the next, changes the outcome of the activities within the same level. However, the design of the program, allows you to shorten or extend the number of years students remain in the same level to suit your specific needs.

STUDENT BOOKS

A consumable *Student Book* is needed for each student in the program. The *Student Books* are a necessary component of the program, because they contain all the pages listed in the teacher's daily plans.

Order the *Student Book* for each student that matches the instructional level where you placed them in the program. *Student Books* include level 2/3, level 4/5, and level 6/7/8. The *Student Book* for level 6/7/8 has directions written specifically to the student, making it more independent.

It is also important to note that project option 2 for the genres is written to correspond with *Book Projects to Send Home* by Lori Sanders and Linda Kimball (Ideal,1999) (McGraw-Hill, 2004). These books are a one time purchase due to the fact that the project directions included in each book are reproducible. The plans for each genre direct you to the matching pages in the project books, so they are very easily used.

Getting Started

Book Projects to Send Home by Lori Sanders and Linda Kimball may be ordered from any retailer that carries McGraw-Hill, Instructional Fair products. The books are moderately priced at approximately $6.00 each. You may also order directly from McGraw-Hill online at www.mhkids.com or by telephone at 1-800-417-3261. If you order directly, use the numbers below that begin with *IFG*.

- Level 2/3 uses *Book Projects to Send Home* for grade 2 (#IFG99160) (ISBN #0-74242-732-3)
- Level 4/5 uses *Book Projects to Send Home* for grade 4 (#IFG99162) (ISBN #0-74242-734-X)
- Level 6/7/8 uses *Book Projects to Send Home* for grade 5 (#IFG99163) Although the project book for level 6/7/8 is listed for grade 5, the projects are very challenging to complete which makes them appropriate for level 6/7/8. (ISBN #0-74242-735-8)

To use project option 2, order one copy of the reproducible *Book Projects to Send Home* for each level that you have students placed in the program.

LITERATURE PACING AND SELECTION

The unit plans are written for 15 days of reading books within the genre and 5 days of working on a culminating project. Day 15 includes both reading and project work time. During the 15 days of reading books within the genre, you individualize the pace at which each student completes the reading of the books you select. You must choose **one** of the following paces for each student in the program:

- 3 books at a pace of 5 reading days each
- 1 book at a pace of 5 reading days & 1 book at a pace of 10 reading days
- 1 book at a pace of 15 reading days

As you select books for each genre, consider the following areas for each student in the program:

- individual interests
- approximate reading level
- ability to understand what is read

Considering the areas listed previously will help you decide whether or not to select the same books for all students in the same level to read.

If you choose for students in the same level to read books that are different from each other, the students can still meet together for their lessons.

However, during the lessons, you will need to "track" answers from more than one book at the same time. Depending on the number of students you have, another option would be to have a separate meeting time with each child even if they are in the same level.

For more help selecting literature, you might want to refer to guidebooks that separate book recommendations into genres and levels. Some examples of such guidebooks are listed below.

• *Books Children Love* by Elizabeth Wilson. (Crossway Books, 1987)
• *Books That Build Character* by William Kilpatrick and Gregory and Suzanne M. Wolfe. (Simon & Schuster, 1994)
• *How to Grow A Young Reader* by Kathryn Lindskoog and Ranelda Mack Hunsicker (Harold Shaw Publishers, 1999)
• *The Read-Aloud Handbook* by Jim Trelaise (several editions)
• *A Landscape with Dragons* by Michael D. O'Brien (Ignatius Press, 1998) This book does not separate titles by genres, but it provides an excellent examination of fantasy books based on a Christian worldview.

You can also utilize the stories in basal readers from any company, if you classify each story by its genre. Then, have students read the stories that match the genre you are teaching.

Remember to go through your own supply of books at home or check books out from the library, prior to purchasing new literature to match a genre.

TIME ALLOTMENT

Level 2/3 requires approximately 25 minutes of teacher directed instruction time as a group for each day. An additional 15 minutes daily for the students to read aloud to you is recommended.

Level 4/5 requires approximately 40 minutes of student work time each day. An additional 20 minutes or more for the students to read their assigned pages is recommended. The teacher meets with students in this level as a group on over half of the days in each unit for approximately 30 minutes. The time spent with the teacher is already included as part of the 40 minutes of daily student work time.

Level 6/7/8 requires approximately 40 minutes of student work time each day. An additional 30 minutes or more for the students to read their assigned pages is recommended. The teacher meets with students in this level as a group on less than half of the days in each unit for approximately 20 minutes.

Getting Started

The time spent with the teacher is already included as part of the 40 minutes of daily student work time.

The daily plans require all levels in this program to meet together as one group on at least 6 of the 20 days in each unit. The group lessons with the teacher last approximately 30 minutes.

For a more detailed overview of when students at each level meet with the teacher, see the *General Daily Format* at the front of this guide.

Appendix

GLOSSARY OF GENRES
(Or categories of literature)

Adventure: Suspenseful stories filled with action and excitement.

Biography: The true story of a notable person's life written by another person.

Fantasy: A fictional story that is not limited by reality.

Folk Tale: Fables, fairy tales, legends, pourquoi or "why" tales, and trickster tales that have been retold and usually have a lesson or a moral.

Historical Fiction: The realistic portrayal of an actual place during a time period from the past.

Humor: Stories, jokes, and poems that have the quality of inciting laughter and are highly entertaining.

Mystery: A story involving a puzzling situation with a problem to be solved.

Nonfiction: Informational books and factual stories based upon real people and events.

Realistic Fiction: An invented story that seems real and is set in modern times.

GLOSSARY OF MAJOR GODLY CHARACTER TRAITS

Brotherly Love: Sincerely caring for others regardless of the circumstance. *Subqualities: compassion, tolerance, patience*

Faith: Having a strong belief that stands firm in the face of opposition. *Subqualities: perseverance, courage, optimism*

Fear of the Lord: Revering the Lord and his commands and believing the Lord can turn harm into good for those who trust in him. *Subqualities: respect for authority, standing against peer pressure, deliberation*

Integrity: Being honest and doing what is right, even when no one else is watching, so that you may be blameless in the eyes of the Lord. *Subqualities: dependability, self-acceptance, leadership*

Joy: Rejoicing, despite your troubles, because God's daily presence within you is not based on your circumstances. *Subqualities: thankfulness, enthusiasm, creativity*

Loyalty: Showing firm, faithful support even in times of trouble. *Subqualities: fairness, discretion, discernment*

Obedience: A willingness to do what is asked or required without complaint. *Subqualities: attentiveness, cooperativeness, meekness*

Responsibility: Being accountable to God and to others as you carry out your duties or obligations in a faithful way. *Subqualities: cautiousness, diligence, initiative*

Virtue: Listening to the promptings of the Holy Spirit to do what is right and good so that you may fulfill God's law. *Subqualities: truthfulness, kindness, self-control*

GLOSSARY OF STORY ELEMENTS

Cause:
A decision, behavior, or incident that happens and produces an effect.

Character:
The people or individuals portrayed in a story.

Compare:
Observing details to note similarities between items.

Conflict:
The issues the characters must face as the pressures in the story continue to mount. Conflicts may be character against character, character against nature, character against society, or character against himself.

Contrast:
Observing details to note differences between items.

Effect:
A consequence that occurs as a result of a cause.

Inference:
Pondering details in the story in order to draw conclusions that make sense of what the text implies.

Main Idea:
The details in the text working together to support one idea. The main idea can be determined for a paragraph, section, chapter, or an entire text.

Mood:
The feeling, sensation, or state of mind created by a story.

Perspective:
How you perceive or view a subject or thing; your point of view.

Point of View:
The author's "voice" or method chosen to tell the events of a story.

Prediction:
Anticipating what will happen next, using clues in the story combined with any background knowledge that you might have.

Setting:
The place where the story happens.

Theme:
The main purpose, lesson, or big idea in the text.

GENRE LOG

Genre: _____

D A T E:	Name:	Title(s):	Pacing	Project
			Circle # days: 5 10 15	Circle Option #: 1
	Circle level #:		Circle # days: 5 10 15	2
	2/3 4/5 6/7/8		Circle # days: 5 10 15	3
D A T E:	Name:	Title(s):	Pacing	Project
			Circle # days: 5 10 15	Circle Option #: 1
	Circle level #:		Circle # days: 5 10 15	2
	2/3 4/5 6/7/8		Circle # days: 5 10 15	3
D A T E:	Name:	Title(s):	Pacing	Project
			Circle # days: 5 10 15	Circle Option #: 1
	Circle level #:		Circle # days: 5 10 15	2
	2/3 4/5 6/7/8		Circle # days: 5 10 15	3
D A T E:	Name:	Title(s):	Pacing	Project
			Circle # days: 5 10 15	Circle Option #: 1
	Circle level #:		Circle # days: 5 10 15	2
	2/3 4/5 6/7/8		Circle # days: 5 10 15	3

Assigned Reading Calendar

Name: _____   **Genre:** _____

Pacing (the teacher checks one box below):
- ☐ 3 books at a pace of 5 reading days each
- ☐ 1 book at a pace of 5 reading days and 1 book at a pace of 10 reading days
- ☐ 1 book at a pace of 15 reading days

Book Title: _____

Number of pages to read daily: _____ pages per day
(the teacher calculates this number)

Day 1	Day 2	Day 3	Day 4	Day 5
p.____ to ____	p.____ to ____	p.____ to ____	p.____ to ____	p.____ to ____

Book Title: _____

Number of pages to read daily: _____ pages per day
(the teacher calculates this number)

Day 6	Day 7	Day 8	Day 9	Day 10
p.____ to ____	p.____ to ____	p.____ to ____	p.____ to ____	p.____ to ____

Book Title: _____

Number of pages to read daily: _____ pages per day
(the teacher calculates this number)

Day 11	Day 12	Day 13	Day 14	Day 15
p.____ to ____	p.____ to ____	p.____ to ____	p.____ to ____	p.____ to ____

Note:
1. Mark an *X* in the box each day after you have read the pages for that day.
2. Update the calendar on days 1, 6, and 11 by writing the assigned page numbers.

READING STRATEGIES: TEACHER'S LIST

Notes:
The strategies listed below range from beginning reading strategies to those that require a higher level of comprehension to apply.

It is important for readers to be familiar with a variety of strategies to try when they come to an unfamiliar word, rather than being "stuck" on a word or being unable to understand what they are reading.

1. **Start the word off right.** Get your mouth ready to form the correct beginning sounds.

2. **Sound out the word.** Model how to blend the sounds of the word together and pronounce it.

3. **Use picture clues.** Look at any pictures on the page for clues to help figure out the unfamiliar word.

4. **Put the word into chunks.** Look for familiar letter chunks in the word. Read each chunk separately. Then, blend the chunks together to form the word (e.g. unfamiliar word: *mahogany,* chunks: *ma- hog- a- ny).*

5. **Look for word patterns, such as little words inside big words, rhyming words, prefixes and suffixes.** (e.g. unfamiliar word: *preschool,* pattern of a little word inside a big word and a prefix: *pre- school).*

6. **Does it make sense? If not, reread it.** Reread the sentence again and think about what word containing those sounds might make sense.

7. **Use the words around it to help make a guess.** Examine the meaning of the text around the unfamiliar word and think about what word might make sense.

8. **Skip the word.** This strategy is acceptable when the unfamiliar word is very difficult and skipping it does not change the meaning of the text (e.g. foreign names or words written in an unfamiliar language).

READING STRATEGIES: STUDENT'S LIST

1. Start the word off right.

2. Sound out the word.

3. Use picture clues.

4. Put the word into chunks.

5. Look for word patterns, such as little words inside big words, rhyming words, prefixes, and suffixes.

6. Does it make sense? If not, reread it.

7. Use the words around it to help make a guess.

8. Skip the word.

QUALITIES OF GOOD READING: TEACHER'S LIST

Notes:
The qualities listed below range from beginning reading qualities to those that require a higher level of fluency and comprehension to apply.

It is important for readers to be familiar with the qualities of good reading, in order to read for understanding and to have confidence when reading aloud.

1.   **Pause at punctuation.** Pause at commas, periods, question marks, exclamation points, hyphens, colons, and semicolons.

2.   **Raise your voice at the end of a question. Exclaim words punctuated with an exclamation point.**

3.   **Emphasize words in all capital letters, bold letters, or italics.** Vary your voice to place emphasis on words that are set apart in a special way.

4.   **Read so the words flow smoothly together.** Use phrasing, or *reading like you are talking*, to build fluency, rather than reading word by word.

5.   **Use expression and proper pitch.** Vary your voice to convey feelings or expressions that fit with the text. Read in a tone that is pleasing to hear, rather than too high or too low in pitch.

6.   **Read at a pace that suits your audience.** Adjust the pace at which you read depending on whether you are reading to yourself, to a younger child, or to a group of people of various ages.

7.   **Use a different tone of voice for different characters.** Change the pitch, volume, accent, or inflection of your voice to match the personalities of different characters. The book is read like a play in order to entertain the listening audience.

QUALITIES OF GOOD READING: STUDENT'S LIST

1. Pause at punctuation.

2. Raise your voice at the end of a question. Exclaim words punctuated with an exclamation point.

3. Emphasize words in all capital letters, bold letters, or italics.

4. Read so the words flow smoothly together.

5. Use expression and proper pitch.

6. Read at a pace that suits your audience.

7. Use a different tone of voice for different characters.

Helpful Hints

1. Find one unfamiliar or strange word in the book you are reading.
    Write the word and the page number where the word is found.

    Word: _____ Page: _____

2. Copy the sentence that contains the unfamiliar word.

    _____

    _____

    _____

3. Read the whole page where you found the unfamiliar word in the
    story.

4. Explain what is happening in the story on the page where you found
    the unfamiliar word.

    _____

    _____

    _____

    _____

    _____

5. Write your guess about what the unfamiliar word means. Make sure
    your guess makes sense with what is happening in the story.

    _____

6. Find the definition of the word in the dictionary and copy it below.

    _____

    _____

    Show the teacher this page when you are finished.

Synonym Search

1. Find three unfamiliar or strange words in the book you are reading. In the chart below, write the three words and list the page number where each word is found.

2. Use a thesaurus to find 3 synonyms, or words that have a similar meaning, for each word you chose. Write the synonyms in the chart below.

Unfamiliar Words	Page	Synonym 1	Synonym 2	Synonym 3
1.				
2.				
3.				

3. For each unfamiliar word, circle one synonym in the chart that could replace the word and make sense in the story.

4. Check to see if the synonyms you circled make sense. For each unfamiliar word, copy the sentence from the story that contains the word. Write the synonym you circled in place of the unfamiliar word in the sentence.

Sentence 1: _____

_____

Sentence 2: _____

_____

Sentence 3: _____

_____

Show the teacher this page when you are finished.

Word Connections

1. Find one unfamiliar or strange word in the book you are reading. Write the word and the page number where the word is found.

   Word: _____ Page: _____

2. In the word written above, circle the root word and draw a line under any prefix or suffix.

3. Copy the sentence from the book that contains the unfamiliar word.

   _____

   _____

4. Find the definition of the unfamiliar word in the dictionary and write it below.

   _____

   _____

5. Use a thesaurus to find a synonym or word that has a similar meaning to the word you chose.

   synonym: _____

6. List an antonym or word that has an opposite meaning to the word you chose.

   antonym: _____

7. Write a new sentence using the unfamiliar word. The sentence needs to show the meaning of the word.

   _____

   _____

Show the teacher this page when you are finished.

Contextual Clues

1. Find an unfamiliar or strange word in the book you are reading. Write the word and the page number where the word is found.

    Word: _____ Page: _____

2. Copy the sentence that contains the unfamiliar word. If it is a short sentence, you need to copy the sentence that comes before or after it too.

    _____

    _____

    _____

3. Draw a box around the unfamiliar word in the sentence.

4. Circle any clue words that were given in the sentence that help you guess the meaning of the unfamiliar word.

5. Write your prediction about what you think the word means.

    _____

    _____

6. Find the definition of the word in the dictionary and copy it below.

    _____

    _____

7. How would you change or add to your prediction in number 5 to make it match the dictionary definition?

    _____

    Show the teacher this page when you are finished.

Resources

Caruso, Beverly; Marks, Ken; & Peterson, Debbie. *Developing Godly Character in Children: A Handbook and Resource Guide for Parents and Teachers.* Lake Elsinore, California: Hands to Help Publications, 1998.

This guide provides numerous Bible references, lists of hymns and choruses, project ideas, and resource lists based on 96 Godly character traits. Each trait is also defined and linked to a key scripture verse. The traits emphasized in *Drawn into the Heart of Reading* are grouped into the same categories as the traits in *Developing Godly Character in Children.*

Kimble, Linda; & Sanders, Lori. *Book Projects to Send Home Grade 2* (revised). Grand Rapids, Michigan: McGraw-Hill Children's Publishing, 2004.

_____. *Book Projects to Send Home Grade 4* (revised). Grand Rapids, Michigan: McGraw-Hill Children's Publishing, 2004.

_____. *Book Projects to Send Home Grade 5* (revised). Grand Rapids, Michigan: McGraw-Hill Children's Publishing, 2004.

Veith Jr., Edward Gene. *Reading Between the Lines: A Christian Guide to Literature.* Crossway Books, 1990.

This is a guidebook that describes the major literary genres. The author discusses how each genre can "portray the Christian worldview". He notes that the "purpose is to promote critical reading, the habit of reading with discernment and an awareness of larger contexts and deeper implications".

Books by This Author:

Little Hands to Heaven
A preschool program for ages 2-5

Little Hearts for His Glory
An early learning program for ages 5-7

Beyond Little Hearts for His Glory
An early learning program for ages 6-8

Bigger Hearts for His Glory
A learning program for ages 7-9
With extensions for ages 10-11

Preparing Hearts for His Glory
A learning program for ages 8-10
With extensions for ages 11-12

Hearts for Him Through Time: Creation to Christ
A learning program for ages 9-11
With extensions for ages 12-13

Hearts for Him Through Time: Resurrection to Reformation
A learning program for ages 10-12
With extensions for ages 13-14

Hearts for Him Through Time: Revival to Revolution
A learning program for ages 11-13
With extensions for ages 14-15

Drawn into the Heart of Reading
A literature program for ages 7-15 that
Works with any books you choose

These books are published by
Heart of Dakota Publishing, Inc.
See the website: www.heartofdakota.com
For placement information, product details, or to order a catalog

For ordering questions, email: carmikeaustin@msn.com
Or, call: 605-428-4068